GEOLOGY BY design

Interpreting Rocks and Their
Catastrophic Record

Carl R. Froede Jr.

Master Books

First printing: September 2007

For information write:
Master Books
P.O. Box 726, Green Forest, AR 72638

ISBN-13: 978-0-89051-503-7
ISBN-10: 0-89051-503-4
Library of Congress Catalog Number: 2007925409
Cover by Farewell Communications

Printed in the United States of America

Previous edition published as *Field Studies in Catastrophic Geology* by the Creation Research Society

Please visit our website for other great titles:
www.masterbooks.com

For information regarding author interviews,
please contact the publicity department at (870) 438-5288

CONTENTS

FOREWORD

The French Revolution of the late 18th century marked another, more subtle revolution — the enlightenment rejection of Christianity in favor of a new world view of secular naturalism. A growing band of intellectuals sought to "free" themselves from the "shackles of religion." One of their most successful victories was the hijacking of the new science of geology in the years following the Napoleonic wars. Guided by the late 18th century works of the Scotsman James Hutton, 19th century geologists imposed a new history of the earth. This history rejected Genesis in favor of long ages of purely physical processes, and was called "uniformitarianism."

Surprisingly, that 200-year-old dogma still persists in modern geology, probably because its version of history supplies a ready excuse to dismiss the Bible and the authority of its God. But after too many years of weak-kneed compromise, Christians in recent decades have begun to respond to the heresies of evolution and uniformitarianism. A small but growing minority has begun to question the geological monolith of uniformitarianism, to the extent that even secular geologists are frantically trying to have their cake and eat it too by insisting that catastrophism is really part and parcel of uniformitarianism!

Why are geologists and "intellectuals" so reticent to even give the Christian explanation a fair hearing? In large part, it is because the Christian challenge is not on the level of scientific facts, or even pet theories, but on the more foundational level of world views. For if the history of Genesis is right, and there was a creation, a Fall, and a Flood, then the whole world view of naturalism must be thoroughly and irretrievably wrong. That is why scientists are fleeing the arena of ideas and resorting to the naked power of judicial force to protect their theories.

But all too many Christians have been slow to grasp the nature of this conflict, and still think and speak in the outmoded "religion vs. science" paradigm, forgetting that without Christianity there would be no science to begin with! Some have awakened to the world view conflict and have begun to criticize Darwinian evolution on those grounds. Science is no longer a successful "cloak" for evolution, in part because Christians have seen the truth of what Jesus said long ago — that a tree is known by its fruit. The fruit of Darwinism has brought only cultural rot. Christians are finally seeing that both evidence and common sense point to a creator — or to "intelligent design" in the modern jargon.

However, the Christian counteroffensive has been much weaker against the older and more deeply entrenched bastion of naturalism in the earth sciences, partly because all too many Christian academics believe that lip service to uniformitarian geology is a magic passkey to "intellectual respectability." But the same philosophical arguments that have proven so effective against evolution also apply to uniformitarianism, and the evidence in favor of a catastrophic global Flood is very compelling. As Christian geologists continue to shed more light on the subject, more people will see just how naked the emperor really is.

Christians fighting in this arena have been labeled "creationists," "young-earth creationists," "Flood geologists," etc. The names matter little — it is the ideas that are powerful. And the idea that garners the most publicity, that invites the harshest attacks from the entrenched elites, and that will prove the most revolutionary to modern thought is that the earth is not 4.55 billion years old. Rather, it is quite young in comparison, with a past marked by tumult and turmoil, not the Victorian stasis imagined by

the gentlemen geologists of old England. John Whitcomb and Henry Morris grasped this essential idea in 1961 with the publication of *The Genesis Flood*, and their definition of the conflict has dominated the discussion ever since.

Now geology can be as simple as a hike down the Grand Canyon, or as complex as steering a drill bit into a narrow reservoir 35,000 feet below the surface. So, although many of the basic ideas are simple, the necessary overhaul of the discipline of geology will be quite complex. But all tasks must start somewhere, and the increasingly innovative work of geologists like Carl Froede Jr. is demonstrating that those adhering to the biblical historical framework can provide explanations for physical phenomena every bit as powerful as those presented by the billions-of-years advocates — as will be demonstrated in the following chapters. These ideas represent nothing less than an ongoing revolution in thought.

This book broadly examines a number of geological phenomena, long thought to be explicable only in terms of "deep time." However, the author demonstrates that all of them are easily understood in the catastrophic context of the Genesis flood and its aftermath. Although the topics are not exhaustively discussed, the author provides a wealth of references that will enable a comprehensive study of each topic by any interested reader. Along the way, you will see that the Flood interpretation is not simply a viable explanation for these geological features — it is the best explanation. As the title suggests, this volume will be a valuable aid for anyone willing to forsake the ivory towers to get out into the field, examine the rocks, and analyze them within the superior biblical framework.

John K. Reed, Ph.D.

5

PREFACE

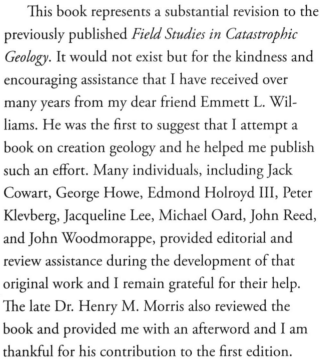

This book represents a substantial revision to the previously published *Field Studies in Catastrophic Geology*. It would not exist but for the kindness and encouraging assistance that I have received over many years from my dear friend Emmett L. Williams. He was the first to suggest that I attempt a book on creation geology and he helped me publish such an effort. Many individuals, including Jack Cowart, George Howe, Edmond Holroyd III, Peter Klevberg, Jacqueline Lee, Michael Oard, John Reed, and John Woodmorappe, provided editorial and review assistance during the development of that original work and I remain grateful for their help. The late Dr. Henry M. Morris also reviewed the book and provided me with an afterword and I am thankful for his contribution to the first edition.

Much has happened in both the secular and Bible-based geological sciences in the ensuing years since the original book was published. Many new ideas have been formulated, tested, and published, and the marketplace of ideas related to the young-earth Flood framework continues its rapid growth. This is an exciting time to be a geoscientist and Bible believer. Many Christians are beginning to discover that the philosophies of naturalism and uniformitarianism have no place in defining earth history within the biblical framework. Research is ongoing in creation science and we are just beginning to realize the power and destructiveness of the global flood of Genesis. However, much work remains to be conducted, and the manner in which this work needs to be performed can be both intimidating and confusing.

This edition remains consistent with the biblical framework of earth history. While many different geologic interpretations are possible, they should all occur within the constraints outlined in the Bible. We live on a young earth, a planet that was created by God from nothing and later reshaped by a global Flood of judgment. We seek to understand its geologic history to the honor of Jesus Christ our Lord and Savior and for the glory of God our Father.

Each of the chapters is intended to provoke thought in contrasting uniformitarian assumptions with the actual rock record. I contend that the biblical framework of earth history provides better answers for resolving geological history. Geology is a dynamic science with both observational and theoretical aspects. Bible-believing Christians need to be able to identify and understand these differences. It is hoped that each chapter will assist the reader in understanding the differences between conceptual ideas and the actual rocks. Many references are cited for those individuals who might wish to pursue the subject matter further.

I am very grateful to the Creation Research Society and all of its members for allowing me to publish my ideas over the years through their excellent organization. I am also grateful to Tim Dudley for helping me publish this book through the New Leaf Publishing Group. Two of my closest friends, Jerry Akridge and John Reed, provided me with wonderful editorial assistance and I thank them both for their time and energy. They provided me with multiple reviews of each chapter and I am exceedingly grateful for their help. However, any mistakes that may occur are my own. I also thank Michael Oard for his assistance and patience in guiding and directing me toward publishing this effort through Master Books. The introduction was provided to me by John Reed and I am grateful for his contribution.

I am very thankful for the continuing support provided to me by my sweet and dear wife, Susan. She is my wonderful helpmeet and a gift from my Lord. Of course, this book would not be possible except for the grace and mercy of my Lord Jesus Christ. He is an awesome Savior and God and worthy to be worshiped and praised.

Carl R. Froede Jr.
Proverbs 3:5–6

CHAPTER 1

Defining the Rock Record within the Context of Biblical History

INTRODUCTION

Earth's geologic history can be constructed from rocks, fossils, radioactive isotopes, ice layers, and other geological features. The manner in which that history is assembled is based on a belief system or world view. In the past, the history conveyed in Genesis was the Western world's foundation for human origins and earth history. Belief in the biblical account focused on the global Flood and individuals who supported this world view were identified as "catastrophists." However, the movement of the Christian Church away from a literal interpretation of the Genesis account, particularly under the influence of the Enlightenment, served to erode confidence in the scriptural record (Laudan 1987). Questions regarding origins could only be answered by a purely naturalistic interpretation — one in which God is omitted. Within this world view of naturalism,[1] the earth's geologic past is defined using natural processes operating in similar settings under processes and rates that we observe today. This concept, that "the present is the key to the past," is known as uniformitarianism. Its icon is the geologic time scale (Figure 1-1). This world view of earth history uses the purported evolution of life and the decay of radioactive isotopes to assign an age to rocks consistent with the geologic time scale.

Can we use the various theories developed in naturalism and framed by their time scale to define a biblical account of earth history? How can we understand earth's geologic history from a biblical perspective when the Bible was not written for that purpose? What should we use in defining a Bible-based geologic history? The simple answer to these questions is that we start from the history that Scripture conveys and work toward understanding its geologic expression in the rocks. Instead of using the conceptualized uniformitarian geological time scale, *we emphasize the biblical account and construct an outline of earth history drawn from the **actual rock record***. This book seeks to lay a foundation for this method. Field examples will show how the scriptural account of earth history presents the most reasonable explanation for the rock record. Two similar Bible-based time scales will also present the framework from which we can define our geologic studies. But first, we must review the uniformitarian time scale based in naturalism to understand its developmental history.

THE DEVELOPMENT OF THE UNIFORMITARIAN GEOLOGIC TIME SCALE

The Enlightenment was a time when many leading thinkers began to reject the Bible. One of their primary targets was its historical reliability, and the new science of geology gave them the perfect weapon. Earth history fell to the philosophies of naturalism and uniformitarianism, which were widely accepted long before they were formalized in 1795 with the publication of James Hutton's *Theory of the Earth* (Adams 1938; Albritton 1986; Gohau 1990; Greene 1982). While catastrophists did represent some of the greatest minds of that period, they were a minority in the battle to define earth history. In fact, it was the catastrophists[2] who produced the first geological maps (i.e., Cuvier and Brongniart's

UNIFORMITARIAN GEOLOGICAL TIME SCALE			
Eon	Era	Period	Age (Ma)
Phanerozoic	Cenozoic	Neogene	23.03
Phanerozoic	Cenozoic	Paleogene	65.5
Phanerozoic	Mesozoic	Cretaceous	145.5
Phanerozoic	Mesozoic	Jurassic	199.6
Phanerozoic	Mesozoic	Triassic	251.0
Phanerozoic	Paleozoic	Permian	299.0
Phanerozoic	Paleozoic	Carboniferous	359.2
Phanerozoic	Paleozoic	Devonian	416.0
Phanerozoic	Paleozoic	Silurian	443.7
Phanerozoic	Paleozoic	Ordovician	488.3
Phanerozoic	Paleozoic	Cambrian	542.0
Proterozoic			2500
Archean			~4550

Figure 1-1. The uniformitarian geologic time scale presents 4.55 billion years of radiometric and evolutionary history. It is assembled from a global patchwork of "type sections" (i.e., rock layers deemed representative for that particular interval of uniformitarian time). The lower 84 percent of the time scale contains little evidence of life and is age-dated solely from radiometric methods. Only in the last 542 million years do the fossilized remains of former life forms become abundant in the rocks where time can be measured by evolution. Not to scale and modified from Gradstein and others, 2004.

final version of their map of the Paris region in 1811, followed by William Smith's map of England, Wales, and portions of Scotland in 1815). However, this work was quickly assimilated into the naturalist world view. In succeeding years, British geologists developed the framework for the modern uniformitarian time scale, which quickly became the standard for ordering and mapping new field data around the world (Rudwick 1985a, 1985b; Secord 1986).

The history and development of the geological sciences can be traced back to the 17th century, when scientists became interested in the lithologic (sediment composition and color) and paleontologic (fossilized organic life forms) content of the sedimentary rock layers. Their analysis of these geologic materials provided no obvious means of determining an appropriate age based solely on the contents or characteristics of the rocks and fossils. However, as field studies of the various sedimentary layers progressed, vertical relationships among the sedimentary layers were noted. Nicolas Steno, a Danish physician working in Tuscany, deduced that the relative age of stratified sediments could be determined using the "law of superposition."[3] Later, certain types of fossilized plants and animals were found in what is interpreted to be a specific succession of changing environments and this led to another concept identified as the "law of faunal succession." This biostratigraphic division of the sediments (based on changes in fossilized plants and animals) was later used to support Darwin's concept of an evolutionary progression of life through time. In turn, evolution provided a "clock" by which geologists could date rock layers.

But even in the turbulent 1800s, not all Bible-believing geologists accepted uniformitarianism (see Mortenson 1997, 2003, 2004). Unfortunately, the geologic work of these Bible-believing Christians failed to develop a scriptural alternative to the geological time scale that could command the same popularity and provide a framework for field research. The momentum of naturalism was too great, and its broad acceptance marginalized these men. As a result, uniformitarianism has dominated the geological sciences (Mortenson 2006). Today, the uniformitarian geologic time scale commands the geological sciences and is the only widely accepted view of earth history (Figure 1-1) (Cohee and others 1978; Berggren and others 1995; Gradstein and others 2004; Harland and others 1990; North American Commission on Stratigraphic Nomenclature 2005; Salvador 1994; Snelling,1985).

If the time scale is the child of uniformitarianism and if uniformitarianism is a part of the world view of naturalism, then Christians cannot simply concede the geological sciences. Fortunately, recent decades have seen a resurgence in biblical creationism and Flood geology following the publication of *The Genesis Flood* (Whitcomb and Morris 1961). A part of that effort has been a critique of the time scale, and several serious flaws have been identified and discussed (see Reed 2001; Reed and Froede 2003; Reed and Oard 2006).

MORE GAPS THAN RECORD

It must be understood that the uniformitarian geologic time scale is a conceptual framework. In very few places do uniformitarian geologists find a stratigraphic section containing most of the major eras of the time scale fitted together. Even then, much of the rock record is missing — periods of tens of millions of years might be represented by only a few thin layers. Often there are many time gaps present (Figure 1-2). A prominent uniformitarian geologist, the late Derek Ager, recognized and noted this perplexing situation over his many years of studying the rock record (1993a). Therefore, it is important to note that the rock layers at any one location on earth are very incomplete time records.

Incomplete history is a tremendous problem for followers of naturalism, because in rejecting

God and the Bible, they are forced to an empirical (i.e., scientifically testable) path to knowledge. No data means no knowledge. Thus, the absence of so much of their historical record means that their confidence in their knowledge of history must also be deficient. Even claiming that their knowledge is based in "science" cannot hide that logic.

Regardless of what can be learned from the rocks, nothing can be understood from the gaps. No matter how geologists might seek to fill those gaps by inference, speculation, and extrapolation, it can never be anything more. Thus, the time scale provides an attractive abstract of their historical narrative, but in many instances it lacks real substance.

Natural History and Science

The incomplete nature of uniformitarian history points to an even more serious problem regarding the differences between natural history and science. History is the study of unique past events. Science is the study of present-day observable processes, relying on repeated observations under

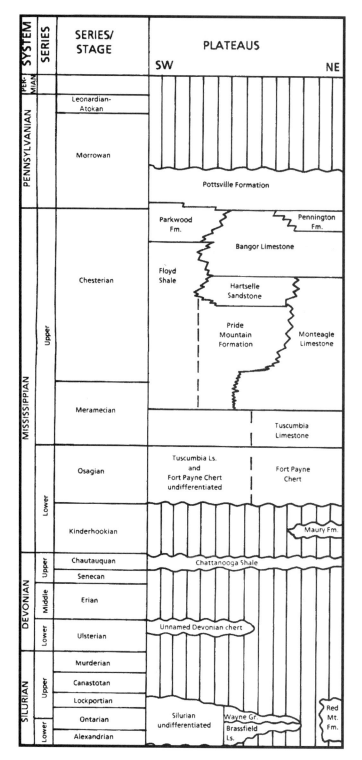

Figure 1-2. There is a dramatic difference between the conceptual time scale and the physical rock record. In most cases, rocks do not represent the entire section of time in which they are defined. Geologists have recognized this discrepancy for many years and have resolved it through the construction of stratigraphic correlation charts. This particular chart is from the plateau region of Alabama (Raymond and others 1988). It reveals both the rocks that are present (assuming long ages for deposition) and the missing time/rock record, represented by vertical lines. This chart does not span the entire stratigraphic section for the Alabama plateau, but shows that much of the area's history consists of no rock record of time. The "youngest" rocks exposed in the area are from the Pottsville Formation, with a time gap of approximately 316 million years between its upper surface and the present. Instead of getting bogged down in the uniformitarian morass, we should focus our investigative efforts on understanding the actual rock record, and interpret it within the framework of the Bible.

controlled circumstances. Thus, natural history is first and foremost *history* and should not be confused with science. However, naturalists attempt to expand science into the domain of history because they equate science and truth. They speak of earth's past with great confidence, even though they have no means of testing and verifying their stories. Their history is an *interpretation* of the rock record within the framework of uniformitarianism. As Christians, we observe the same rocks, sediments, and fossils, but we would interpret these geologic materials within the constraints of the biblical time scale. While we should use scientific methodology to help us develop and define models of historic geology, we need to realize that natural history (where not directly observed) is based on interpretation.

For example, finding a sand deposit exposed at an outcrop would allow us to scientifically test the physical properties and characteristics of the individual sand grains. We can drop the grains into either moving air or water and document how they are deposited. This is experimental science as we can test ideas and observe the results. However, when we move back to the exposed outcrop of sand and speculate how it was formed, we move from the realm of science to historic interpretation. Science might tell us that the sediments were transported by water, but it is our world view that tells us whether this was a rolling river millions of years ago or the Genesis flood in the recent past. Ultimately, the interpretation of the entire rock record will depend upon the world view of the individual and their preconceived ideas — not science (Figure 1-3).

DEVELOPING A CREATIONIST TIME SCALE

The uniformitarian view of earth history never advertised its connection to naturalism, and because it was thought to be merely "scientific," it gained favor inside the Church. Many church leaders sought compromise with the new popular ideas being presented in geology (see discussions in Morris 1985 and Taylor 1991). Unfortunately, this trend usually occurred as the biblical record was conceded. Christians were hoodwinked for decades by the false dilemma of "religion versus science." Those not intimidated into silence were led into error by the "science" they were taught in school, never realizing the philosophical conflicts beneath the surface.

Even some young-earth creation scientists have attempted to synthesize the uniformitarian time scale and a young-earth Flood framework (e.g., Austin 1994; Coffin and Brown 1983; Hedtke 1971; Holt 1996; Morris 1996; Northrup 1986, 1990a, 1990b; Oard 2006; Rugg 1990; Scheven 1990; Silvestru 2006; Snelling 1997; Snelling and others 1996; Tyler 2006; Tyler and Coffin 2006). In addition to the philosophical problems, none of these proposals has proven consistent in application outside of a very local area. The root of the problem lies in this: uniformitarianism was established precisely to rid history of the Genesis flood. How then can its time scale be integrated with the Bible? Where could the Flood fit within the various eras, periods, epochs, and stages? Several creationists have also attempted to set Flood boundaries within the uniformitarian geologic time scale[4] (Figure 1-4) (e.g., Anonymous 1995; Austin 1994; Austin and Wise 1994; Garner 1996a, 1996b; Garton 1996; Robinson 1996; Tyler 1996, 2006). However, in each case, they are left with the problem of requiring multiple large-scale post-Flood events never mentioned in the Bible. In many instances, hemisphere-to-global-scale tectonic, sedimentary, and extinction events would be necessary to explain the remaining Paleozoic, Mesozoic, or Cenozoic overburden created during the post-Flood period. Although these creationists all reject the long ages of the time scale, they believe that they can use its linear framework to define a Flood-based stratigraphy (Snelling and others 1996; Snelling 1997). Unfortunately, they

Figure 1-3. Exposed along this escarpment are cross-bedded quartz sands and invertebrate shell layers that reflect deposition by water. These geologic materials could be collected and carried into the laboratory with the sedimentary bedding reproduced in a flowing water tank. This is experimental and reproducible *science*. The sand/shell outcrop could then be *interpreted* within a uniformitarian perspective as having formed within a number of different former aqueous environments operating over hundreds to thousands of years, potentially even longer based on historic changes in the former sea level position. Notice how we moved from the scientific aspect of the deposit (i.e., sand and shells deposited in flowing water — based on experimentation) to the interpretive (uniformitarian historical narrative). The history of this exposure does not equate to science — but it is easy to confuse the two concepts. This confusion occurs at almost every rock outcrop where the actual conditions of deposition were not observed, and assumptions are made within a specific world view. In reality, this exposure containing cross-bedded sands and shell layers formed in a matter of minutes with the entire exposed section forming in just a few hours (Froede 2006a). We know this because these sedimentary materials were added to the beach during recent renourishment activities. Water-transported and deposited sediments compose this man-made rock record. From this small outcrop, we can imagine how this process would have occurred on a global scale, depositing in places thousands of feet of antediluvian sediments over a brief period of time. Scale is divided into six-inch (15-cm) units.

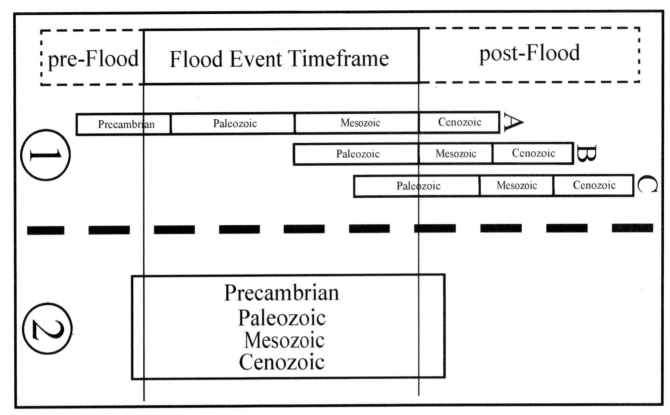

Figure 1-4. Some creationists have attempted to unify the uniformitarian geologic time scale and biblical history, while others propose to define the rocks solely from the biblical perspective. These two different concepts are presented here: 1) The linear progression of time conveyed by the uniformitarian time scale welded to the Flood event. Several Flood/post-Flood boundaries (A, B, C) have been correlated to the uniformitarian geologic time scale, but none successfully extend outside of the local area in which they are defined. 2) This is an alternative approach that does not support the idea that the uniformitarian geologic time scale is linear and which provides the flexibility necessary to define the physical rock record within a biblical framework. Since almost all of the earth's crustal rocks were either formed or altered by the global flood of Genesis, we would expect that the majority of the uniformitarian geologic time scale would occur within the Flood Event Timeframe in no particular order.

fail to understand that the time scale is a conceptual framework rather than an empirical reality (Froede 1997a; Reed and Froede 2003; Reed and others 2006b). To date, all attempts to integrate the Bible and uniformitarian geology end up sacrificing the biblical account in favor of natural history.

But the problems with these attempts are also empirical. A study conducted several years ago tested these boundaries against actual sediments infilling the northern Gulf of Mexico basin (Froede and Reed 1999). This basin has been extensively investigated for oil and gas deposits found within the subsurface. The stratigraphy of the area has been well defined within the uniformitarian geologic time scale. The creationist investigation assessed potential end-of-Flood boundaries at the time scale's Paleozoic/Mesozoic and Mesozoic/Cenozoic contacts, and near the top of the Cenozoic (see Figure 1-5). Our results suggest that the volume and nature of the sediments above even the "youngest" uniformitarian boundary would require many large-scale sedimentary events and/or special geological

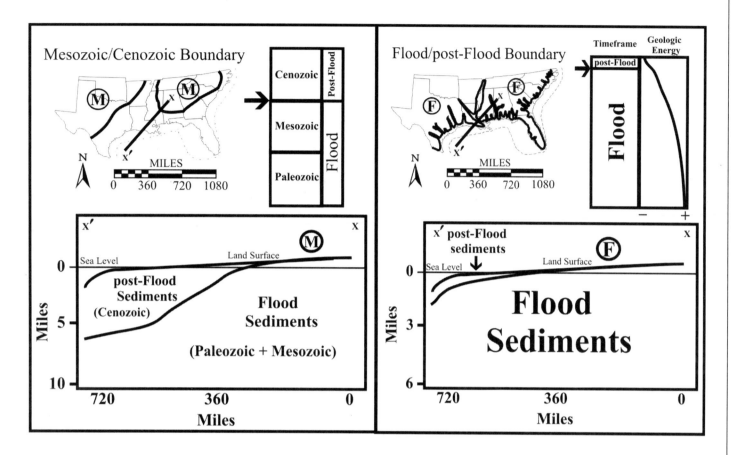

Figure 1-5. The northern Gulf of Mexico basin provides a well-defined geological setting in which to test the possible unification of the uniformitarian geologic time scale and biblical record. In our analysis, emphasis was placed on determining if a Flood/post-Flood boundary could be correlated to the Paleozoic/Mesozoic, Mesozoic/Cenozoic, or a late Cenozoic (i.e., Pliocene/Pleistocene) boundary (for additional information see Froede and Reed 1999). Two different boundaries are presented in this diagram: 1) the Mesozoic/Cenozoic-Flood/post-Flood boundary, and 2) a biblical interpretation outside the bounds of the uniformitarian time scale (modified from Froede and Reed 1999, Figure 4 and Figure 6). Regarding the possible Mesozoic/Cenozoic (K/T) boundary — note the tremendous volume of sediments that would have been eroded from the continent, transported laterally off the Gulf of Mexico coastal plain and deposited out into the basin within a *post-Flood* setting. Is this a reasonable expectation from biblical history? While the Bible does not provide us with much geological information, is this interpretation consistent with the biblical narrative? Should we expect such large-scale geologic activity following the Flood? We believe that this interpretation is unreasonable, and to accept the K/T boundary as the Flood/post-Flood boundary for this location requires greater geological activity than what might be expected in the post-Flood world. We need to redefine basin-filling strata within the constraints of biblical history, and in doing this, we believe that the best approach is to completely ignore the uniformitarian geologic time scale. Our focus should be consistent with the scriptural account and within reasonable and expected levels of geologic activity.

conditions *after the Flood*. Since none of the proposed boundaries were successful, we concluded that any attempt to define the Flood through application of the uniformitarian time scale would fail. Rather than continuing to seek conformity to the uniformitarian framework, we need to shift our emphasis toward the biblical record and define earth history accordingly (Figure 1-6) (see Froede 1997a; Reed and Froede 2003; Reed and others 2006a, 2006b; Woodmorappe 1981).*

WHAT IS THE ROCK RECORD?

This leads us to another important conclusion: the rock record and the uniformitarian time scale are not one and the same. The time scale is a template constructed from a patchwork of stratigraphic-type sections scattered across the globe. Naturalists assert that these rock/sediment sections represent specific locations where the strata have accurately recorded a specific period of earth history. Compiling these individual type sections into a single vertical rock column then purportedly reflects earth's 3.8-billion-year history.[5] Counter to this perspective, Christians can be confident that the Bible provides

*Note: In this book, the capitalized, one-word term "Timeframe" is used by the author to denote his concept of a biblical geological time scale, defining specific geologic time intervals as opposed to other secular designations. The five divisions therein are also capitalized in this book: Present Age, Ice Age, Flood Event, Antediluvian, and Creation Week.

TIMEFRAME	DIVISION
Present Age	Upper
Present Age	Middle
Present Age	Lower
Ice Age	Upper
Ice Age	Middle
Ice Age	Lower
Flood Event	Upper
Flood Event	Middle
Flood Event	Lower
Antediluvian (Pre-Flood World)	
Creation Week	Day Seven
Creation Week	Day Six
Creation Week	Day Five
Creation Week	Day Four
Creation Week	Day Three
Creation Week	Day Two
Creation Week	Day One

Figure 1-6. This biblical geological time scale (Froede 1995b) defines specific geologic time intervals and provides a broad framework for testing models about geologic history. Though flexible with regard to the interpretation of the rock record, the overarching biblical framework is consistent (Reed 2001; Reed and Froede 1997). Varying levels of geologic activity are believed to be reflected within the site-specific rock record and this information can be interpreted to reflect the various "time frames" in which the materials were formed or deposited based on Scripture.

us with the only accurate account of earth history. From it we learn that the rock record is certainly not billions of years old, but no more than 10,000 years old and probably closer to 6,000 years old.

Many young-earth creationist geoscientists are beginning to understand that the uniformitarian time scale has no place in a biblical outline of earth history (Froede 1995b; Reed and Froede 2003; Reed and Oard 2006; Reed and others 1996, 2006b; Walker 1994; Woodmorappe 1981). Focusing on the actual three-dimensional rock record frees the investigator from the philosophical straitjacket of uniformitarianism and allows for an objective analysis of the physical data (Reed 2005). This new perspective facilitates a young-earth creationist to interpret the rocks based on changes in geologic energy (e.g., hydraulic, sedimentary, tectonic, thermal, and climatic) before, during, and following the Flood.

For example, the Navajo Sandstone is a large layer of sandstone that extends across portions of four southwestern states in the United States. It is a mappable unit identified by its lithology and stratigraphic position, and as such, it conforms to the definition of a "formation" (North American Commission on Stratigraphic Nomenclature 2005). Uniformitarian scientists consider this massive sandstone as being all of the same age. That is probably not true. From a creationist perspective, the Navajo Sandstone was formed during the Flood Event Timeframe, prograding outward from an unknown source — possibly the uplifted and submerged Appalachian Mountains (Froede

Navajo Sandstone

2004a). Experimental laboratory work conducted and reported by Julien, Lan, and Berthault (1993) and Berthault (1994) suggests that massive horizontal sheets of sand — like the Navajo Sandstone — should not be considered a lithologic unit of equal age. The hydrodynamic transport, sorting, and settling of sediments across the submerged North American continent during the Flood would create prograding horizontal deposits of similar lithologic composition that are actually not of

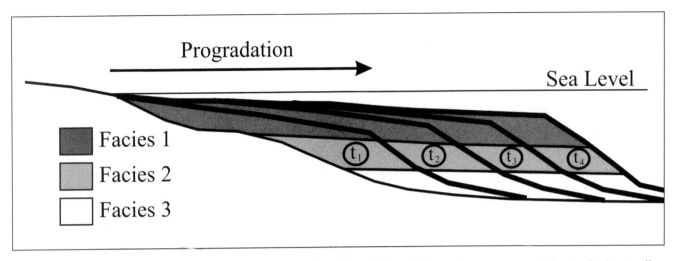

Figure 1-7. Laboratory work by Julien, Lan, and Berthault (1993) has demonstrated that lithologically similar sediments can develop one on top of another as materials are added to the front of a prograding delta. This is reflected in the horizontal "facies." The Navajo Sandstone is a horizontal sheet of quartz sand that is consistent with this view. However, time is actually defined by the slope of the prograding surface and the diagonal stack of varying materials — represented by t_1, t_2, t_3, and t_4. From this perspective, the Navajo Sandstone "facies" should *not* be considered of equal age. This approach to understanding stratigraphic relationships between sedimentary layers has great relevance to the Flood model. Many of these revolutionary ideas have been incorporated into the new field of sequence stratigraphy (modified from Berthault 1994, Figure 1).

equal chronological age (Figure 1- 7) (see Berthault 2002, 2004; Julien, Lan, and Berthault 1993). This new concept of prograding sedimentation and time serves to redefine massive lithologic units like the Navajo Sandstone and it challenges several uniformitarian geologic principles (e.g., law of faunal assemblages, law of faunal succession, law of original continuity, law of horizontality, law of superposition), suggesting that these concepts may be less useful to creationists. Flood geology requires innovative thinking, focusing on field data rather than simply repeating uniformitarian interpretations. The Flood demands a different perspective for most of the rock record that is consistent with waterborne transport and deposition occurring over a brief time.

As a result, we should focus on sedimentary features reflecting changes in the hydraulic conditions because that better characterizes Flood-related processes than do slowly changing paleoenvironments. This is illustrated by Figure 1-8, which shows different ways of interpreting sediments formed by a prograding delta. The sediment source area is to the left and sediments are being transported to the right. Box A reflects the simplistic "layer cake" approach to interpreting the stratigraphic record. The numbers on the right of the drawing reflect the layering sequence and lateral spread of strata of equal ages. This approach is consistent with many uniformitarian stratigraphic laws (e.g., original continuity, horizontality, superposition, faunal assemblages, faunal succession) and assumes that the age of the strata decreases with each new layer of sediment. Box B is derived from the tenets of sequence stratigraphy,[6] a new approach based on *Walther's law* in defining stratigraphy reflective of changes in sea level position. While many of its principles hold great promise for creationist studies, its inherent assumptions remain uniformitarian.

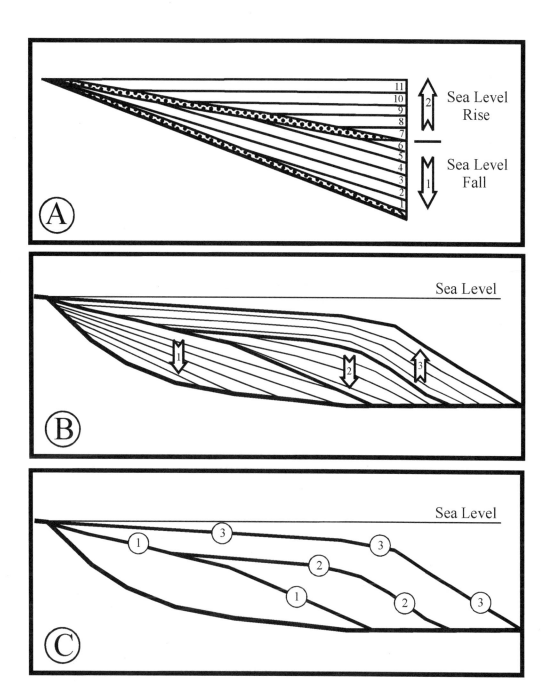

This concept of stratigraphy has been largely discarded due to geophysical work at many of the large sedimentary basins around the world. Box B represents new ideas from sequence stratigraphy. This conceptual approach emphasizes defining sedimentary units grouped into parasequence sets, sequences, and unconformity-bounded system tracts. Sea level changes affect the construction of these sedimentary packages. The arrows indicate sea level conditions during the deposition of that group of sediments and the numbering refers to the progression of development bounded by unconformities (the heavier line). Box C represents a modified sequence stratigraphic approach to Flood geology. Areas of greatest interest probably occur along unconformity boundaries, which imply changing geologic conditions during the course of the Flood. Creationists would tend to focus attention on the sedimentary changes marked by the unconformity boundaries. The numbering refers to the age progression of the unconformities. See text for further information.

Figure 1-8. Three different ways of understanding the development of a stratigraphic sequence. Boxes A and B emphasize uniformitarian envisioned changes in sea level position while box C focuses on Flood conditions. Box A represents an outdated layer cake model. The sedimentary layers are age-dated from the bottom (oldest) to the top (youngest). A sandstone layer marks the base and top of the sea level fall series and only occurs along the base of the sea level rise series (modified from Grabau 1960, Figure 151).

Young-earth creationists can use this conceptual approach, but must remain aware of its limitations within the biblical framework (Froede 1994a, 1998a; Klevberg 1999, 2000). Box C reflects a creationist adaptation of sequence stratigraphy. Our emphasis would be on the unconformity boundaries, which reflect changes in geologic energy instead of sea level changes over purportedly long periods of time. These boundaries might reflect differences in sediment source areas, floodwater conditions, and even tectonism. They would probably not be correlative outside of their depositional basin. This approach would place less emphasis on individual parasequence sets and sequences and more on systems tracts. Less value would be placed upon paleontological content or the lithology of the strata. Changes in organic materials and sediment would not be used to assign age, but would point to possible hydrologic and sorting conditions or possible source areas. Although this example is a delta, other flood settings would be interpreted using similar principles.

This emphasizes the distinction between our focus on the rock record and the uniformitarian time scale. Most of the sedimentary strata thought by uniformitarian geoscientists to have been deposited over hundreds of millions of years were in fact laid down in the Flood Event Timeframe (see Figure 1-4, Number 2). Rock units defined by uniformitarian scientists as an orderly march from the Precambrian to the Cenozoic, in reality, were deposited at the same time or even out of order. Every created kind[7] has existed on earth from the creation week, and we would not expect the rock record to show evolutionary order. Rather, the formation of most of the *rock record* would be the end product of Flood-derived erosion, transport, and deposition reflective of changes in hydraulic energy, tectonics, sediment type, and accommodation space (other factors apply but only these are listed). The arbitrary divisions within the uniformitarian geologic time scale, based on changes reflected by fossilized organic life or radioactive daughters, are meaningless within our understanding of earth history. As a result, it should be easy to understand why the uniformitarian geologic time scale, with its linear arrow of time derived in support of the purported evolution of life, cannot be welded to the biblical account of earth history (see further discussion in Froede and Reed 1999; Reed and Froede 2003; Reed and others 2006a, 2006b; Reed and Oard 2006).

A BIBLICAL APPROACH TO DEFINING EARTH HISTORY

The Bible provides only an outline of geologic history because it was not written as a geologic textbook. However, it is an excellent textbook of ancient history, the only one carrying God's stamp of truth. Thus, the sparse geologic-related information that it does provide is absolutely reliable, and several Bible-believing geoscientists have proposed geologic chronologies based on the biblical record.

In the mid-1990s, two biblical geologic time scales were proposed (Walker 1994; Froede 1995b). In 1996, several of us published a chart of geologic energy versus time based on the Genesis account (Reed and others 1996). Since these conceptual models follow the biblical account, they are a good starting point for geological investigations. All of these ideas focus on the actual rock record rather than trying to find accommodation with uniformitarian assumptions or methods.

THE WALKER TIME SCALE

In 1994, Dr. Tasman Walker, an Australian engineer and geologist, published what is certainly the most detailed Bible-based geological time scale to date (Figure 1-9). According to Walker (2005), the time scale is divided into four parts identified from the biblical record. The creation event lasted six days and the Flood event about one year. The 1,700-year

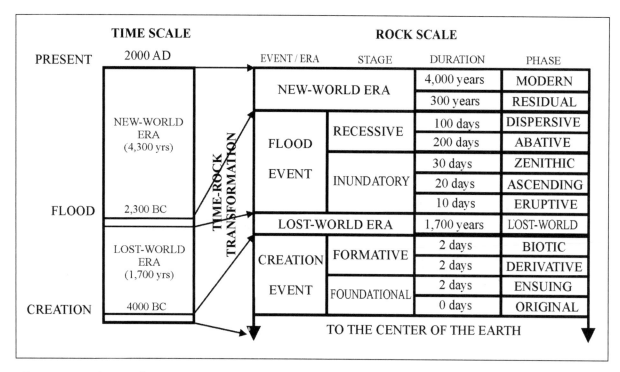

Figure 1-9. The Walker biblical geological time scale (1994) is composed of two parts, a rock- scale on the right and a time scale on the left. Most geologic activity occurred during the creation event and the Flood event. Although not explicit, the rock-scale also defines time intervals in light of changing geologic energy. This time scale is divided into great detail based on expected hydraulic conditions that occurred and are recorded in the rock record during the course of the Flood.

period between the creation event and the Flood event is called the Lost-World Era, while the 4,300-year-period from the Flood event to the present time is called the New-World Era.

The term "event" corresponds to a significant happening that occurred within a short period of time, whereas the term "era" is for a much longer period of time. These terms reflect the variation in geologic intensity for different times in the past because most geological activity happened during the short events, rather than the longer eras. The time duration of this time scale runs parallel with the events based on the biblical chronology developed by Ussher (1658).[8]

The rock-scale is correlated to the time scale via the time-rock transformation. Older rocks underlie the younger in the same manner in which they occur on earth. The lengths of the rock-scale units conceptually correspond to the quantity of rock material found on earth today and stand in marked contrast to the length of the units of the time scale.

This concept of time-rock correlation is fundamental to this biblical geologic time scale and reflects the non-uniform effect of historical events on the geology of earth. Emphasis is placed on the geologically significant processes and not time. The correlation between these two columns is indicated by arrows. Although the creation and Flood events occurred quickly and were of rather short duration, they were responsible for almost all the sedimentary rocks and a considerable volume of basement rocks present on earth today. The two long eras that make up virtually the entire time scale column did not contribute significantly to the development of the rock-scale column. Because these eras have such little impact on the rock-scale, the exact dates for the creation and the Flood, within reason, are not critical to the model.

Walker has successfully applied his geologic time scale to sites in New Zealand (Walker 2001) and Australia (Walker 1996a, 1996b). This time scale has also been used to define strata for several locations in the United States (Klevberg 2005; Klevberg and Oard 2005; Oard and others 2005; Spencer and Oard 2004).

THE FROEDE TIME SCALE

My own concept for a Bible-based geological time scale (Figure 1-6) was developed in 1993/1994 and published in 1995 by the Creation Research Society (Froede 1995b). Earth history is divided into five geologic time periods: 1) Creation Week Timeframe, 2) Antediluvian Timeframe, 3) Flood Event Timeframe, 4) post-Flood Timeframe, and 5) Present Age Timeframe. It is presumed that the post-Flood Timeframe would be *geologically* dominated by the post-Flood ice age. Therefore, the entire post-Flood interval is identified as the Ice Age Timeframe. The term "Timeframe" is used because it has no uniformitarian geologic connotations. This time scale is not as finely divided as Walker's because present knowledge is not sufficient to support such specificity. Several sites across the southern United States have been investigated and correlated to this time scale (Akridge 2000; Akridge and Froede 2005; Akridge and Williams 2001, 2005; Froede 1997d, 2005a; Froede and others 1998a, 1998b, 1998c; Froede and Williams 1999).

Several questions emerge when dividing earth's geologic history with the Bible. Some of these issues may be resolved through further study and some may never be known:

1. The first question involves the magnitude of the geological processes that occurred during the six days of the creation week. For example, the withdrawal of water from the land surface (on day 3) implies considerable geologic activity (e.g., erosion, transport, deposition, tectonism, and possibly even volcanism). However, if present laws of nature were not in effect, then the resulting earth materials would be created in place and only exhibit the appearance of having been developed by real geologic processes. Perhaps future investigation can resolve this question if Creation Week Timeframe sediments and strata can be identified in the rock record. However, the differences between strata formed by actual geologic activity and strata created *in situ* with the same features could prove to be unresolvable.

2. We can only speculate about geologic processes and paleoenvironmental settings during the Antediluvian Timeframe because we do not know precisely what the conditions were like during this interval of time. Many ideas have been put forth (e.g., no rain, no glaciers or ice sheets, no high mountains, one continental land mass, more uniform lower-energy geologic processes), but these are, at best, educated guesses. The eventual identification of one or more antediluvian environments and possibly *in situ* fossils might help in accurately determining the geologic setting and climatic conditions during this interval of earth history.

3. Did the "breaking of the fountains of the deep" have a terrestrial or extraterrestrial cause? Some individuals invoke the breaking of earth's crust by terrestrial forces (e.g., Austin and others 1994; Brown 2001; Horstemeyer and Baumgardner 2003), while others have suggested that the breakup might have been initiated by meteoric impact (e.g., Auldaney 1992, 1994; Faulkner 1999; Fischer 1994; Froede 2002a;

Froede and Brelsford 1998; Froede and DeYoung 1996; Parks 1990; Spencer 1994; Unfred 1984). The answer to this question has important connotations for understanding the likely condition of earth's crust, beginning with and extending throughout the Flood Event Timeframe.

4. The majority of the rock record was created by the global Flood and has yet to be specifically correlated to a biblical geologic time scale. Only a few areas have been investigated using this approach. A lot of work is waiting for anyone interested in undertaking this challenge. I believe that presently, the smallest interval of time that can be discerned from the rock record is at the "Division" level (Figure 1-6). Further research should result in the creation of additional smaller subdivisions of geologic time.

5. The geologic time interval identified as the Flood Event Timeframe extended longer than the year-long Flood documented in Genesis. The withdrawal rate of Flood water from each of the continents has yet to be determined. It is not likely that Flood water withdrew from every continent on earth at the same rate to expose all of them at the same time. There is geological evidence to support the idea that Flood water remained on portions of some of the continents well after the year-long event recorded in Scripture. Evidence in support of this proposal occurs as fossilized *in situ* invertebrate communities are found in life position along the southern end of the former North American epeiric seaway (Froede 1995a) and across various portions of the United States Gulf Coastal Plain (Froede 1997c). Additional evidence comes from exposed reef corals that are tens of feet above present-day sea

level in areas such as the Florida Keys (Froede 1999, 2006b). Many questions still remain regarding the duration and range of the multiple global sea level changes that would have occurred throughout the Ice Age Timeframe as a function of tectonism, isostasy, and polar ice sheet glacial expansion and contraction. These eustatic changes could also create problems in determining where Flood-created marine deposits terminate and where overlying marine strata age-dated to the Ice Age Timeframe might begin. A combination of geological and archaeological evidences could prove useful in defining the termination of the Ice Age Timeframe (see Rucker and Froede 1998).

6. Finally, only with the establishment of a somewhat stable modern climate and a general reduction/cessation of large-scale tectonism can we ascertain which deposits represent the Present Age Timeframe. During this time, sea level position would moderate with alpine glacial advances and retreats (see Karlén and others 1995) and measured differences would only deviate from the present eustatic level within tens of feet (several meters) (see Fairbridge 1961, 1976). Most continental volcanic eruptions would be subaerial. Resulting ash deposits would reflect wind patterns consistent with our modern weather patterns. Lava flows would follow the land surface that we observe today. The creeks, streams, and rivers initiated following the withdrawal of Flood water and developed within the varying atmospheric conditions during the Ice Age Timeframe would begin to reach equilibrium with the land surface. The world's coastlines would also begin to move toward equilibrium, as sea level would stabilize

within a general tidal range. For most locations, the proper determination of this stratigraphic boundary will probably occur near the top of the rock record due to the expected reduction in geologic energy and climatic stability for most settings. The resulting layers of Present Age Timeframe sediments and fossils should correspond to a more uniform environment similar to our modern geological settings.

THE REED, FROEDE, AND BENNETT GEOLOGIC ENERGY CURVE

In 1994/1995, I met several times with two colleagues to discuss the role that geologic energy played in biblical history. We quickly realized that, from a geologic perspective, the Flood interval would have experienced the greatest levels of geologic energy necessary for building the rock record through sedimentary, tectonic, thermal, and hydraulic processes (Figure 1-10). Our ideas were published in the *Creation Research Society Quarterly* (Reed and others 1996). The energy curve is less specific in its divisions of geologic time when compared to the two earlier proposals, but it remains a very important tool for understanding the expected magnitude of geologic forces in operation over the course of biblical history. It has been applied to the geologic history of the North American Midcontinent Rift (Reed 2000), as well as other locations (Reed 2001, 2002, 2004). This curve provides a conceptual means of translating global geological activity to the rock record.

CHOOSING A BIBLICAL GEOLOGIC TIME SCALE

The Walker and Froede geologic time scales can be used to define the rock record in accordance with Scripture. Other geological models are possible and beneficial as long as they are constrained by the literal biblical record. Conceptual ideas (i.e., models) are important tools for earth history research. However, they must be validated by field results. Creation geoscientists must test their ideas and report their findings to support their theories. This work must begin at the outcrop and proceed toward understanding the stratigraphy and sedimentology of the site, area, or region. Every attempt should be made to examine the entire stratigraphic column (surface outcrops, subsurface cores, and well logs) within an area of investigation. This is necessary to accurately determine the physical properties of the rocks in question. This knowledge can then help in determining the creationist time frame in which they originally formed. Some areas may contain a rock record that spans one or more biblical geologic time frames. The investigator should also pursue related literature resources, both secular and creationist. With this detailed information, the researcher must then discern between the physical rock record and uniformitarian interpretation. All that remains is the interpretation of the rock record within the biblical framework. This is how the biblical outline of earth history should be developed.

CONCLUSIONS

The world view of naturalism and its component of uniformitarianism have given us a distorted view of history encapsulated by the uniformitarian geologic time scale: a construct that has no place within the biblical account of earth history (Froede 1997a; Reed 2001; Reed and Froede 1997, 2003; Reed and others 2006b). We do *not* need to waste further time and effort attempting to unify these mutually exclusive concepts. This planet is six to ten thousand years old, not 4.55 billion. All life was created in six days, and not over the course of billions of years.

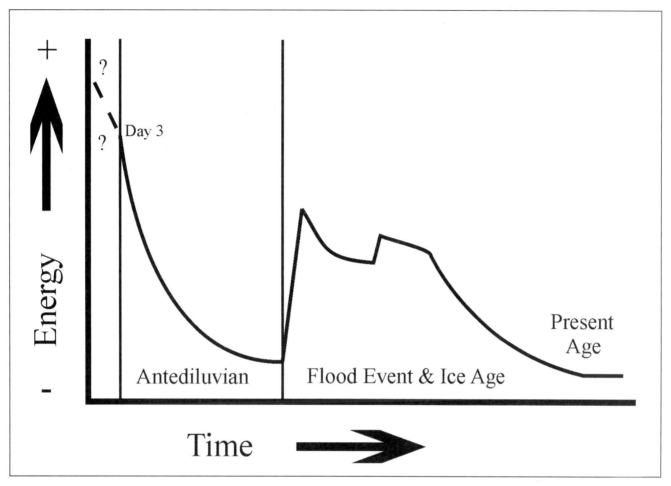

Figure 1-10. Another tool for investigating Flood strata is a geologic energy curve (Reed and others 1996). It can also be used to help define geologic conditions expected during the course of earth history, and corresponding changes in energy levels (modified from Reed and others 1996).

Most of the rock record was deposited in a year-long Flood, and not over billions of years. Any effort to join these two different accounts of earth history will only come from sacrificing one world view for the other.

Our approach to defining the geologic time scale along biblical lines would not recognize the time-rock gaps noted by uniformitarian scientists. Our interpretation of the stratigraphic record for any particular area would expect it to be relatively complete unless erosional features suggested otherwise. Any changes in sedimentary composition and content in the vertical stacking of the rock layers might easily reflect hydraulic

conditions during transport or possibly changes in the sediment source areas, rather than slow accumulations over eons. Additionally, our historical interpretation of the rock record would be drawn from the framework provided by Scripture. We have no common ground with either naturalism or uniformitarianism.

Young-earth creationists should start with the scriptural account and apply it to the rock record by focusing on geologic energy levels of widely varying magnitudes and the effect that this has had on rocks, sediment, and fossils.[9] Interpreting the rock record within any one of the Bible-based time scales reviewed in this chapter should enable us to better define and understand earth's geological history. This new approach will provide the creationist geoscientist the freedom to conduct research away from the confines of the uniformitarian geologic time scale and eliminate the confusion that occurs when the two world views are mixed together. It is time to get started in defining the rock record within the biblical framework of earth history.

Endnotes

1. Naturalism is also referred to as materialism, secularism, secular humanism, and evolution (see Reed 2001).

2. While identified as "catastrophists," many of these individuals were compromising biblical truth to try to keep pace with the new science, abandoning the biblical chronology and the uniqueness of Noah's flood.

3. The *law of superposition* states that younger strata will be found on top of older strata unless disrupted by later events. This geologic term along with many others is defined in the glossary.

4. Three different Flood/post-Flood boundaries have been proposed within the uniformitarian geologic time scale (Figure 1-4, Numbers 1A, 1B, and 1C). In order for any one of them to succeed as a definitive boundary, they must correlate between the uniformitarian column and biblical history at every appropriate uniformitarian boundary location on earth. All of them fail in their application to strata filling the northern Gulf of Mexico basin (a test case). Therefore, they should all be rejected.

The uniformitarian column has no place in the scriptural account of earth history. Rather, an alternative approach is proposed (Figure 1-4, Number 2) based on our expectations within the Flood framework of earth history. We should abandon the linear arrow of uniformitarian time and redefine the physical rock record consistent with the biblical narrative.

5. Earth is reportedly 4.55 billion years old based on the age-dating of meteoric materials which are assumed to be of the same age as the earth. However, the oldest rocks on earth have been age-dated to approximately 3.8 billion years.

6. Emphasis has moved away from many of the old assumptions and laws of stratigraphy toward understanding the depositional setting in which these sedimentary units build parasequence sets, sequences, and eventually system tracts (see Emery and Myers 1996; Catuneanu 2006). The individual system tracts in this sequence (with a stable sea level position) generally conform to a sigmoidal curve (i.e., a clinoform).

7. The Genesis "kinds" are not the same as Linnaean species. After the Flood, new "species" might have appeared as the basic kinds migrated outward to fill the post-Flood earth.

8. Archbishop James Ussher is widely ridiculed for his biblical chronology, yet it is one of the greatest works of scholarship ever published.

9. What is proposed here is not new. Rather, this conceptual framework follows what others such as Gish (1995), Morris (1985), Whitcomb (1988), Whitcomb and Morris (1961), and Woodmorappe (1993) have already recognized. These gentlemen have stated that fossil-containing strata and radiometric dating, as defined within the framework of the uniformitarian geologic time scale, do not define *time* from a biblical perspective.

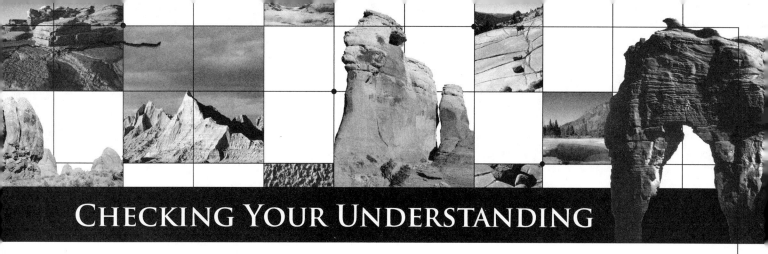

CHECKING YOUR UNDERSTANDING

1. Read Genesis, chapter one.

   A. What days within the creation week suggest geological activity?

   B. How does this account of earth differ from the uniformitarian account?

   C. Is there a way to reconcile the two accounts, working from Genesis, chapter one?

2. If we cannot unify the biblical account with naturalism, then which version should we trust? Why?

3. Explain the differences between a world view, history, and science? How does one affect the other?

4. How do we know if our world view is consistent with scientific principles? Does it have to be?

5. What is the difference between the physical rock record and the uniformitarian geologic time scale?

6. Can we interpret the actual rock record outside of the framework of the uniformitarian geologic time scale?

7. How can we age-date earth's rocks, sediments, and fossils from a biblical perspective?

CHAPTER 2 — *Uniformitarian Envisioned Paleoenvironments Defined in Biblical History*

INTRODUCTION

Uniformitarian scientists contend that geologic time can be defined and divided using rocks, sediments, and fossils. Radiometric dating and biological evolution provide the necessary framework from which their patchwork of strata can be joined to their conceptual geologic time scale (see Figure 1-1). The passage of time is purportedly documented by changes in sediments and fossils moving both laterally and vertically through successive sedimentary layers. Environments that we see today — swamps, beaches, reefs, deserts, etc. — existed in a slowly evolving montage over millions of years, to be preserved in the rocks as they were gradually buried and replaced by other environments. Even though the rocks only record a small fraction of earth's supposed history, uniformitarian scientists contend that their reconstruction is accurate enough to see evolution in action.

Young-earth creationists present a different geologic history, one based on the eyewitness testimony found in the Bible (see Figure 1-6). We believe that earth was created and filled with life in the first six days of the Creation Week Timeframe. That created biosphere continued with little change throughout the Antediluvian Timeframe, but rapid and dramatic changes occurred during the Flood. It was an event of such cataclysmic geologic energy that it completely reshaped earth's surface. The Flood buried or eroded the many and varied pre-Flood environments. Existing materials (inorganic and organic) were transported and deposited across broad areas. New geologic materials were added by volcanic processes, chemical precipitation, and meteoric impacts.

Given the magnitude of the event, it is only logical to conclude that the majority of the rock record is a result of the vast amount of geologic energy expended during the Flood Event Timeframe.

Since the majority of the earth's rock layers were rapidly deposited during the Flood, it stands to reason that none of the uniformitarian envisioned "paleoenvironments" ever existed. This perspective marks a profound point of departure for Flood geologists as we seek to define earth's geological history within the context of Scripture.

THE UNIFORMITARIAN VERSION OF EARTH HISTORY

Although uniformitarian history is completely conceptual, it is widely accepted as fact and we must understand it in order to identify its flaws. As noted, the uniformitarian investigation of earth's past involves the reconstruction of perceived historical environments derived from the rock record. To frame their time scale, uniformitarian geoscientists look to lithology, paleontology, radiometric dating, and unconformities in the rock record (Figure 2-1). Lithologic similarity between sediments allows the assumption that these materials were all being deposited across the earth at the same time. For example, the Cretaceous Period is equated to chalk or carbonate sediments while "red beds" are common to the Permian Period and thick halite deposits are typically linked to the Jurassic. Likewise, changes in the types of fossilized organisms can mark one or more boundaries in the uniformitarian time scale. For

Figure 2-1. The northern wall of the Grand Canyon. Uniformitarian scientists think that each layer represents a distinct time in earth's distant past. An alternative explanation is that the strata were derived from various antediluvian sources and deposited during the Flood (see Austin 1994).

Figure 2-2. Uniformitarian diorama of an early Cambrian setting based on the fossils found in the Burgess Shale from a quarry in Field, Canada. This stratigraphic setting marks the "Cambrian Explosion," an important event to evolutionists in establishing the supposed beginning of all life forms on earth (Morris 1998). Gould (1989) proposed that the preservation of this unique setting resulted from turbidity currents that transported these delicate marine creatures along with their fine-grained matrix into deep waters where burial ensured preservation. From a biblical perspective, we could assign the formation of these deposits to the lower division of the Flood Event Timeframe. This former antediluvian marine setting was transported a short distance, rapidly buried, and preserved until tectonics during the upper division of the Flood Event Timeframe served to uplift and expose these lithified shales in the Canadian Rockies. It should be noted that the Burgess Shale and associated fossil assemblage may not have actually existed as naturalists envision them because the sedimentary materials and fossilized life forms may have been derived from more than one paleoenvironment and mixed together during deposition. Great care must be taken in assuming the naturalists' paleosetting and interpretations are appropriate or correct. Height of the exhibit is approximately 4 feet (1.2 m). From the National Museum of Natural History, Smithsonian Institution, Washington, D.C.

example, the end of the age of dinosaurs marks the end of both the Cretaceous Period and the Mesozoic Era. The end of the trilobites (a marine arthropod) is used to mark the end of the Permian Period and the Paleozoic Era. All fossil-based time markers support evolutionary assumptions. Unconformities can also be used to define either minor or major time boundaries. These features are said to indicate time gaps. For example, the Mesozoic-Cenozoic boundary in the United States Gulf Coastal Plain is identified by an erosional unconformity. The new ideas in sequence stratigraphy use unconformities to provide time boundaries both above and below packages of sediment (i.e., systems tracts) rather than emphasizing the individual layers of strata. Where available, radiometric dates are believed to provide absolute time markers for their time scale.

Uniformitarian geoscientists seek to construct earth history consistent with their geologic time scale and they do this by examining the rock record and imagining the varied ancient environments. This forensic reconstruction between sediments and fossils found within a given historical formation includes a comparison with modern geologic analogs. Hence, present-day geological settings and processes are typically extrapolated back into the past. An enormous amount of time, money, and effort has been expended in this type of research, which has generated libraries of literature supposedly documenting the passing of billions of years and supporting the *story* of evolution. The same story is told in virtually all natural history museums[1] and conveyed through a multitude of nature documentaries on television (Figure 2-2). All of the information is crafted to present a confidence in *history* as though the former plants, animals, and their ancient environments can now be known just as surely as we know that objects fall to the ground by the attraction of gravity.

UNIFORMITARIAN PALEOENVIRONMENTAL CONSTRUCTION

The uniformitarian paleoenvironmental presentation is based on lithologic (sediment characteristics) and paleontologic (fossils) information (Figure 2-3). To reconstruct any environment from the rock record, geologists begin with an examination of the geologic materials (e.g., sand, silt, clay, and carbonates) that compose the layers of sediment. At the same time, they identify features and structures formed by the sedimentary materials, such as cross-bedding, imbrication, load features, or lateral pinch-outs. This work is valid because certain styles of sedimentation can be produced by varying hydraulic conditions. However, it is a leap beyond empirical science to move from saying that a given sand was deposited in a moving current to saying that it was deposited in a river flowing 200,000,000 years ago. Uniformitarian scientists get around this difficulty by comparing characteristics of the rocks to observations of those that were developed in modern environments (Allen 1982; Harms and others 1975, 1982; Middleton 1965; Rubin 1987; Selley 1988). However, there is a leap in logic, too. It is not valid to take *one* possible scenario and then present it as the *only* possible conclusion. Yet all too often this is exactly what happens.

The identification of fossils, both macro- and micro-scale organisms, in the sediments is typically the next step in the analysis of the rock record (Figure 2-4). From biological information, scientists will estimate the diversity of plants and animals, their probable communities, differences among nutrient levels, water depth, salinity, clarity, and whether it was underwater (subaqueous) or on land (subaerial). In addition to sediments and fossils, geologists also examine any trace fossils preserved in the sediment (Figure 2-5). These organically derived features, such as tracks, trails, and burrows, can be used to determine probable environmental conditions based on animal behavior (Bromley 1990; Crimes and Harper 1970, 1977; Curran 1985; Frey 1975). For example, the variation in the traces found along a rock outcrop could indicate changing environmental conditions. Trace fossils are useful in providing information about a paleo-setting that would not be readily apparent from the rocks alone. The combination of trace fossils, plant fossils, and animal fossils are then used by uniformitarian scientists to present a paleosetting within naturalism (e.g., Ager 1963; Braunstein 1973; Curran 1985; Dodd and Stanton 1990; Frey 1975; Hallam 1981; Imbrie and Newell 1964; McKerrow 1978; Schäfer 1972).

Figure 2-3. This outcrop of carbonate rock contains an assortment of fossils assigned by their evolutionary status to the Middle Devonian Period (Conkin and others 1998). Using the many and varied fossils found at this outcrop, naturalists have recreated a purported inland tropical sea. They contend that the accumulation of carbonate muds buried succeeding environments until eventually everything was buried by clay-rich carbonate muds. However, nothing about the fossils or associated carbonate mud matrix suggests *in situ* development or the passage of extensive periods of time. Rather, it would be more reasonable to interpret these layers as having been derived from an antediluvian environment, transported some distance, and deposited in a depression that was rapidly filled and covered, thereby ensuring preservation. The eventual removal of the overburden began with retreating Flood water and continued in association with the establishment of the ancestral Ohio River. During the Ice Age Timeframe, large volumes of water derived from heavy rain and glacial melt eroded the river banks and eventually exposed these now-lithified, fossil-rich carbonate layers. The location of this outcrop is along the Ohio River at the Falls of the Ohio State Park, Clarksville, Indiana. Scale in six-inch (15-cm) divisions.

The final step in any paleoenvironmental reconstruction is the comparison of the imagined setting to a modern one. This need for comparison between ancient and modern geologic environments has resulted in the extensive investigation of modern depositional settings and their geologic processes (e.g., Braunstein 1974; Cant and Hein 1987; Curtis 1978; Reading 1996; Rigby and Hamblin 1972; Scholle and Spearing 1982; Scholle and others 1983; Walker and James 1992; Wilson 1975). However, remember that the ancient environment that is interpreted from the rock record only exists in the mind of the geoscientist who imagined it. There can be other possible interpretations depending upon the individual's geologic perspective or world view (for examples, see Akridge and Froede 2000; Froede and Akridge 2003; Froede and Cowart 1996; Froede 2002).

Despite the seeming straightforwardness of this course of study, problems exist. The detailed study of many purported paleoenvironments reveals no suitable modern counterpart. For example, geoscientists are well aware that using modern coral reef environments (Figure 2-6) to characterize the geologic past is a bad analogy for ancient carbonate sedimentation (Ager 1993a, 1993b; Braithwaite 1973; Dunham 1970; Froede 2006b; Nevins 1972; Roth 1995; Whitmore 2007; Woodmorappe 1980). Not having a modern carbonate setting comparable to the postulated ancient environment then forces the interpretation along modern lines. This is how many uniformitarian scientists persist in evaluating carbonate environments (e.g., Asquith 1979; Cys and Mazzullo 1978; Friedman 1969; Scholle and others 1983; Wilson 1975).

A Young-Earth Flood Framework

Naturalists have been working for almost 200 years to redefine earth history apart from the

Figure 2-4. Numerous dinosaur bones are exposed in this upturned bed at Dinosaur National Monument, Utah. Uniformitarian scientists think that the dinosaurs drowned while crossing a flooded river (West and Chure 1994). It is more likely that this sediment was deposited in the lower division of the Flood Event Timeframe, with the death, transport, and burial of the dinosaurs. This would explain their burial below any erosional scour level, as would be expected if the river story were true. Note person in lower left for scale.

Figure 2-5. Trace fossils from a sandstone layer near Lake Champlain, New York (Smith 1994). Trace fossils like this one are typically created by a creature passing across or through soft sediment substrate and that disturbance is preserved. Traces formed in this manner reflect animal behavior and have a place in helping us interpret and understand the Flood-formed rock record (Cowart and Froede 1994; Froede and Cowart 1996). An unknown animal that moved across a submerged sandy sea floor created these traces (Sullivan and Voss 1991). Water movement created the ripple marks. Creationists would interpret this sandstone layer as having formed during the Flood. This example is at the National Museum of Natural History, Smithsonian Institution, Washington, D.C. Scale in inches and centimeters.

biblical record. What can we expect in constructing a geologic history from the biblical perspective? Can we use any of the uniformitarian data or do we have to throw everything out and start anew? How do we begin and where should we start? The simple answer is that we start by setting firm boundaries within biblical truth.

Next, we proceed to the actual rock record and interpret the geologic materials within the context of scriptural history (Figure 1-6) (see Froede 1995b; Reed and others 2006; Walker 1994). We will need

to examine existing sources of information and separate the physical data from any uniformitarian interpretation. Often this is more difficult than imagined because layers of uniformitarian assumptions are closely intermingled with the data, sometimes very subtly. In many instances, the amount of data extracted may be very small. But it is essential to extract the physical from the metaphysical.

For example, a coral reef exposed at the quarry on Windley Key (Figure 2-7) is composed of the same types of coral species that occur offshore in

Figure 2-6. An aerial view of the Western Sambo coral reef in the southwestern Florida Keys. The dive boat to the right is approximately 30 feet long. The spur and groove coral reef structure (vertical bands of light and dark in the center of the picture) is clearly visible and is the preferred end state of a healthy stand of Elkhorn coral (*Acropora palmata*). Other modern corals do not form this type of coral reef structure. Uniformitarian scientists contend that this same spur and groove structure was formed by corals now extinct. As in many cases, the data can be interpreted in several ways and do not verify any particular history (see Froede 2006b).

the modern reef. Based on radiometric dating, the coral found within the quarry is 95,000 years old (Pasley 1972). It is believed to have developed during the Pleistocene when sea level was higher than it is today. That is the uniformitarian story. But from a biblical perspective, we would counter that the former higher sea level position was the result of Flood water slowly receding from this portion of the North American continent (Froede 1999). The fact that the fossilized coral species are the same as the modern reef would support our contention that the

ancient reef is recently formed. We reject the radiometric age assigned to the coral because its assumptions and methods are flawed (Austin 1994; Vardiman and others 2005; Woodmorappe 1999). While it is possible to interpret the elevated coral reef found at Windley Key Quarry to a higher sea level position during the Ice Age Timeframe, I believe it is more reasonable to look to conditions expected at or near the end of the Flood, when geologic energy was decreasing and there was sufficient time and opportunity for coral reef development (Froede 1999,

Figure 2-7. A coral head exposed in the quarry on Windley Key, located in the upper Florida Keys. The gap in the middle of the coral was created by former quarrying operations. This brain coral (*Diploria* sp.) is also found in the modern coral reef tract (Smith 1971). Naturalists contend that this coral head and associated reef formed 95,000 years ago when sea level was high enough to accommodate coral growth. Creationists would propose that this coral reef developed while Flood water was still slowly receding from this portion of the North American continent. Missing from the Florida Keys coral reef rock record is a sufficient thickness of coral to defend the purportedly extended periods of uniformitarian time cited for the growth and development of the original Pleistocene age reef (Froede 1999, 2006b). Scale in six-inch (15-cm) divisions.

2006c). The total thickness of coral reef rock in the Florida Keys is consistent with its formation in just a few hundred years.

Another consequence of working within biblical boundaries (Figure 1-6) is that the rocks considered by uniformitarian scientists to be *prehistoric* marine and terrestrial paleoenvironments were largely derived from the remains of the former pre-Flood world. The Flood redistributed antediluvian sediments and organic materials by means of geologic forces beyond our comprehension. The rock units that we see today were the result of this global event (see Woodmorappe 1983), and not as a series of paleoenvironmental changes happening over long eras.

During the Flood, changes in geologic energy (Figure 1-10) would have restructured earth's surface. Some areas were uplifted and eroded while other locations experienced subsidence and deposition. Wide variations in the local and regional levels of geologic energy during the course of the Flood would make the correlation of sediments, fossils, or unconformity boundaries virtually impossible on a global scale. It is highly unlikely that a single event would have occurred during the Flood that would span the entire planet and therefore serve as a chronostratigraphic marker. Perhaps a global event marker can be identified when extended research supplies an expanded database, but that work remains to be conducted. So another consequence of biblical geology is the need to concentrate on interpreting specific areas first, and then speculate about global conditions. That alone will exclude many of the methods — lithostratigraphy, biostratigraphy, allostratigraphy, etc. — that uniformitarian geologists have used to build their own geologic time scale.

With the decrease in geologic energy in the latter stages of the Flood (upper Flood Event division), erosion would have decreased and various marine creatures would have reestablished themselves on the still-submerged portions of the continents. Probably the first organisms to attempt to establish themselves in this highly turbid environment would have been the trace makers (Cowart and Froede 1994). Then other marine creatures could have colonized as the sea water became less turbid. These marine communities would have then retreated with the receding Flood water. Fixed and submerged communities, unable to move basinward with the withdrawing marine water, were buried by sediments derived from the exposed continents. For example, marine communities that previously existed within the North American epeiric seaway were eventually

Figure 2-8. An outcrop of the Demopolis/Selma Chalk in northeastern Mississippi. Prehistoric oyster shells (*Exogyra* sp., now extinct) are found in their original growth position. This locale contains a large number of oyster shells that developed in the upper division of the Flood Event Timeframe. This community of invertebrates was killed and later buried under a thin sedimentary cover by retreating Flood water. Similar sites from across the Gulf Coastal Plain support the concept that Flood water slowly withdrew from this area. Scale in inches and centimeters.

destroyed by the additional deposition of sediments along with the withdrawal of Flood water (Figure 2-8) (Froede 1995a).

However, not all marine communities were adversely affected by slowly retreating Flood water. Some of the saltwater environments that originated during the latter stages of the Flood have survived into our present day. For example, carbonate environments far removed from active areas of clastic sedimentation gave coral reef builders the opportunity to thrive to the present in areas like the Florida Keys, the Bahama Islands, and Australia's Great Barrier Reef. Hence, some marine environments survived and even thrived, depending on their location as modern sea level equilibrated.

CONCLUSIONS

The uniformitarian concept of deep time is populated by a slow, continual succession of changing paleoenvironments. However, it is impossible to reconcile this picture of the past with that framed by the Bible. The uniformitarian perspective is merely an interpretation into which data are forced to conform. As we noted in the last chapter, the time scale is a template, not a summary.

A biblically devised time scale divides the rock record into time intervals consistent with anticipated changes in geologic energy. The formation of the largest portion of the rock record was caused by the Flood. Therefore, changes in rocks, sediments, and fossils for any given section of the rock record do not reflect any former paleoenvironments — with the possible exception of very rare preserved antediluvian settings. Rather, the rock record is a summary of changes in the sources of sedimentary material and various life forms, as they were affected by widespread variations of geologic energy during the Flood. The scarcity of fossils in any particular section could reflect their absence from the original source area or their lack of preservation following deposition. The vertical variability in sedimentary layers could reflect differences in source areas or hydraulic sorting during transport. These often-subtle changes in the rock record can tell us much about true geologic history if we will only carefully examine them in the light of the Flood.

There is no evidence from the rock record that forces Christians to concede earth history to the advocates of naturalism. Slowly evolving paleoenvironments are a consequence of that world view, not the rocks themselves. Therefore, we should embrace empirical study of the rocks and embark on a new course of discovery, one guided by Scripture. Now we need to get out into the field and begin the work.

Endnotes

1. Happy exceptions are the ICR museum in southern California and the AIG museum near Cincinnati, Ohio.

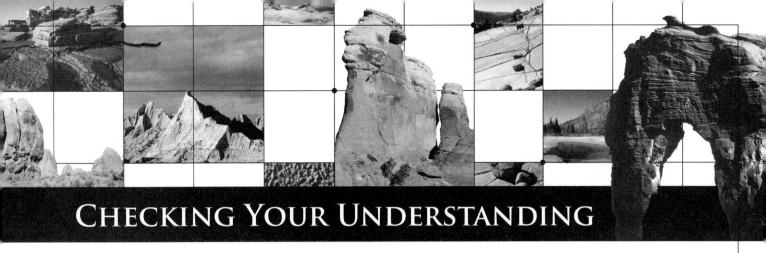

CHECKING YOUR UNDERSTANDING

1. The reconstruction of earth history by uniformitarians is captured by what icon?

2. How does the uniformitarian geologic time scale relate to evolution? Is there another way of discovering earth's history? How does the Bible portray the establishment of life on earth?

3. What information can sediments, sedimentary features, and fossilized life forms tell us about earth history? How do world views affect their use in historical reconstructions?

4. Can we reconcile slowly changing paleoenvironments occurring over millions of years with the biblical account of earth history? Why not?

5. What would we expect to see from the rock record if the biblical account of a global Flood is true? Is there a way that we can apply scientific methods to test this world view? What might be some examples?

6. Is there anything in the rock record that forces us away from the biblical account and requires that we accept and defend the uniformitarian view of earth history?

7. Can we use any of the existing uniformitarian geological work as we seek to define earth history consistent with the scriptural account? What should be accepted or rejected?

CHAPTER 3

Defining Tempestites in Biblical History

INTRODUCTION

Uniformitarian and creationist geologists agree that the rock record contains sedimentary deposits that record past storm activities. Uniformitarian scientists have identified many storm deposits, or tempestites, throughout their geologic time scale. Of course, we are told that these deposits represent small-scale, local events. Creationists must view them differently. In a sense, the entire Flood could be considered a global storm with all of its resulting rocks and fossils then labeled as tempestites. But this would be unproductive and so it is recommended that tempestites be defined to require deposition associated directly with atmospheric disturbances.

Much of the rock record formed during the high-energy conditions of the Flood (Froede 1995b; Reed and others 1996; Walker 1994). As the Flood waned, the geologic energy responsible for the vast thickness of sediments was reduced in both intensity and geographic extent. Continents were uplifted and the ocean basins were deepened, providing gravitational assistance to drain Flood water from the continents. While questions remain regarding the rate of Floodwater withdrawal from many of the continents, there is fossil evidence that marine life began to establish itself in some of the epeiric seas.

Flood water that continued to cover low-lying portions of some of the continents would have been stirred by passing storms, which were generated during climatic adjustments from the close of the Flood through the Ice Age Timeframe. Developing marine communities in these shallow waters would have been disturbed by each passing storm. Larger

Figure 3-1. A sand dune ridge scarp located on Dauphin Island, Alabama, showing the fossil-rich storm layer in cross-section. Scale in six-inch (15-cm) divisions.

storms, such as hurricanes, would scour large volumes of sediment and invertebrate shells from the sea floor. This material would have been reworked and then deposited across a broad area. We can see the results of these events in the fossiliferous tempestites found in coastal plain sedimentary deposits in the rock record.

There are many storm layers (sedimentary and fossiliferous) awaiting identification in the rock record. In some instances, these deposits have been misidentified by uniformitarian scientists as deposits formed in low-energy settings. If we are aware of the likelihood of these deposits and of their characteristics, then we can properly identify and describe them. Following this, we can then place them within the biblical geologic time scale.

STORM DEPOSITS ARE RECOGNIZED BY UNIFORMITARIAN SCIENTISTS

Many uniformitarian geologists have described modern storm deposits in an effort to recognize these types of sediments within their geologic time scale.[1] In the process of doing so, they have come to see the importance of storm energy as an agent of both erosion and deposition.[2] A single passing storm can deposit multiple layers of stratified sediments that could easily be misunderstood as separate and distinct paleoecological and paleoenvironmental settings existing over expanses of time (e.g., Boyajian and Thayer 1995; Westrop 1986).

Modern storm deposits are typically thin units that occur within a generally localized area. They form due to regional atmospheric disturbances that stir water in coastal zones. Young-earth creationists concur with the modern mechanism and resulting deposits created from localized storm systems. However, the biblical geologic framework of earth history would also predict larger-scale storm deposits. Tempestites in the rock record could have been derived from any number of atmospheric disturbances such as experienced today in the form of hurricanes and cyclones. It is also probable that multiple tempestites could have developed both vertically and laterally from the force of a single massive storm (i.e., hypercane). Several examples will show how storm deposits can be interpreted within the biblical geologic framework.

A RECENT STORM DEPOSIT ON DAUPHIN ISLAND, ALABAMA

Dauphin Island, a 14-mile-long barrier island located approximately five miles offshore from southwestern Alabama, became segmented during the course of Hurricane Katrina in 2005. As a fragile barrier island in the northern Gulf of Mexico, it experiences varying levels of coastal erosion from passing storms or cold fronts. In 1994, beach erosion along the eastern seaward portion of the island created a small cliff face along a foredune. The exposure revealed stratified sand along with a layer of shell debris in a silty-sand matrix (Figure 3-1). The shells contained within this layer did not show a

Figure 3-2. A close-up of the storm layer on Dauphin Island revealing the jumbled nature of the shells within the silty-sand matrix. No specific orientation of these shells was noted, suggesting deposition during a single wave surge rather than a sustained current. Scale in centimeters and inches.

Figure 3-3. A portion of the Tuscahoma clay exposed along Hurricane Creek, Alabama. A layer of shell debris is observed between layers of gray clay. It is likely that the bounding gray clay layers are also a part of the tempestite. Scale in six-inch (15-cm) divisions.

preferential orientation,[3] nor did they exhibit graded bedding (Figure 3-2).

It is likely that one or more large storm waves surged landward during the course of Hurricane Frederic (September 22, 1979), carrying shells and sediment across the top of the preexisting dune field (Froede 2006d). This surge created a storm deposit that was 6 to 8 inches thick, and approximately 5 feet (1.5 m) above today's high tide level. It measured approximately 200 feet (61 m) wide by 50 feet (15 m) deep along the shore-facing cliff scarp.

The organic materials within the tempestite primarily consist of oyster shell (*Crassostrea virginica*) pieces with a few (<1 percent) clam and snail shells. These materials were probably derived from oyster reefs located to the north of the island in the Mississippi Sound, adjacent to Mobile Bay. Tidal forces coupled with occasional eastward directed storm water flow transported the shell materials out of Mobile Bay and onto the Mobile Bay ebb-tidal delta. During the course of Hurricane Frederic, the shell debris and silty sand were eroded and transported northwestward from the ebb-tidal delta. Storm waves eventually washed the materials ashore forming this tempestite.

After the storm, the shell layer was buried with sand derived from natural and man-made (beach renourishment) sources. The eventual landward migration of the shoreline, in association with a period

Figure 3-4. A close-up of the shell event layer exposed along the banks of Hurricane Creek, Alabama. The shells exhibit normal grading (i.e., largest shells on bottom and smallest on top) suggesting deposition in an active current of water. Scale in inches and centimeters.

of rapid beach erosion for this portion of the island (Douglass 1994; Froede 1995c, 1997b; Sanchez and Douglass 1994), exposed the storm layer at the foredune cliff scarp. Subsequent hurricanes impacting the island since Hurricane Frederic removed more of the foredune ridge (Froede 2005b, 2006e). On August 29, 2005, Hurricane Katrina completely overwashed this portion of Dauphin Island and stripped this tempestite from the rock record. This illustrates the challenge of understanding any high-energy event: it can both erode and deposit sediments, and because of erosion, the final product may show very little of all that actually occurred.

An Ancient Storm Deposit along Hurricane Creek, Alabama

Having observed what modern hurricanes can do, let us move to an example that has been preserved in the rock record. This tempestite is located along Hurricane Creek in southeastern Alabama (Figure 3-3), approximately 100 miles north of the Gulf of Mexico (Hastings and Toulmin 1963; Toulmin 1977). Stratigraphically, the deposit occurs within the Tuscahoma Sand. According to Hastings and Toulmin (p. 17), this fossil-rich exposure is:

. . . gray firm silty fine-grained sand and gray thin-bedded silty clay or shale. A discontinuous irregular fossiliferous layer consisting largely of more or less worn and abraided [sic] shells and phosphorite pebbles indicate current-type deposition in a near-shore area. Some shells are little worn and must have been transported a short distance. The fossils are similar to those in the Bells Landing Marl Member near the middle of the Tuscahoma Sand in exposures on the Alabama River. The most common and conspicuous fossils are large *Ostrea compressirostra* (i.e., *Ostrea sinuosa* Rogers and Rogers), *Venericardia aposmithii*, *Turritella postmortoni* (oyster, clam, and snail shells, respectively), and the colonial coral *Haimesiastraea conferta* (parenthesis mine).

Like the Dauphin Island example, the high concentration of shells in this layer is an indication of storm deposition (Figure 3-4). The normal grading exhibited by the shells, along with what appears to be imbrication for some of the large oyster shells (i.e., *Ostrea sinuosa*), suggests flow from the southwest. A powerful storm scoured these invertebrates from nearshore sediments. Oblong and rounded clay clasts (clay is very difficult to erode) included in the shell deposit indicate significant storm energy. This fossiliferous tempestite was created when Flood water still covered this part of southeastern Alabama. The size and extent of the deposit suggests a storm as large as a hurricane, or perhaps even larger, created this shell-rich layer.

HYPERCANES AND THE ROCK RECORD

Recently, atmospheric scientists have suggested the existence of hypercanes — super hurricanes — that occurred in the past. They would have formed when unusual heating of both the atmosphere and oceans followed large meteoritic bombardments or underwater volcanic eruptions (Emanuel and others 1995; Emanuel 2003). The idea fits well into biblical history (Vardiman 2003; Woodmorappe 1998). A combination of meteoritic impact and volcanism during the Flood could have created the heat necessary to warm both the oceans and atmosphere. Hypercanes would be expected during the Flood Event Timeframe and likely continued to occur through the Ice Age Timeframe.

The depth of Flood water on the continent at the time of a hypercane's passing would have been an important limiting factor in the storm's ability to erode unconsolidated materials from the sea floor. Tempestites formed from such a large-scale event could potentially be both widespread and massive. Geoscientists have only begun to identify these super storm deposits in the rock record. What follows are two examples where evidence of hypercane deposits exists in the rock record. The dimensions of these deposits reflect a much larger-scale storm than would occur under present-day atmospheric conditions.

REGIONAL FOSSILIFEROUS STORM DEPOSITS ACROSS ALABAMA

The previously discussed tempestite exposed along Hurricane Creek contains shells considered to be from the late Paleocene. In reality, these faunae were probably an epeiric sea shelf community that developed late in the Flood. Retreating Flood water in this part of southeastern Alabama created ideal conditions for the development of this community of organisms. We know from the Hurricane Creek rock record that a large-scale storm killed, transported, and eventually buried many invertebrates. More interesting is the presence of similar fossiliferous deposits across a wide area. At the time of the Hurricane Creek event, other communities of the same organisms existed at other locations on the submerged continent where similar conditions would allow for their development. Several outcrops, extending from the Chattahoochee River on the east to the Tombigbee River on the western side of the state, exhibit many of these same species of invertebrates that we find at Hurricane Creek.

In southwestern Alabama, this same group of invertebrate species is found in a thick sequence of multiple shell layers. If these invertebrates were originally one broad community, then the deposits may well have been formed by a *single* hypercane that moved across the submerged Gulf Coastal Plain during the later stages of the Flood. The massive storm would have passed over southern Alabama (approximately 200 miles wide) with an intensity sufficient to scour both sediments and invertebrates from the submerged sea floor. The storm would then have carried sediment and shells across the shelf, dropping both into low-lying areas. In this manner, a single hypercane could rapidly form multiple fossiliferous deposits across a very broad area. This could also explain the similarity of the isolated invertebrate faunas found across the Alabama coastal plain. Rather than taking millions of years to develop, these shell deposits were probably created in a matter of hours! While this interpretation is only one possible scenario, it demonstrates how large storms, such as hypercanes, could have generated multiple and widespread tempestites preserved in the rock record.

A Massive Fossiliferous Storm Layer at Alum Bluff

Hypercanes could have also scoured sediments and faunae from several different

Figure 3-5. The Apalachicola River has eroded into its bank, creating the 172-foot (52-m) high Alum Bluff. At the base of this exposure is the Chipola Formation, which contains approximately 10 feet (3 m) of shell-rich material.

Figure 3-6. The fossiliferous Chipola Formation at Alum Bluff contains a variety of abundant shell material that readily weathers out of the surrounding silty-sand matrix. The concentration and condition of the sediments and shell material suggest the unit was created during a large storm, transported a very short distance, and deposited and preserved. Scale in inches and centimeters.

locations, transported them some distance, and then deposited them in one concentrated, shell-rich deposit. This would create a single, thick fossiliferous layer with many different types of organisms. Uniformitarian scientists might see this deposit as an evolutionary progression in a single marine environment, but we need to remember that a person's view of history is going to drive their interpretation of the rocks.

One of these fossil-rich outcrops is at Alum Bluff along the Apalachicola River in the panhandle of Florida (Figure 3-5) (see Dunbar and Beardsley 1961; Gardner 1926-1944; Schmidt 1986). A close examination of the 10-foot thick fossiliferous layer, the Chipola Formation, suggests that most of the invertebrates were transported a short distance and quickly buried. The shells show little evidence of abrasion associated with transport (Figure 3-6). Variation in both fossil types and sediments can be attributed to their diverse source areas prior to being uprooted and redeposited by the passing storm.

High-Energy Sedimentary Deposits Devoid of Life

Storm-generated sedimentary deposits can also form without containing any fossils — whether body fossils or pre- or post-event behavioral traces.

The lack of body fossils in a tempestite suggests several possibilities: (1) the source sediments were possibly devoid of life, (2) the organic material was not preserved, or (3) there was insufficient time to create a community of organisms that could be preserved. As creationists, we would expect to find fewer shell accumulations within tempestites, as the only available time for invertebrate community development would have occurred as Flood water began to slowly recede from the continents.

From a uniformitarian perspective, all tempestites should contain numerous invertebrate body fossils due to having thousands of years available for community development before conditions might change (e.g., basin fills, sea level drops, sediments change) where invertebrate communities could no longer live. However, finding tempestites devoid of body or trace fossils is largely the norm in the rock record. That sedimentary layers typically exhibit high-energy sedimentary features and are missing any evidence of life or post-event traces suggests that high-energy conditions were in operation during and following their formation. This is also consistent with the observations of Derek Ager, who noted that the rock record largely preserves the catastrophic sedimentary event (1993a, 1993b). Tempestites without body or trace fossils are expected due to the short time available for community development with receding Flood water.

One of the diagnostic features of lifeless storm deposits is a type of sedimentary bedding that geologists call hummocky cross stratification (e.g., Bourgeois 1980; Duke 1985; Hamblin and Walker 1979; Harms and others 1975; Walker 1984). Typically, these features are of limited scale (both vertically and laterally) and little effort has been expended to correlate areas that display hummocky cross stratification with adjacent areas that do not. This is due to the uniformitarian assumption that storm event beds are of a limited scale.

Sedimentary features reflective of high-energy deposition (Figure 3-7) are seen in many of the exposed sidewalls in the open pit kaolin mines near Americus, Georgia (see Froede 2005a). The absence of body fossils and scarcity of trace fossils suggest that the deposition of these sedimentary layers occurred during a short period of time in a high-energy setting. Interestingly, these types of deposits occur across a broad area in southwestern Georgia at relatively the same stratigraphic position and elevation. Uniformitarian scientists would probably point to many storm events because of their perception of long periods of time, but it is entirely possible that these deposits were formed from a single massive storm event during the waning stages of the Flood (Upper Flood Event Division).

A YOUNG-EARTH FLOOD FRAMEWORK

Understanding modern tempestites can provide clues for interpreting similar features in the rock record, and our knowledge of the progression of the Flood provides a framework within which we can place our observations (Figure 1-6). However, it might be difficult to determine the age of a specific fossiliferous storm deposit due to the unknown duration of Flood water over the area under investigation. A careful examination of the strata both above and below the storm deposit can help constrain the time. For example, a storm deposit sandwiched between marine deposits could imply its creation during the Flood Event Timeframe — when marine water still covered this portion of the continent. The size of the tempestite might extend beyond this limited outcrop, thereby suggesting that it formed in deeper water and across a broader area. These issues can be resolved with the examination of adjacent strata.

Perhaps the most important issue for the creation geologist to resolve in identifying fossiliferous storm

Figure 3-7. Cross-bedded sand exposed in a mining pit (Fowler Mine) near Americus, Georgia. These sedimentary layers are devoid of both trace and body fossils. The cross-bedded sands suggest that these strata were rapidly formed under high-energy conditions. These conditions are more consistent with the expectations of rapid formation during the Flood rather than forming over the course of millions of years. Persons in lower left of image for scale.

event layers is to differentiate between: (1) Flood-event generated deposits which exhibit storm-like features and (2) actual storm deposits. The identification of storm deposits requires that an actual environment existed both before and after the short-term storm event. Marine communities would begin to establish themselves on the submerged portions of continents as the Flood water receded toward the ocean basins during the later stages of the Flood. These communities were established in the tens to hundreds of years of sea water withdrawal as opposed to the millions suggested by the receding epeiric seas defined by uniformitarianism.

Large storm systems associated with the close of the Flood event and the onset of the Ice Age (Oard 1990) moved across these areas covered by shallow water, and would have disrupted these marine communities. These storms would have winnowed, concentrated, transported, and deposited the invertebrate shells across portions of the then-submerged continents. Additional sedimentary deposition (both clastic and carbonate) following the storm event would then bury the tempestite layers until they were later exposed. With the decreasing levels of expended geologic energy associated with this post-Flood period extending into our present age, we would expect to find a decrease in the number, thickness, and lateral extent of storm layers in the rock record.

The young-earth Flood framework would predict a greater role for catastrophic geological processes operating in the past. The greatest energy released for the generation, erosion, transport, and deposition of sediments, including dead floras and faunas, would have occurred during the Flood (Figure 1-10) (Reed and others 1996). The high-energy environment associated with the Flood probably resulted in the deposition of entire facies in very short periods of time.[4] This high-energy setting must be differentiated from the post-Flood setting of greatly reduced geologic energy, and local-to-regional scale storm sedimentation as a function of climatic events.

CONCLUSIONS

Proponents of the Flood must carefully examine the rock record and interpret it within biblical constraints. This effort cannot occur unless traditional uniformitarian methods of reconstructing paleoenvironments are abandoned. A possible alternative is a hydraulic approach, where changes in hydraulic energy are used to reconstruct the conditions of deposition (Julien and others 1993; Berthault 1994; Froede 1995b; Reed and others 1996). This new approach may also help determine the scale of storms that generate tempestites.

Understanding tempestites requires a broader knowledge of the geology and stratigraphy of the area. Actual storm layers are defined as having formed from atmospheric disturbance and not as a result of a Flood-associated process. Within the biblical geologic framework, we would expect that storm deposits were formed during the later stages of the Flood (Upper Flood Event Division) through the Ice Age Timeframe when atmospheric disturbances swept up sediment and organisms from epeiric seas. The resulting strata should reveal sedimentary features reflective of temporary high-energy conditions spanning a spectrum from hummocky cross stratification through fossiliferous sediments to laminated undisturbed clay layers.

Endnotes

1. There are far too many articles and books to comprehensively list them here as examples. All follow the conceptual uniformitarian geological time scale. A few examples that demonstrate this approach can be found in Aigner 1985; Aigner and Reineck 1982; Andrews 1970; Davis and others 1989; DeCelles 1987; Goodbred and Hine 1995; Hayes 1967; Hayes and Boothroyd 1969; Hunter and Clifton 1982; Isphording and Isphording 1991; Keen and Slingerland 1993; Kreisa 1981; Kumar and Sanders 1976; Morton 1988; Specht and Brenner 1979; and Tsujita 1995.

2. Excellent examples reflective of the relationship between storm energy and the generation of strata can be found in Ager 1993a; Brett and Baird 1997; Clifton 1988; Dott 1983; Dott and Bourgeois 1982; Duke 1985; Duke and others 1991; Lee and others 1994; Seilacher 1984a; and Seilacher and Aigner 1991.

3. Shell orientation can sometimes provide a greater understanding of the conditions of deposition, such as wave or current direction (e.g., Ager 1963; Allen 1982; Austin 1994; Dodd and Stanton 1990; Müller 1979; Parsons and Brett 1991; Potter and Pettijohn 1977; Schäfer 1972; Wise and Austin 1995).

4. This type of high-energy depositional setting has actually been suggested by uniformitarian scientists (Specht and Brenner 1979) for a locale along the western interior epeiric seaway of North America. The vertical and lateral variation of these facies would give the appearance of a change or shift in depositional environments and play into the uniformitarian interpretation of changing paleoenvironments, but where none formerly existed.

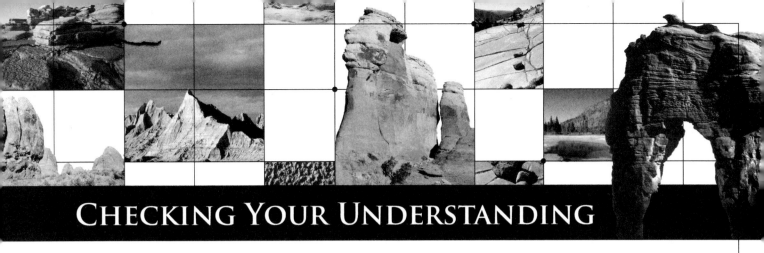

CHECKING YOUR UNDERSTANDING

1. Define a tempestite. Why should we limit them to sedimentary deposits formed through atmospheric disturbance?

2. How much of the Flood-formed rock record would we expect to be defined as tempestites?

3. What is the difference between a hurricane and a hypercane? Should we expect that atmospheric conditions during the Flood Event Timeframe (Figure 1-6) were able to generate hurricanes and hypercanes?

4. What sorts of sedimentary deposits should we expect to find in association with tempestites? Would we always find shell materials in association with tempestites? How fast would tempestites form?

5. Explain how a single hurricane or hypercane can create storm deposits across a broad area such as the U.S. Gulf Coastal Plain? What do isolated fossiliferous layers convey about the physical setting of the former submerged marine environment?

6. Can we expect multiple layers of storm deposits from a single atmospheric system? If so, explain how this might occur.

7. Finding a highly cross-bedded sand with no evidence of any bioturbation conveys what sort of history about this deposit? How do we know that it formed underwater and not as a sand dune on the beach?

CHAPTER 4 *Defining Paleosols in Biblical History*

INTRODUCTION

Uniformitarian scientists claim to have identified ancient soils throughout their geologic time scale. These fossil soils, or paleosols, are thought to have taken thousands to millions of years to form. If that is true and there are paleosols of different stratigraphic ages, then the Bible's chronology is false. Paleosols cannot exist, or if they do, they cannot be as old as uniformitarians claim and still fit a young-earth Flood framework. Therefore, creationists need to address the nature of paleosols, understand how they might form, and recognize the criteria by which they can be identified in the rock record. If they exist, then we need to determine how they might fit in the scriptural view of earth history.

PEDOLOGY: THE STUDY OF SOILS

The science of pedology is defined as the study of the genesis, morphology, and classification of soil types (Bates and Jackson 1987). Typical characteristics used to classify soil types include: (1) structured soil horizons (or zones), (2) pans/caliche/crusts, (3) color changes, (4) root traces, (5) insect burrows, and (6) organic debris layers (Brewer 1976; Buol and others 1980; Clarke 1957; U.S. Department of Agriculture 1975, 1993, 1994). See Tables 4-1 and 4-2 and Figure 4-1.

Soils develop when exposed geologic materials interact with acidic atmospheric gases (Kimberley 1990). Most pedologists view soil formation as a top-down process, one where chemically active fluids move down from the surface gravitationally through surface materials. Important elements in this process include: (1) time, (2) composition of the parent material, (3) topography, (4) climate, and (5) associated floras and faunas (Jenny 1941). Ground water also plays an important role in soil development (Buurman 1980; Twidale 1990). Uniformitarian pedologists claim that different soils form because of variations in geomorphology and associated climatic factors (Akin 1991; Büdel 1982; Colman and Dethier 1986; Daniels and Hammer 1992; Driese and others 1992; Ellis and Mellor 1995; Goudie 1995; Hunt 1972; Paton and others 1995; Robinson and Williams 1994; Steila and Pond 1989; Wilson 1983).

TABLE 4-1
Nomenclature of Soil Horizons

Horizon	Characteristics
O	Upper layers dominated by organic material above mineral soil horizons. Must have >30% organic content if mineral fraction contains >50% clay minerals, or >20% organic if no clay minerals.
A	Mineral horizons formed at the surface or below an O horizon. Contains humic organic material mixed with mineral fraction. Properties may result from cultivation or other similar disturbances.
E	Mineral horizons in which main characteristics is loss of silicate clay, iron, or aluminum, leaving a concentration of sand and silt particles of resistant minerals.
B	Dominated by obliteration of original rock structure and by illuvial concentration of various materials including clay minerals, carbonates, sesquioxides of iron and aluminum. Often has distinct color and soil structure.
C	Horizons, excluding hard bedrock, that are less affected by pedogenesis and lack properties of O, A, E, B horizons. Material may be either like or unlike that from which the solum presumably formed.
R	Hard bedrock underlying a soil.

Horizons can be divided into subhorizons by adding Arabic numbers (e.g., A1, A2,... A12, B2, C3). See Figure 4-1.

Adapted from the U.S. Department of Agriculture Soil Survey Manual (1993), and modified from Ritter et al. (1995, p. 66).

The amount of time deemed necessary to create a soil varies widely. Jenny (1941) estimated that a soil could form from most parent materials in as little as 10 to 50 years. Other soil scientists, such as Paton and others (1995), suggest that it takes 100 to 1,000 years. Foss and Segovia (1984) estimated that the formation of soils could take from 50 to 3,000 years. Weaver (1989) suggested that some soil horizons represent 100 million years of weathering! The nature of the parent material, erosion, and climate are all considered factors that constrain the time frame necessary in the formation of a soil (Holliday and others 1993), but uniformitarian bias clearly places an emphasis on time.

Soil horizons are created by the dissolution, transport, and precipitation of various minerals within the unconsolidated material. Basically, there are three soil horizons: (1) the eluvial (uppermost and/or surface) horizon which is subject to loss of minerals via dissolution or leaching; (2) the illuvial horizon, immediately beneath, where the dissolved minerals precipitate; and (3) the parent horizon from which the overlying soil horizons are derived. Specific types of soils and horizons within them can

TABLE 4-2

**Common Descriptive Symbols Used in Conjunction
With Major Soil Horizons**

Symbol	Meaning
b	Buried soil
g	Strong gleying
h	Illuvial humus
ir	Illuvial iron
k[5]	Accumulation of calcium carbonate; commonly $CaCO_3$
cs	Accumulation of calcium sulfate ($CaSO_4$)
cn	Accumulation of concretions or nodules with sesquioxides
m	Strong cementation including ortstein, caliche, and duripan
p	Plowing or other disturbance (used only with A)
sa	Accumulation of salts more soluble than $CaSO_4$
si	Cementation by siliceous material; sim if continuous (used only with C horizon)
t	Illuvial clay (used only with B horizon)
x	Fragipan—a firm, brittle, high-density layer

These symbols are often combined with the other soil horizon designations (e.g., B3t, B1h, Ck/Cca, Cg).

The symbol "k" replaces the former designation "ca" which is used in much of the older literature.

Adapted from the U.S. Department of Agriculture Soil Survey Manual (1993) and modified from Ritter et al.(1995, p. 67) and Akin (1991, p. 251). This is not a comprehensive list of symbols and the interested reader should review the most current U.S. Department of Agriculture Soil Survey Manual for additional information.

be identified by changes in composition and zonation, respectively. However, *most modern soil horizons cannot be identified accurately in the field and require laboratory analysis.* For example, Ritter and others (1995, p. 66) stated:

> The horizons established by the Soil Conservation Service [see Table 4-1] . . . are so precise that laboratory analysis may be required before certain zones or horizons can be identified.

A detailed discussion of pedology is well beyond the scope of this brief chapter, and for additional information the interested reader should consult the various cited references (e.g., Birkeland 1999; Ellis and Mellor 1995; Paton and others 1995; Schaetzl and Anderson 2005; Singer and Munns 1991).

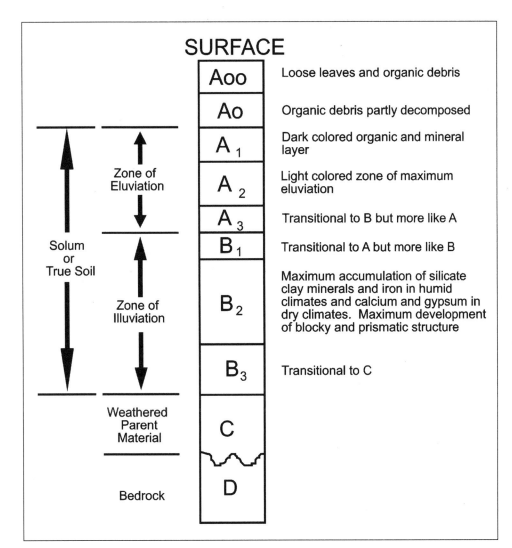

Figure 4-1. A Hypothetical soil profile showing all the principle horizons (modified from Akin 1991, p. 248). Very few soils have all of these horizons. The exact identification of each of these zones/horizons usually requires laboratory analysis. Hence, field determinations are speculative. Many paleopedologists follow this soil classification system.

It is important to note that those who study paleosols (paleopedologists) tend to follow modern soil science methods that are not always directly relevant to paleosols, thus introducing ambiguity into their interpretation (Kraus 1999; Retallack 1981).

PALEOPEDOLOGY: THE STUDY OF PALEOSOLS

Paleopedology is the study of ancient soils and involves the identification of buried soil horizons. Ruhe (1965, p. 755) provided some basic definitions:

A paleosol (from Greek, *palaio* ancient, and Latin, *solum* soil) is a soil that formed on a landscape of the past. *Relict soils* are soils that formed on pre-existing landscapes but were not buried by younger sediments. Formation of such soils dates from the time of the initial landscape. *Buried soils* also formed on pre-existing landscapes and were subsequently covered by younger sediment or rock. *Exhumed soils* are those that were buried but have been re-exposed on the land surface by erosion of the covering mantle.

Paleopedology was originally developed by uniformitarian scientists to address fossil soils in the Quaternary Period (Birkeland 1999; Boardman 1985; Machette 1978; Mahaney 1978; Valentine and Dalrymple 1976; Yaalon 1971). The first pre-Quaternary paleosols to be widely documented were associated with coal deposits, especially those from the upper

Figure 4-2. Exposed bentonitic clays of the Aguja Formation in Dawson Creek, Big Bend National Park, Texas. Lehman (1989, 1990) claimed that several paleosols exist in this formation, but many are based on changes in clay mineralogy and color that can be caused by ground water interaction with the saturated sediments. It should be noted that the clays are very acidic and prevent plant growth.

Carboniferous (Wright 1992a). Paleopedologists have since identified paleosols back as far as the Precambrian (Kraus 1999; Martini and Chesworth 1992; Retallack 1981, 1992a). Research focuses on environments in which soils might form and be preserved, such as alluvial, fluvial, deltaic, and volcanic settings (Figures 4-2, 4-3, 4-4, and 4-5) (e.g., Bown and Kraus 1981a, 1981b; Kraus 1992; Reinhardt and Sigleo 1983; Retallack 1983a, 1983b, 1986; Wright 1986, 1992a).

The identification of a paleosol in the subsurface requires that at some point in the past a soil formed only later to be buried and preserved. An important factor in the identification of a paleosol is the preservation of enough of its original features and structure that it can be identified in the subsurface.

However, problems arise with this concept as paleosols can alter in the subsurface (Gerasimov 1971; Martini and Chesworth 1992; Retallack 1990; Ruellan 1971; Working Group on the Origin and Nature of Paleosols 1971).

The identification of paleosols within the subsurface can be an extremely difficult process requiring expert skill in a discipline that pedologists typically do not possess. According to Retallack (1997, p. 1):

> Unusual soil-forming conditions of the past and alteration of soils after burial can create paleosols very different in appearance than surface soils. The recognition of paleosols is thus a task requiring special expertise.

Figure 4-3. Contact between two distinct volcanic deposits near Ashfork, Arizona. The absence of a paleosol or erosional surface between the volcanic layers suggests that little time elapsed between their deposition. Contacts like this one in volcanic strata appear to refute the "deep time" assumptions of the uniformitarian framework. Scale in inches and centimeters.

Figure 4-4. Cerro Castellan in Big Bend National Park, Texas. According to uniformitarian scientists, this large feature exposes approximately 470 feet (143 m) of volcanic strata deposited over tens of thousands of years. No uniformitarian work to date has identified any paleosols along any of the lithologic contacts. This volcanic environment would have been conducive to the creation and preservation of many soil horizons. That no paleosols are found is expected in our biblical framework of earth history.

Due to their complexity, Retallack (1997) has proposed three important features that are characteristic of paleosols: (1) traces of life, (2) soil horizons, and (3) soil structure (Figure 4-6). One or more of these features in the subsurface can suggest a paleosol, but identification can still be uncertain, even when bounded between quite different sediments (Retallack 1997).

The evolutionary stage set by fossils is also used to age-date paleosols (Frye and Leonard 1967) and, in many instances, the kinds of fossils and numbers of paleosol horizons are used to reconstruct a former environment and document its changes over the purportedly vast expanse of time (e.g., Retallack 1984, 1986, 1992b; Retallack and others 2000).

The deep time assumption of uniformitarianism can create its own problems in dealing with the development of paleosols. For example, not all paleosols have developed due to

Figure 4-5. According to uniformitarian scientists, lava flowed from the Merriam Crater and overtopped the Little Colorado River at Grand Falls, Arizona, 150,000 years ago. The contact between the 150,000-year-old lava and the underlying Kaibab Formation (approximately 245 million years old) should show a well-developed paleosol. However, no paleosol is present, which is consistent with the young-earth Flood framework (see Froede and Williams 2003). Scale in six-inch (15-cm) divisions.

atmospheric processes. According to Kimberley (1990, p. 2011):

> Although natural acids (largely dissolved carbon dioxide) are almost entirely supplied by the atmosphere during modern soil formation, that does not seem to have been the case with all paleosols, particularly the most ancient paleosols and those that are associated with ore deposits.

Following evolutionary history, Kimberley (1990) asserts that since plants and earth's atmosphere were completely different in the past, other processes must have been important in creating paleosols. What those conditions might have been is a matter of conjecture, based on assumption rather than empirical science.

An extensive investigation on paleosols across central Oregon illustrates some of the problems with the supporting science. Retallack and others (2000, p. 22) stated:

> Interpretation of many of the beds in Eocene and Oligocene sequences of the Painted Hills as paleosols is well supported

by many lines of evidence gathered in both the field and the laboratory. Some of this evidence is merely compatible with a paleosol interpretation, and is not compelling in itself. Laboratory data may appear impressive but are not always convincing.

Hence, the identification of a paleosol in the rock record can be subjective, depending on an individual's perspective of earth's history. While paleosols may exist, their proper identification clearly drifts from science into the arena of world views.

HOW TO IDENTIFY A PALEOSOL

Presently, there is no standardized methodology used to identify paleosols. Some investigators prefer modern soil science methodology while others have developed their own schemes (Lewis and McConchie 1994; Martini and Chesworth 1992; Retallack 1981). The variety of techniques encourages a highly interpretive framework (see Fenwick 1985; Wright 1992b) and illustrates the subjectivity in paleopedology.

Even today, paleopedologists cannot agree on what constitutes a paleosol, even though several excellent articles and books have been published in an attempt to standardize the procedures and methods (e.g., Mack and others 1993; Martini and Chesworth 1992; Reinhardt and Sigleo 1988; Retallack 1990; Weide 1985; Wright

Figure 4-6. Exposure of the Tobacco Road Formation southwest of Aiken, South Carolina. Note the plant roots and root traces. If this soil were buried, it would show diagnostic features of a paleosol. Scale in one-inch (2.5-cm) divisions.

1986). Ongoing research continues to advance the science of paleopedology (e.g., Bown and Kraus 1987; Fedo and others 1995; Kraus 1987; Kraus and Bown 1993; Lehman 1989, 1990; Retallack 1983a, 1983b, 1993, 1994; Retallack and Germán-Heins 1994; Schiebout 1979; Verosub and others 1993). However, its dependence on uniformitarianism and its assumptions regarding deep time forces an element of speculation into every investigation.

A Young-Earth Flood Framework

Given these uncertainties, it is not surprising that rules for identifying paleosols in the rock record are not set in Flood geology. It is certainly possible that ancient soils may have existed within several biblical geologic time frames (Figure 1-6):

1. An *Antediluvian Timeframe* soil could have survived the erosion associated with the Flood by being rapidly buried and preserved.

2. Soils could have formed immediately following the withdrawal of Flood water from the continents (*Upper Flood Event — Lower Ice Age Divisions*) and subsequently been buried.

3. Soils could have formed rapidly during the wet weather *Ice Age Timeframe*, especially in alluvial, fluvial, and deltaic settings with each soil layer being rapidly buried by new pulses of sedimentation, forming a vertical succession of paleosols.

4. Paleosols could have been buried by localized, rapid sedimentation (e.g., river flooding) or by volcanic eruptions during the *Ice Age Timeframe* or the *Present Age Timeframe*.

However, the few thousand years since the Flood would suggest that the likelihood of finding multiple well-developed, stacked paleosols within the subsurface would be unexpected.

An excellent series of articles on the subject of soils and paleosols have been published by several creation geoscientists (Klevberg and Bandy 2003a, 2003b, in press; Klevberg and others 2003, 2007). They examine soil-forming processes and discuss the definitions of soils and paleosols. These articles provide an excellent starting point for research in paleopedology from a biblical point of view, directing investigations toward the expected rapid development of soils following the Flood, and the limited development of paleosols within the young-earth framework. Perhaps the most important point made by these authors is that an individual's world view is the most important factor influencing the identification of paleosols in the rock record.

Creationist Observations Regarding Paleosols

Uniformitarian scientists believe that layers of strata reflect the passage of time (Figure 4-7). If so, and if these layers were deposited under subaerial conditions, then we should expect to find numerous stacked paleosols as new soils developed over time on each of the changing former environments. A biblical framework would predict limited paleosols, mostly within the youngest strata.

The best sedimentary environments for soil development and preservation occur in alluvial, fluvial, deltaic, or volcanic settings. The absence of stacked paleosols within these settings suggests support for relatively short time intervals between events and is better explained within the biblical framework. If earth's surface has been subject to terrestrial conditions since the draining of Flood water from land surfaces several thousand years ago, then we would expect to find only a few paleosols in the uppermost layers within the local rock record.

Soil preservation within the creationist model would be based on the burial potential of a given

Figure 4-7. This particular location is along the Rio Grande River just north of Lajitas, Texas. The river flowed across this region and deposited stacked fluvial deposits, which were later covered by rhyolite lava. No paleosols are present, either in the fluvial deposits or at the contact with the overlying lava. This is consistent with the biblical view of history. Pole in foreground is approximately 3 feet (90 cm) high.

environment. For example, a soil that developed near an active volcano would have a greater chance of preservation than a soil formed in a stable area that is minimally affected by deposition and erosion. Within the post-Flood period, the repeated burial of a soil by volcaniclastics could result in the generation of several paleosol horizons. But these horizons might be hard to identify because diagenetic changes of a volcanic ash could easily be mistaken for paleosol horizons. After all, paleosols are often identified in the field based on criteria as simple as a change in color or a change in clay content with depth (see Howe and others 2003).

Any researcher must take care to correctly identify a paleosol. Root traces (Figure 4-8) or distinctive animal/insect burrows (Figure 4-9) remain the best available means to identify a former soil horizon. However, the problem with these indicators is that they are most often limited to the upper soil horizons. Hence, a deeper horizon might not contain these indicators, leaving the identification to be tentatively based on a change in color and/or an accumulation of minerals — both of which could be the result of diagenetic alteration of the sediments caused by ground water.

THE ROLE OF GROUND WATER

Environmental concerns have stimulated a surge in the study of ground water. Researchers have discovered that ground water moving through the shallow subsurface can alter the sediments in a way that mimics soil development (Kraus 1999; Pimentel and others 1996; Twidale 1984, 1990). Differences in ground water geochemistry and soil types can lead to either the dissolution or precipitation of minerals. Organic materials in the sediments also play an important role by creating acids that leach minerals from sediments within the subsurface. Ground water can dramatically alter the composition and appearance of sediments, creating features like those formed by subaerial exposure (e.g., laterites and kaolins — see Froede and Rucker 2006). However, these interactions are not widely known, and ground water-soil interaction remains a poorly developed part of pedology. Paleopedologists unaware of this knowledge have improperly identified paleosols when, in fact, the sediment in question has merely been altered by ground water.

Several creationists have written about the effects of ground water on shallow subsurface sediments (Howe and others 2003; Klevberg and Ban-

Figure 4-8. Rhizoliths (fossil casts of roots) from San Salvador, Bahamas, are all that remain of a former soil. The plants developed during the Ice Age Timeframe, after Flood water receded enough to expose the island. The plant seeds and soil-forming dust were transported from Africa by storm winds (see Froede 2003). Hundreds to thousands of years of growth in a well-developed soil is not conveyed by these rhizoliths. Rather, all of these plant roots could have developed over the course of a few decades. Missing is the evidence of the deep time assumptions within uniformitarianism. Scale in inches and centimeters.

Figure 4-9. One of the important features that can be used to characterize paleosols is evidence of life. These insect traces exposed in a cliff on San Salvador, Bahamas, should supply us with information about the former soil. The carbonate sediments were not cemented when the insects constructed their dwelling. Subsequent hardening of the limestone occurred with exposure to air and precipitation. No obvious soils are visible. Insect traces are not always diagnostic of soils and this example presents the rather subjective nature of using insect traces to define either a soil or paleosol. The traces were created by sweat bees that were carried from Africa to the island on winds during the Ice Age Timeframe (see Froede 2003). Scale in inches and centimeters.

dy 2003a, 2003b; Klevberg and others 2003). First and foremost, they have shown that these altered sediments are not paleosols. Most of the changes to the sediments did not occur until terrestrial conditions were established following the Flood. Soils began developing when acidic rain flushed marine Flood water from the surface sediments. The breakdown of organic material within or above the sediments created acids that accelerated the development of one or more soil horizons. Ironically, these diagenetic changes within the zone of ground water fluctuation created the appearance of multiple paleosol horizons.

Today, ground water continues to play an important role in the subsurface alteration of sedimentary material. Creationists should evaluate the likelihood of ground water diagenesis when faced with apparent paleosols in the field (e.g., Curtis 1976; Gautier 1986; McIlreath and Morrow 1990; Scholle and Schluger 1979). Diagenesis is an ongoing process in the subsurface, and its products are not paleosols, even though the appearance can be similar.

Conclusions

Uniformitarian scientists predict paleosol horizons at every terrestrial paleosetting, while creationists predict true paleosols would be rare and found primarily in the youngest sediments. Given the difficulty in identifying true paleosols, it is clear that the interpretation in the field will be driven by the individual's assumptions regarding earth history. The time scale and conditions suggested by uniformitarian geoscientists regarding terrestrial conditions in the past are not supported by the sparse number of paleosols actually found in the rock record. Paleosols are purported to reflect the passage of extended periods of geologic time on what was once a subaerial ground surface. If a ground surface were exposed for millions of years to weathering, we would expect to find well-developed soil horizons. Additionally, the

slow input of sediments over an existing soil during the course of millions of years should result in an upward-creeping soil profile. A periodic pulse of sedimentation should result in the occurrence of multiple (stacked) paleosols. This physical evidence is not demonstrated in the rock record.

The claim by paleopedologists that paleosols can provide a window into earth's climatic past is therefore questionable, especially since diagenesis can produce similar features. If we do not know the original condition of the buried soil, then it is hard to understand how it could possibly serve as a climatic recorder. Additionally, the use of evolutionary age-dating methods (e.g., radiometric, paleontologic, or palynologic) as a means of establishing the age of any paleosol is also not acceptable within the biblical framework.

Ground water alteration of shallow subsurface soils has not been widely recognized or acknowledged by paleopedologists. A better understanding of diagenesis may result in a general decrease in the number of paleosols claimed by uniformitarian scientists. Changes to sediment caused by ground water do not require deep time. Rather simple pH/Eh changes can have profound effects within decades or centuries — well within the time constraints of biblical history.

Our biblical framework does not preclude the existence of paleosols. Rather, our time scale suggests that the majority of soils that might be preserved as paleosols would have developed following the withdrawal of Flood water from the continents. The possibility exists that some antediluvian soils might have been preserved due to burial and they may exist within the subsurface as paleosols. However, either due to the short period of time available for the development of a soil or in its subsequent burial, our model would predict fewer paleosols in the rock record.

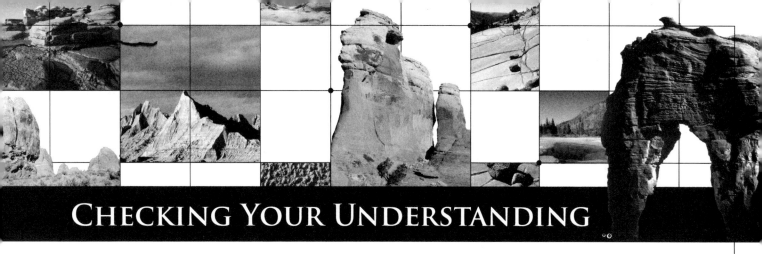

CHECKING YOUR UNDERSTANDING

1. Define a paleosol. What features must be present to make a buried soil a paleosol?

2. How far back in time have uniformitarian scientists identified paleosols? How does this fit within the biblical account of earth history?

3. What environments provide the best geologic conditions for the formation of a paleosol? Why?

4. What methods do paleopedologists use to identify a paleosol? What are the key indicators?

5. Why is the world view of the individual important in identifying paleosols in the rock record?

6. Where might creationists expect to find paleosols?

7. What do paleosols tell us about biblical history?

CHAPTER 5
Defining Laterites and Ferricretes in Biblical History

INTRODUCTION

Laterites and ferricretes are sedimentary features commonly found in soils. Many uniformitarian scientists contend that they form over the course of thousands to millions of years and are the result of intensive weathering under tropical or forested warm-to-temperate climates. This premise is based on their conceptual model, which is outside the realm of testable science. Laterites actually comprise several types of sedimentary materials which can form at the ground surface and/or within the subsurface. Although laterites are defined in different ways by uniformitarian geologists, geomorphologists, and soil scientists, all of the theories are heavily weighted to long periods of time.

One might think that our knowledge of laterites is now settled and that young-earth creationists should accept the uniformitarian understanding. However, this is not necessary. We need to replace the conceptual model that presupposes a multibillion-year-old earth with one consistent with the biblical framework. In addition, we must highlight uniformitarian assumptions that do not have any sound scientific basis. In the case of laterites and ferricretes, we find that they can develop in a short period of time in a manner consistent with the expectations of the biblical framework.

HISTORY OF LATERITES

Buchanan (1807) was the first person to use the term "laterite" to describe an iron-rich sedimentary deposit found within the shallow subsurface that hardens upon oxidation (Figure 5-1). The investigation of these unique sediments was predominately

Figure 5-1. These locally derived blocks of quarried laterite were used in the construction of an early American industrial mill at Arcadia Mill Park, in Santa Rosa County, Florida. Scale in six-inch (15-cm) divisions.

the work of geologists. However, studies by Oldham (1893), followed by Glinka (1914) and Harrassowitz (1930), suggested that laterites formed as soils, thus their studies emphasized pedology. Then Campbell (1917) discovered that laterites could form under the influence of ground water migration, and the emphasis shifted again to the study of chemical processes in the shallow saturated subsurface. This dual perspective continues today. Soil scientists interpret laterites as soils while geologists emphasize hydrogeologic processes. More recently, geomorphologists have incorporated laterites as tools in defining the development of various landforms using both pedological and hydrogeological concepts.

DEFINING LATERITES

Buchanan (1807) defined the iron-rich laterites that he examined based on their color and hardness. Subsequent investigators (McFarlane 1976) have defined laterites largely by their varying chemical content (e.g., iron, alumina, desilicification, and silica-sesquioxide ratios).

Many early investigators thought laterites formed by intense weathering of rocks over extended time. For example, Russell (1889) proposed that laterites were simply residua remaining after the removal of the more mobile minerals. Defining laterites as residuum expanded the group to include other sediments that exhibit desilicification, such as kaolin and bauxite. The increasing number of sedimentary features identified as laterites resulted in confusion. According to Ollier (1991, p. 166):

> Laterite is a very confusing term, being used for soil ("laterite is the common soil of the tropics"), for hard or potentially hard material ("temples at Chiang Mai are built of laterite"), for nodular ferricrete ("laterite used for road building in Uganda is known as murram"), and often in relation to a weathering profile ("the laterite profile includes pallid and mottled zones").

Pullan (1967) attempted to clarify the definition by distinguishing between lateritic ironstones and ferruginous soils on the basis of their morphology. But his approach has since created even more confusion (Bourman 1993a; Bourman and Ollier 2002).

Pedologists were the first to abandon the term "laterite," choosing instead to reclassify the many profiles into specific soil categories. However, geologists and geomorphologists continue to use the term "laterite" and have largely focused on the ground water aspects of its formation and iron content.

A typical lateritic profile (Figure 5-2) consists of a ferricrete crust overlying a mottled zone which in turn overlies a pallid zone. The ferricrete typically forms in sedimentary materials that unconformably overlie the mottled zone (Ollier 1991).

Today, a laterite is defined as:

> . . . a highly weathered red subsoil or material rich in secondary oxides of iron, aluminum, or both, nearly devoid of bases and primary silicates, and commonly with quartz and kaolinite. It develops in a tropical or forested warm to temperate climate, and is a residual product of weathering. Laterite is capable of hardening after a treatment of wetting and drying, and can be cut and used for bricks (Jackson 1997, p. 359).

Perhaps the simplest definition for a laterite profile comes from Ollier and Galloway (1990) who proposed that it consists of a ferricrete layer overlying a saprolite (a highly weathered residuum, commonly of crystalline rocks).

Laterites can develop through two different processes: (1) soil development and (2) changes in ground water chemistry. Wang (2003) claimed that the two types of laterites can be differentiated, but the ability to do so depends on the scientific perspective (i.e., pedologist or geologist) of the researcher.

LATERITES IN SOIL SCIENCE

Pedologists believe that the intense weathering of surface to near-surface sediments in humid and tropical climates can result in laterite formation. Rain dissolves minerals in the topsoil and then transports them downward, precipitating them lower in the soil horizon. All of this occurs above the water table. The resulting highly weathered soil profile has historically been defined as a laterite (Alexander and Cady 1962; Maignien 1966). Today, soil scientists now classify laterites within the oxisols and ultisols (Buol and others 1980). In some instances, the weathering forms iron-cemented layers in the subsurface. These iron-enriched layers are identified as hardpans or ferricretes. A lateritic profile can contain one or more relatively

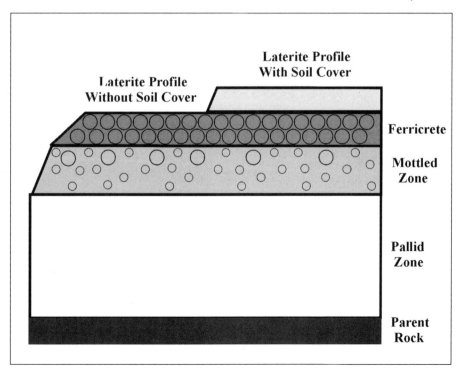

Figure 5-2. Diagram of the idealized laterite soil profile. Note that the ferricrete is typically not derived from the underlying mottled zone; rather, it lies unconformably above it (modified from Ollier 1991).

flat-lying ferricretes above bleached and mottled zones. These zones often overlie the parent material (Milnes and others 1985). Iron in the ferricrete is believed to be derived from either overlying or underlying iron-containing geologic materials (MacFarlane 1976; Singer 1975; Bourman and Ollier 2002).

The flat landscape overlying laterites and ferricretes is considered old (Schaetzl and Anderson 2005). Laterites have been used as evidence of plate tectonic motion across tropical/temperate zones (Tardy 2003), in addition to providing evidence of the paleogeography and paleoclimatology of the region. For example, Tardy (2000, p. 602) stated:

> Laterites are products of tropical weathering, formed *in situ* on old continent shields, regions that are tectonically stable and relatively well preserved from mechanical erosion. Lateritic profiles can be up to several tens of meters thick, and have generally been formed over periods of tens of millions of years. Most laterites are polygenetic, having been formed and transformed under various types of climatic successions. Laterites thus serve as continental archives and are excellent indicators of change in palaeoclimatic or palaeogeographical conditions.

Wang (2003) suggested that long periods of landscape evolution are responsible for laterites formed by both soil and ground water processes. He believes that laterites can only form by extended subaerial exposure, tectonic quiescence, and climatic stability.

LATERITES AND GROUND WATER

Despite its popularity among pedologists, their theory cannot explain the iron-rich deposits or the residuum when the source of the iron could not have been locally derived (Maignien 1966; Ollier 1991; Bourman 1996). The resolution of this problem has been the identification of anaerobic and acidic ferrous ground water flow within the subsurface (Bourman 1993b; Bourman and others 1987; Froede and Rucker 2006; McFarlane 1976; Milnes and others 1985; Twidale 1984, 1990). Ground water can leach and precipitate minerals as pH and Eh conditions change in the subsurface. Iron is especially subject to dissolution, transport, and precipitation under these conditions (Peterson 1971; Norton 1973; Mann and Ollier 1985). Sediments within the ground water zone can be leached of minerals until they appear deeply weathered, developing a lateritic profile totally unrelated to normal soil-forming processes (Figure 5-3). The oxidation of iron-rich ground water within the subsurface can also create ferricretes (Figure 5-4).

FERRICRETE DEVELOPMENT BY GROUND WATER ACTIVITY

Lamplugh (1902) used the term "ferricrete" to describe the cementation of geologic materials in the shallow subsurface by iron precipitated from ground water. A year earlier, Ransome (1901) identified iron cement precipitating from ground water as originating from the weathering of iron sulfides associated with silver ore bodies near Silverton, Colorado. He correctly reasoned that when acidic, anaerobic, and ferrous ground water entered local creeks, it was oxidized, forming iron oxide cement.

Since then, this process has been noted at many locations (e.g., Chan and others 2000; Bourman 1993a, 1996; Ferguson and others 1983; Furniss and others 1999; Mann and Ollier 1985; Milnes and others 1987; Ollier 1991; Ollier and Galloway 1990; Phillips and others 1997; Phillips 1999, 2000; Wright and others 1992). In some instances, surrounding areas have been eroded, leaving the ferricretes higher than their surroundings. These elevated areas are known as inverted relief surfaces (e.g., Froede and Rucker 2006; Milnes and others 1985; Pain and Ollier 1995; Schwarz 1994).

Figure 5-3. A ferricrete from Iron Mountain, Santa Rosa County, Florida. This outcrop is consistent with the idealized laterite profile and demonstrates an unconformity between the ferricrete and underlying mottled zone (see Froede and Rucker 2006). Scale in inches and centimeters.

Groundwater-formed ferricretes can neither be correlated laterally nor be used to define their time of formation. They should not be used to infer past climatic conditions or viewed as having been derived directly from either over or underlying geologic materials (Bourman 1993b; Bourman and others 1987; Milnes and others 1985; Pain and Ollier 1992, 1995).

How long does it take a ferricrete to form either at the surface or within the subsurface? Several studies have documented this process occurring over surprisingly short periods of time, ranging from ongoing areas of precipitation to those that develop over several years, all dependent upon the changing geochemistry of the ground water (e.g., Ferguson and others 1983; Furniss and others 1999; Pain and Ollier 1995; Perse 2000; Phillips 2000; Phillips and others 1997; Plumlee and others 1995).

Figure 5-4. The multiple ferricretes at this location in southwest Georgia formed as a result of an oscillating paleo-water table, probably in a very short period of time. They reflect the former oxidation surface of iron-saturated ground water. Scale in six-inch (15-cm) divisions.

Figure 5-5. This sloped ferricrete in a clay pit near Holly Springs, Mississippi, demonstrates that neither ferricretes nor laterites should be viewed as purely horizontal features. Scale in inches and centimeters.

FERRICRETE SURFACES

Many uniformitarian scientists believe that ferricretes form in the subsurface parallel to a relatively level (horizontal) ground surface (e.g., McFarlane 1976; Schaetzl and Anderson 2005; Wang 2003). This has proven to be false. Several studies have shown that they can form on hillsides and along stream beds (Figure 5-5) (Clare 1960; Bourman 1993b; Furniss and others 1999; Phillips 1999, 2000; Phillips and others 1997), or in subsurface depressions and channels (Pain and Ollier 1995). Ferricretes can also follow joint sets creating a highly varied surface (Figure 5-6) (Mann and Ollier, 1985). With a changing ground water table, ferricretes can develop multiple horizons. Due to the complexity of surface processes and ground water fluctuation, it would be unwise to assume and generalize that ferricretes were once horizontal surfaces that have subsequently been tilted.

A YOUNG-EARTH FLOOD FRAMEWORK

Although laterites, especially in association with one or more ferricretes, suggest intense, prolonged weathering and precipitation, new research is demonstrating other options. Deep time is not necessary; laterites and ferricretes can both form rapidly. Within the constraints of our biblical framework (Figure 1-6), laterites could form from the intense leaching created by acidic and anaerobic fluids, both during and after the global Flood. Following Flood water withdrawal, the presence of organic materials within the subsurface would produce acidic conditions in an oxygen-depleted setting. Furthermore, some of the sediments may have generated acids with their decomposition (e.g., volcanic materials, hydrothermal deposits, metalliferous deposits). Ground water moving within the subsurface would leach soluble minerals and concentrate others, thus forming laterites and ferricretes.

Ferricretes are important sedimentary features in our framework as they likely reflect processes in association with the transition from Flood water to fresh water (i.e., Ice Age Timeframe) (Figure 1-6). The movement of charged and mineral-laden fluids from areas undergoing uplift to low-lying adjacent areas would occur within the subsurface. The flushing of those fluids by fresh water, itself charged by the breakdown of organic and geologic materials, would also leach the more soluble minerals from the sediments. Where migrating ferrous-rich fluid encountered oxidizing conditions, the dissolved minerals would precipitate, forming one or more ferricrete layers within the subsurface. This process occurs today as acidic and anaerobic ground water encounters an oxidizing environment.

CONCLUSIONS

Laterites and ferricretes are unusual sedimentary and soil-related features, long thought to provide evidence in support of uniformitarianism — the products of long, slow weathering in warm and wet environments. However, as with many other phenomena, the bias of the researcher plays an important role in the interpretation of these features. While the uniformitarian model for laterite and ferricrete development forces the assumption of deep time, it is now clear that other possibilities exist. Scientists are now discovering that both of these features can form in a short period of time.

This new way of understanding the development of laterites is consistent with the geological/ geochemical processes that we would expect as landforms, climate, and ground water regimes moved toward a new equilibrium after the Flood. The generation and movement of chemically charged fluids within the subsurface would be expected with the initiation of the Flood. The eventual draining of Flood water from the continents, coupled with organic decomposition and freshwater flushing, would provide the chemical conditions necessary to develop laterites and a lateritic soil profile below the former ground surface.

Laterites and ferricretes provide important information about the establishment of freshwater conditions within the subsurface. They represent post-Flood sedimentary deposits developed from the movement of acidic and anaerobic ground water. They can also assist in determining the paleo-ground water movement direction and subsurface lithology, especially where these features now form inverted relief structures (e.g., Froede and Rucker 2006). Most importantly, and not surprisingly, they do not require intense surface weathering and can form in a short period of time in the subsurface.

Figure 5-6. Joints developed within this massive sandy clay in southwest Georgia have exposed iron-saturated ground water to oxidation, resulting in this strangely shaped ferricrete layer. This feature would be difficult to explain by soil-forming processes. Scale in six-inch (15-cm) divisions.

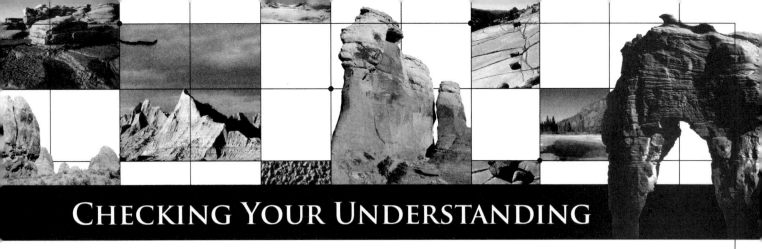

CHECKING YOUR UNDERSTANDING

1. What is the difference between a laterite and a ferricrete?

2. What does their formation tell us about sea level position and how does this relate to the Flood?

3. What are the two competing processes used to explain the creation of laterites and ferricretes within the subsurface?

4. Where might we expect to find laterites and ferricretes today?

5. What was the source of the iron that formed ferricretes when surrounding sediments contain no iron source materials?

6. What are the subsurface depth limits to either laterite or ferricrete development?

7. How quickly can ferricretes form within the subsurface today? And also laterites?

CHAPTER 6

Defining Seismites in Biblical History

INTRODUCTION

Seismites are sedimentary features that can form in minutes or even seconds due to violent ground movement. Some of these features have previously been misinterpreted by uniformitarian scientists because of their bias towards a deep-time interpretation of earth history. But seismites reflect short-term catastrophic events. They are useful tools, providing information about the seismic history of an area. This chapter will review several forms of seismites in an effort to understand their origin and place within the young-earth Flood framework.

SEISMITES

Seismites are paleo-seismograms (Seilacher 1969) and include such features as clastic dikes, syneresis mudcracks, ball-and-pillow structures, molar-tooth structure, and septaria (Anand and Jain 1987; Ettensohn and others 2002; Froede and Howard 2002; Plaziat and others 1990; Pratt 1994, 1998a, 1998b, 2001; Seilacher 1969). Other sedimentary features have also been attributed to seismic forces, including dewatering structures, slumping sediments, fault-graded bedding, turbidite structures, convex-down stacking of shells, and even current-orientation in wave-ripple accumulations (Seilacher 1969, 1984b). All of these sedimentary features formed from either the liquefaction/fluidization of sediment or through soft sediment deformation (Einsele 1998). Ongoing research continues to identify new examples of seismites in the rock record — a matter of interest to creationists. We will review several types of seismites and discuss their relevance to the biblical framework of earth history.

Clastic Dikes

Uniformitarian geoscientists have been investigating and reporting on clastic dikes for more than a century (e.g., Diller 1889; Hobbs 1907; Munson and others 1995; Newsom 1903; Pavlow 1896; Smyers and Peterson 1971; Waterston 1950). Young-earth creationists have also studied these sedimentary features (e.g., Austin and Morris 1986; Froede 1998b; Morris 1994; Whitmore 2005; Woodmorappe 1993).

Two different ideas have been proposed for their genesis. The first concept suggests that a hydraulically confined, unlithified layer is compacted by overlying sediments until it becomes over-pressurized. This could occur during rapid sedimentation, by differential compaction, or from hydrostatic pressure differences between the sedimentary layers. Whatever the cause, the over-pressurized layer instantaneously erupts upward, or possibly downward, through fractures or other zones of weakness into or possibly through the confining layers, creating clastic dikes.

The second theory proposes that the unlithified, hydraulically unstable layer is pressurized by tectonic strain, seismic activity, or impact from a pounding wave or meteorite. As before, the over-pressurized layer erupts through the confining layer (Figures 6-1 and 6-2) either by rupture of the confining layer or by injection when the confining layer becomes thixotropic.

If conditions are right, the erupting sand can extend upward through the overlying sediments eventually reaching the ground surface, forming sand volcanoes (Neumann-Mahlkau 1976; Reineck and Singh 1980). Later, the clastic dikes might be subject to cementation and if the surrounding clay weathers or is eroded away from the dikes, they can form sandstone walls (Figure 6-3) (see Morris 1994). Conversely, if a deeply buried over-pressurized layer experiences some seismic disturbance, it can rupture downward into

Figure 6-1. A sandstone dike has penetrated from a lower sand-rich layer through silts and clays in a sidewall of Laundry Creek near the Chattahoochee River at Fort Benning, Georgia. Scale in inches and centimeters.

an underlying layer forming downward protruding clastic dikes (Whitmore 2005).

Of the two ideas used to explain clastic dikes, the rapid sedimentation/compaction model is not favored by uniformitarian scientists because they assume that sedimentation occurred over the course of millions of years. This extended time would have prevented the sedimentary layers from experiencing over-pressurization from either rapid sedimentation or compaction. It is also likely that during this long duration, the sedimentary layer would have lithified and no longer be subject to soft-sediment

Figure 6-2. A sandstone dike has penetrated upward through silts and clays. This dike is exposed along Uchee Creek, southwest Georgia. Scale in inches and centimeters.

deformation by over-pressurization. Therefore, the mechanical strain model is more commonly cited by uniformitarian scientists as the cause for clastic dike formation.

Source layers in the subsurface that are likely candidates for developing clastic dikes require an outside force to over-pressurize them into eruption. This is a reasonable requirement and in many instances these clastic dikes are found in areas that have historically experienced seismic activity. The creation of clastic dikes through the process of seismic activity occurs on the order of seconds to minutes. Once ruptures are initiated through the confining layer by seismic action, the over-pressurized, unlithified siliciclastic sediment quickly moves into the breaches to form clastic dikes. Additional seismic activity would serve to create new clastic dikes. Work performed by Tuttle and Schweig (1995) within the area around the New Madrid Seismic Zone has verified the formation of multiple generations of clastic dikes with continued earthquake activity.

DISCREPANCIES IN UNIFORMITARIAN THEORIES

Uniformitarian scientists assume that sedimentation occurs over extended periods of time, slowly

Figure 6-3. This massive sandstone dike, located along the Chattahoochee River near Fort Benning, Georgia, forms a wall measuring nearly two feet in width and almost three feet in height. Erosion of the confining clayey-silt from around the clastic dike has created this rather large feature. Scale in six-inch (15-cm) divisions.

building layers of sand, silt, and clay one upon another. Then the sediments are compacted, diagenetically altered, and eventually lithified. However, this conceptualization is inconsistent with what Whitmore (2005) found in the Grand Canyon. Clastic dikes originating in the Coconino Sandstone extend downward into the Hermit Formation by as much as 30 feet. They were instantaneously formed. But the seismic event supposedly occurred approximately 200 million years *after* the Coconino Sandstone was deposited and subsequently buried.

Another inconsistency between the physical and conceptual occurs in the scarcity of clastic dikes in areas of known historical seismic activity. If sedimentation occurred over millions of years in these seismically active areas, then we should find a great number of clastic dikes cutting across strata of different ages. Uniformitarian explanations for the rarity of clastic dikes in these settings include fewer historical earthquakes and conditions different in the past. Both are ad hoc explanations, especially in areas with known historical seismic activity.

Septaria

A septarium (septaria is the plural) is a unique concretion. According to Bates and Jackson (1984, p. 458), a septarium is defined as:

> A large spheroidal concretion, generally of impure limestone or clay ironstone, cut into polyhedral blocks by radiating and intersecting cracks which have been filled (and the blocks cemented together) by a mineral material, generally calcite.

Three ideas have been proposed to explain the development of septaria:

1. Concretions form within the shallow subsurface near to the sediment-water interface (Duck 1995; Hesselbo and Palmer 1992; Raiswell 1971; Raiswell and Fisher 2000; Wetzel 1992). Septarian cracks are opened by either geochemical dehydration or the over-pressurization of the interiors of the concretions. Dissolved calcium carbonate from the surrounding sediments passes through the case-hardened exterior and precipitates calcite cement in the open cracks within the interiors, forming a septarium.

2. Septaria form at depth due to rapid burial and over-pressurization (Astin 1986; Hounslow 1997). The cracks that develop within these deeply buried concretions are tensile features. However, Hounslow (1997) suggested that crack development could occur at depths less than 33 feet if tensional failure resulted from locally high pore pressure. Scotchman (1991) proposed that septarian cracks developed soon after burial, just below the sediment-water interface, with growth continuing over a long period of time as the developing septaria are buried to greater depths. Multiple cracks (which are later filled with calcite and other cements) are believed to reflect multiple episodes of burial (Astin 1986; Scotchman 1991).

3. Septarian cracks can form by the passage of seismic waves through developing concretions (Pratt 1996, 2001). These waves create instantaneous, chaotic, and elevated stresses which cause shrinkage, fracturing, and/or brecciation inside the developing concretions. As a result, septaria exhibit features best explained by the passage of seismic waves through water-saturated sediments. These include: (a) lenticular shrinkage cracks, (b) broken macrofossils, (c) broken, dislodged, and shingled macrofossil fragments from loss of shear strength in the matrix, (d) flaky surface of shrinkage cracks, (e) parallel-sided cracks cutting the matrix and first

Figure 6-4. Exposed dissected septaria from Hannahatchee Creek (southwestern Georgia). These rather large features have been eroded to expose the septarian cracks that are consistent with a seismic origin. Scale in inches and centimeters.

stage of cement, (f) breccia fragments of matrix and first stage cements, (g) reticulate arrays of parallel-sided cracks, (h) branching cracks, (i) en échelon sigmoidal cracks, (j) plumose cracks, and (k) geopetal sediment injected from outside the concretion after the first stage of fibrous calcite cementation has occurred in the shrinkage cracks (Pratt 2001).

Site-specific conditions will dictate which of these three concepts is most appropriate. However, while all three models can be used within the biblical framework, the seismic formation of these sedimentary features is of significant interest (Figures 6-4 and 6-5). Septaria would then represent a paleo-seismic recorder where no other record of seismic activity might have been preserved (Froede and Howard 2002; Pratt 2001).

MUDCRACKS

Everyone has seen mudcracks form in a drying patch of clay. These same features are found throughout the rock record. Uniformitarian scientists have historically interpreted mudcracks as desiccation features formed under dry climate conditions. However, mudcracks can also form underwater. Mudcracks that form under saturated conditions at or near the water-sediment interface are called "syneresis cracks." These are small-scale features that form from the geochemical desiccation of smectite clay due to the introduction of a saline solution (Burst 1965). Creationists have also sought to explain mudcracks, but within the context of the convulsive flood of Genesis (e.g., Froede 1994b; Oard 1994). Both uniformitarian and creationist geoscientists have focused on syneresis cracks and the difficult and controversial question of their origin. Recently, scientists have switched their focus from chemical desiccation to seismology.

Probably the first identification of mudcracks in turbidites was by Dzulynski and Walton (1965). They postulated that these sedimentary features might have formed due to some effect of seismicity. Pratt (1998a) noted mudcracks in turbidite deposits in the Canadian Rockies. He interpreted them as intrastratally (i.e., formed between sedimentary layers) derived dewatering features reflective of past seismic activity. The old idea that they formed in a dry, subaerial setting did not fit the depositional setting.

Figure 6-5. A septarium with cracks filled by calcite crystals that developed in water-saturated conditions. From Hannahatchee Creek in southwestern Georgia. Scale in inches and centimeters.

Instead, they were dewatering features created nearly instantaneously by seismic waves passing through the sediments. Likewise, Tanner (1998) interpreted interstratal mudcracks as the products of both seismicity and compaction dewatering.

At present, the development of mudcracks in a subaqueous setting is viewed as occurring within the shallow subsurface and not at the water-sediment interface (Figures 6-6 and 6-7) (Pratt 1998a; Tanner 2003). These interstratal dewatering structures are believed to result from the geochemical alteration of smectite clays coupled with the dewatering of sediments from either above or below due to seismicity and/or compaction. The size and form of the polygonal cracks is related to a number of factors, including bed thickness, rheology, and anisotropy (Tanner 2003).

Naturalists and creationists can both agree that the formation of mudcracks within the rock record no longer requires a subaerial dry climate. Mudcracks as interstratal dewatering structures provide important information to the investigator regarding depositional setting, rate of sedimentation, sedimentary source area, compaction, and seismicity.

BALL-AND-PILLOW STRUCTURES

Ball-and-pillow structures form as a result of a physical shock being applied to semi- to unconsolidated layered sediment. The shock causes rupture to occur to the sedimentary layer resulting in a loss of its stability in relation to the underlying sedimentary layers (Blatt and others 1972; Collinson and Thompson 1989; Dzulynski and Walton 1965; Pettijohn 1975; Pettijohn and Potter 1964; Pettijohn and others 1987; Reineck and Singh 1980; Ricci-Lucchi 1995). Following deposition and initial consolidation, sedimentary layers are subjected to an external force that destabilizes and separates the individual layers. Individual lobes then move downward into an underlying layer forming the "pillow" (Figure 6-8) or, in some instances, the clay flows upward between the individual sedimentary lobes (Figure 6-9). In many cases, the sand pillows retain their original bedding even when surrounded by the underlying sediments.

One of the most comprehensive works to address these structures is that of Potter and Pettijohn (1977, p. 201) who described the ball-and-pillow structure thus:

Characteristically the structure is confined to one bed — being present neither in the overlying or underlying beds. Several such disturbed beds, however, may be present in the same outcrop. The bed is broken

Figure 6-6. Seismically derived syneresis mudcracks are exhibited along a clay bedding plane in a large slab of lithified sandstone in the Sequatchie Formation from Ringgold, Georgia. Scale in inches and centimeters.

Figure 6-7. Another surface of the Sequatchie Formation from Ringgold, Georgia, with large polygonal cracks created by sand injection into a clay under the influence of seismic forces or possibly by compaction-related dewatering. Rock hammer for scale.

into a series of hassock- or pillow-shaped masses. They are rarely spherical, more generally they are hemispherical or kidney-shaped, ranging from a few inches to very large bodies several feet in size. The bed involved will thus vary from less than a foot to 8 or 10 feet in thickness. The pillow structure is commonly found only in the lower part of the bed and grades upward into ordinary undisturbed sandstone. The bed, therefore, appears to have a sharp but highly undulatory base and a flat top. In extreme cases the pillows become isolated in a matrix of shale and fail to form a continuous bed. The underlying shale is very much deformed and appears to be wrapped around the pillows, to be squeezed in between them and to extend as thin tongues up into the sandstone bed.

The identification of the cause and effect relationship between the clay and overlying sand layer was only finally resolved through laboratory experimentation. This complex structure was duplicated in the laboratory by Kuenen (1958), Owen (1996), and others (see Allen 1982) by applying a shock to multilayered strata — usually a sand layer over a clay layer. On a larger scale, this force could be applied by earthquakes, meteoric impacts, and volcanic eruptions (see Pope and others 1997).

Figure 6-8. Large ball-and-pillow structures developed in the Eutaw Formation in southwest Georgia. The individual ball/pillow structures have separated from the original silty-sand layer. Scale in six-inch (15-cm) divisions.

A YOUNG-EARTH FLOOD FRAMEWORK

The effects of seismic activity on recently deposited sediments are of great interest to young-earth creationists. The Flood provided the perfect combination of both factors, with ongoing sedimentation, tectonism, volcanism, and extraterrestrial impacts. Seismic activity would have continued into the Ice Age Timeframe and to a lesser extent into the Present Age Timeframe. Sediments deposited during the Flood could have remained unlithified for many years (and in many instances still remain unlithified). Seismic waves would cause some of these unlithified sediments to form seismites. The short duration and reduction in the scale and intensity of energy sources are reflected in the rock record by the size and number of seismites found.

Clastic dikes usually develop within seconds to minutes under high-energy conditions. One means of dating clastic dikes is using the "law of crosscutting relationships" — the dike would be younger than the beds it penetrates. Determining which strata are cut by the dike could help in identifying the age of both the strata and the dikes, and possibly aid in understanding the biblical age (Flood Event, Ice Age, or Present Age Timeframes — Figure 1-6) in which the clastic dike formed. One major difference between the two world views is that uniformitarian scientists discount sedimentary loading as a means of creating clastic dikes because they think everything happened over long ages. Creationists should retain sedimentary loading for clastic dike development because sediments could rapidly accumulate to great thickness due to Flood transport and deposition, and the destabilization and dewatering of those sediments by compaction and settling could account for the formation of some of the clastic dikes.

Septaria are a unique form of paleo-seismic indicator. While septarian crack formation would be instantaneous, the precipitation of cements within those cracks would have extended over some period of time. Initiated from a subsurface concretion in highly porous silt and clay deposits, septaria offer evidence of historic earthquake activity where they are preserved. Also, the orientation of septaria can possibly provide evidence in support of subsurface dewatering pathways and define areas with exceptional organic content that enhance methanogenesis and sulfate reduction (Froede and Howard 2002).

Syneresis mudcracks present a new frontier to young-earth creationists. Their formation in the subsurface, either within sedimentary layers

Figure 6-9. Ball-and-pillow structures in the Blufftown Formation in southwest Georgia. The underlying clay rapidly penetrated upward between sections of the overlying silty-sand layer. Scale in inches and centimeters.

or along bedding contacts as a result of seismic energy, is consistent with the expectations of the biblical record of earth history. Interestingly, Pratt (1998a) noted a greater abundance of these seismically derived features in the lower sections of various sedimentary layers that he examined. As with clastic dikes, the formation of syneresis cracks could also occur due to the rapid loading of sediment and the eventual destabilization and dewatering of those sediments by compaction and settling (Tanner 1998). Expulsion of water along bedding planes could also account for the formation of these features apart from seismicity. Mudcrack formation by sediment dewatering should remain a consideration within our Flood framework.

Ball-and-pillow structures require high-energy forces operating over seconds to minutes. The Flood was a geologically short period of intense diastrophic activity in which the semi-consolidated nature of the strata, as well as the physical forces necessary to create the ball-and-pillow structures, were present. Seismic energy expended throughout the Ice Age and Present Age Timeframes could also have created ball-and-pillow structures where the strata remained semi- to unconsolidated and completely water-saturated.

CONCLUSIONS

Seismites reflect the passage of seismic energy through semi- to unconsolidated sediments. Their presence in the rock record is a testimony to the combination of rapid sedimentation of extensive seismicity that would have been present during the Flood. In seismically active areas, we would expect these features to be abundant in the rock record and in many instances they are not. What does this imply for those who hold to the uniformitarian world view?

The young-earth Flood framework contends that the majority of the rock record was created during the Flood. This period of earth history would have experienced tremendous seismic activity which would have decreased over time through the Ice Age and the Present Age Timeframes. Therefore, we would expect to observe seismites exhibited in many of the Flood deposits due to past seismic activity.

These sedimentary features can aid in understanding syndepositional and post-depositional seismic forces in a study area and can provide a means of understanding their relative age through crosscutting relationships. Seismites provide an important tool in defining the rapid sedimentation and unstable conditions associated with the Genesis flood.

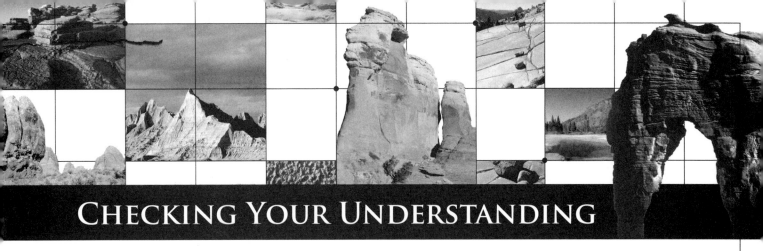

CHECKING YOUR UNDERSTANDING

1. Define seismites and explain what they can tell us about earth's past.

2. What kinds of features have been identified as seismites?

3. How quickly can seismites form?

4. What types of sediments do they form in?

5. What do the sizes of seismites tell us about seismic events?

6. What period in earth's biblical history probably had the highest levels of seismic activity?

7. What can we learn from seismites when they are concentrated in one area or occur in a linear manner across an area?

CHAPTER 7 *Defining Rounded Sedimentary Structures in Biblical History*

INTRODUCTION

Much of the rock record can be interpreted as the result of catastrophic forces and processes that occurred mostly during the Genesis flood. Many rounded sedimentary structures in strata exhibit evidence of catastrophic formation. Uniformitarian scientists interpret these features as concretions formed by diagenetic processes in low-energy depositional settings over extended periods of time. However, Potter and Pettijohn (1977) noted that concretion research is far from complete. Other interpretations are clearly possible. While concretions can develop in association with the breakdown of organic material, this is not the only manner by which rounded sedimentary features can form. In some instances, processes acting within a high-energy setting better explain them. This chapter will explore both explanations. Creationists need to determine how these features fit within our young-earth Flood framework.

CONCRETIONS AND ROUNDED SEDIMENTARY STRUCTURES

Concretions are common throughout the rock record. Research suggests they form contemporaneously within the enclosing sediments or shortly thereafter. In either instance, concretions are believed to form diagenetically (Collinson and Thompson 1989; McLane 1995; Pettijohn 1975; Ricci-Lucchi 1995). Some concretions are found to contain organic material; its decomposition creates changes in pH/Eh conditions that cause the precipitation of mineral cements in a radial manner around the organic mass. This process serves to entomb the decomposing material and form a concretion. However, not all concretions indicate that they formerly contained organic material.

Concretions typically form in sediments composed of silt- to clay-size particles. In many cases, they occur in well-defined stratigraphic layers. Sometimes the composition of the surrounding matrix differs from that of the concretion. Uniformitarian scientists generally assume that concretions form in low-energy environments over the course of thousands of years since none have been found developing today.

How can we determine the validity of this interpretation? Is this the only way that rounded concretions can form? Laboratory experiments have certainly demonstrated that the decomposition of organic matter within sediments can form concretions, but is that the only process? Is every rounded sedimentary feature a concretion?

Despite the empirical restrictions (no one has actually seen them form), there are sedimentary features that can help differentiate between organically derived concretions and rounded sedimentary structures. Some of these include the presence of erosional contacts, armoring,[1] and dissimilarities in composition between concretions and the surrounding matrix. We will see that some of the rounded features are not concretions, but form during transport and deposition of sediments.

ROUNDED SEDIMENTARY BOULDERS IN THE BASHI FORMATION, MISSISSIPPI

Exposures of the Bashi Formation just to the south of Meridian, Mississippi, can provide insight into how rounded structures can form depositionally. According to Ingram (1991, p. 12) the Bashi Formation:

> . . . varies in thickness between four and five feet in eastern Mississippi. Boulder-size concretions characterize this unit, and outcrops of the Bashi Formation in Mississippi and western Alabama are easily recognized by their presence. The Bashi marine unit is composed of white fine- to medium-grained quartz sand, and medium-grained glauconite. In places, a very fossiliferous sand is present below the concretions. The contact [with the underlying layer] is abrupt and undulates, showing that it was *an active scouring surface* which truncated the underlying beds. (Brackets and emphasis mine.)

The glauconite clay within the Bashi Formation contains fossilized shells throughout its thickness. At outcrops in Meridian, the lower scour surface of the upper marine unit of the Bashi Formation contains coral, snail and clam shells, shark teeth, stingray crushing plate pieces, alligator teeth, snake vertebrae, and an Omomyid primate tooth and jaw fragment (Dockery 1980, 1986; Ingram 1991). According to Dockery (1980, 1986), fossil mollusks are most abundant along the base of the numerous Bashi concretions, suggesting that they formed as a lag material.

Rounded boulders found within the Bashi Formation were first reported by Foster in 1940. They are often called "Bashi balls" or "Bashi boulders" (Figures 7-1 and 7-2). The combination of a scoured surface covered by fossil-rich sands capped by Bashi boulders suggests a high-energy environment, possibly a former channel with the sands and fossils forming lag deposits. In fact, uniformitarian scientists have proposed that the boulders formed in this manner and were rolled by tidal forces (Mississippi Geological Society 1983).

While some of the Bashi boulders (e.g., those found at the type section in southwestern Alabama) might well be large concretions, others appear to have been formed depositionally in a high-energy setting. Once formed as a clay layer, it was subject to erosion in a manner that removed large sections

Figure 7-1. Bashi boulders near Meridian, Mississippi, have been placed adjacent to one another as a result of road construction. The boulders average approximately 3.5 feet (1.0 m) in diameter.

Figure 7-2. Several Bashi boulders along the side of a road south of Meridian, Mississippi. Approximately 3.5 feet (1.0 m) in diameter, they are abundant in this area.

Figure 7-3. Close-up of the outer surface of one of the Bashi boulders from Meridian, Mississippi. Note the many clamshell impressions across the clay surface caused by rolling and armoring during transport. In some instances, all that is left of the original armor is a shell impression, while in other cases, shells and other debris are imbedded in the clay surface. Scale in one-inch (2.5 cm) divisions.

of the soft clay. Water currents rolled the large clay masses into 3.5-foot-diameter rounded features within existing channels. Today, we can see the many rounded and armored clay structures along the sides of some of the roads south of Meridian (Figure 7-3).

This interpretation is based primarily on Bashi boulders in Mississippi because of (1) invertebrate shells armoring their outer surface, and (2) they lie on material that appears to be a channel lag. On the other hand, the Bashi boulders exposed at their type locale in southwestern Alabama appear to be actual concretions because (1) they occur within a clay layer, and (2) they do not have the same type of armoring or associated channel-lag deposits as the boulders in Mississippi. Not surprisingly, the high-energy environment necessary to explain the rounded boulders found in Mississippi is not present or even conceivable in modern coastal processes. However, this energetic setting is expected within the Flood framework.

Rounded Sedimentary Structures in the Aguja Formation, Texas

The Aguja Formation (upper Cretaceous) in Big Bend National Park, Texas, contains rounded-to-oval-shaped sedimentary structures that appear

Figure 7-4. Aguja Formation rounded sandstone structures at Croton Springs, Big Bend National Park, Texas. The composition of the boulders varies slightly from the surrounding matrix, suggesting that the matrix is not the source material for the boulders. These boulders were found within a limited area that suggests a former channel. Note person in upper left for scale.

to have formed prior to deposition. These features were created in high-energy conditions associated with nearby volcanic eruptions, all within a sub-aqueous environment. These rounded sedimentary features formed as the materials were transported to lower elevations and subsequently buried (Figures 7-4 and 7-5). According to Maxwell and others (1967, p. 79–80), the Aguja Formation clay at Chisos Pen:

> . . . contains concretions up to 3 or 4 feet in diameter; some are in layers and others are irregularly scattered through an interval 50 feet thick. Most of the concretions are reddish-brown ironstone. . . .

The rounded structures found within the Aguja Formation have a slightly different composition from the surrounding matrix. The internal composition of some of these rounded structures suggests that they are composed of fine-grained sandy silt or clay. No fossils or organic matter have been noted within them.

Rounded Sedimentary Structures in the Fort Union Group, North Dakota

Another setting exhibiting large-scale rounded sedimentary features can be found in the northern segment of Theodore Roosevelt National Park, North Dakota (Chronic 1984; Ellwood 1996; Feldmann 1990). These rounded structures weather out of the Fort Union Group (Paleocene) clays. These clays probably originated from subaqueous volcanic activity. Although a diagenetic origin for these "cannonball" concretions has been suggested (Chronic 1984), it is more likely that many formed underwater by rolling action caused by moving Flood water. When the current energy decreased, the balls were deposited and buried under additional subaqueous volcanic materials (Figure 7-6). Following their burial, diagenesis served to harden them *in situ*. Today, erosion exposes these cannonball features at various locations within the park.

Figure 7-5. Aguja Formation with rounded-to-oblong-shaped sandstone boulders found along contacts in Dawson Creek, Big Bend National Park, Texas. The composition of the sandstone boulders differs significantly from the volcanic bentonitic material that encases them. This suggests that they were not diagenetically derived, but are reflective of the high-energy conditions associated with the deposition of the sandy-ash layer under subaqueous conditions during the Flood. Scale in six-inch (15 cm) divisions.

ROUNDED SEDIMENTARY STRUCTURES IN A VOLCANIC SETTING

The theory that rounded sedimentary features can form within a high-energy subaqueous volcanic setting is counter to the uniformitarian theory of concretion development. However, the creationist concept is based on solid evidence — the presence of these rounded structures in volcanic settings that would have provided sediments that were cohesive enough to form large clasts, subject to rounding under high-energy subaqueous conditions.

If the volcanically derived rounded clay boulders were armored, there would be no discussion about the rolling action necessary to explain them. But the absence of obvious armoring and slight differences in composition between the rounded boulders and surrounding sediments allows uniformitarian scientists to conclude that they are concretions — the result of diagenesis — even without evidence of any former organic material inside the features. Caution should be observed when interpreting rounded sedimentary structures found in the rock record because some are likely organically derived, while others reflect formation by rolling under the high-energy

Figure 7-6. A cannonball concretion, approximately 5 feet (1.5 m) in diameter, exposed in front of the clay from which it has weathered (Fort Union Group). This locale is in the northern segment of Theodore Roosevelt National Park, North Dakota, an area of probable subaqueous volcanic activity during the Flood. Many of the boulders became rounded and armored as they rolled under the force of Flood water. However, some may have also formed by diagenesis. Only by careful examination can the origin of these rounded features be determined.

conditions associated with moving Flood water (see Froede 1997e). Further site-specific investigation is required to determine which interpretation might be appropriate.

A Young-Earth Flood Framework

The current-derived Bashi boulders were formed while Flood water still covered the Gulf Coastal Plain (Froede 1995a, 1997d). Several depositional settings are possible, but it is likely that these Bashi boulders formed as Flood water began to retreat from the area. Large channels would have been created across the southeastern Coastal Plain. These channels would have accelerated water movement, creating the energy necessary to incise downward into semi-lithified strata such as the Bashi Marl. Large sections of clay would have been eroded (some possibly by undercutting) and giant clay clasts rounded as they rolled along the channel. As the currents waned, the rounded clay boulders were deposited in the former channels. The addition of sediments within this marine environment would bury the boulders and channel lag deposits. This interpretation is consistent with the expectations of the Flood framework.

Rounded sedimentary features in the Aguja Formation reflect subaqueous volcanic formation as large-scale eruptions across this area created conditions of uplift from which pyroclastic materials were released into the surrounding water. During this volcanic activity, the volcanic materials would be transported toward adjacent low-lying areas. Some of the material was cohesive enough to form into rounded structures. Many of these features have a silty-sand surface and they are usually found in layers of a different (i.e., more silty-to-clayey) composition. These rounded features have not been found to contain any fossilized organic material. The same can be repeated for a number of the cannonball concretions from the Fort Union Group.

Concretions are present in the rock record. But many of them may have a depositional origin rather than a diagenetic one. Each occurrence of concretions should be examined carefully to determine their origin. The young-earth Flood framework invokes short-term, high-energy forces that would create conditions responsible for the rapid formation and burial of many of these rounded sedimentary features. We must look beyond current uniformitarian interpretations and seek the best empirical reconstruction of the rock record within the constraints of the young-earth Flood framework.

The Flood Event and Ice Age Timeframes were periods of intense diastrophic activity. A careful examination of site-specific conditions will be required to accurately determine the appropriate creationist time frame for the formation of the original strata (e.g., Flood Event, Ice Age, or Present Age Timeframe — Figure 1-6). However, only short periods of time would be necessary to form and deposit these rounded sedimentary structures within this postulated high-energy setting.

Conclusions

While the organically driven diagenetic formation of concretions remains a valid alternative, in some instances other interpretations are clearly possible. The formation of concretions via organic decomposition is not unreasonable within both the young-earth Flood and uniformitarian frameworks. However, the high-energy depositional formation of rounded sedimentary structures would be more consistent with the creationist perspective.

The presence of rounded sedimentary structures within the rock record raises at least three issues for the creationist stratigrapher:

1. Are they diagenetic in origin or were they possibly formed by water transport?

2. If they were formed from water transport, then what levels of energy might have been necessary to erode and transport them?

3. What distance have they traveled?

In some instances, we can demonstrate that rounded sedimentary features have formed as a result of water transport. Our understanding of these features will vary greatly from the uniformitarian interpretation of millions of years of changing paleoenvironments, low-energy sedimentary processes, and long-term diagenesis. One example is the Bashi boulders found in Meridian, Mississippi. They probably formed when a preexisting clay layer was eroded, and the resulting clay clasts were rounded, transported, and eventually deposited in submerged channels along with other channel lag deposits. Later, they were buried by additional materials derived from both the shallow marine shelf and upland terrestrial areas.

Another potential source of boulders was from the subaqueous volcanic eruptions during the Flood. Volcanic ash, flowing downhill underwater, could have formed large clasts that would have been rounded before deposition. These semi-lithified materials were transported by water currents in effect at the time to adjacent areas where burial and subsequent diagenesis served to further lithify them into cohesive strata. Today, these inappropriately labeled "concretions" weather from the surrounding clays as rounded-to-oblong sedimentary objects, and in many instances they are lithologically different from the surrounding matrix. While post-depositional compaction and diagenesis have played a role in further shaping and lithifying these rounded sedimentary features, they were originally created under high-energy processes.

Young-earth creationists need to consider more than one alternative when defining rounded sedimentary features in the field. While some are of diagenetic origin, others could have formed in association with subaqueous transport, deposition, and burial. Our Flood framework requires that we define the rock record consistent with the biblical perspective of earth history. As a result, many of the uniformitarian assumptions regarding these rounded features will be rejected. Rounded sedimentary features can provide valuable information related to the hydraulic conditions for a particular locale at a specific time during the Flood Event Timeframe.

Endnotes

1. Armoring occurs as a semi-lithified mass of sedimentary material is rolled (and rounded) across the surface of another sedimentary material, thereby coating the outer surface of the rolled mass and providing protection from further mechanical erosion. An example is where a clay ball would roll across a sand, pebble, or shell surface and the particles become embedded around the clay ball, affording it protection from further erosion.

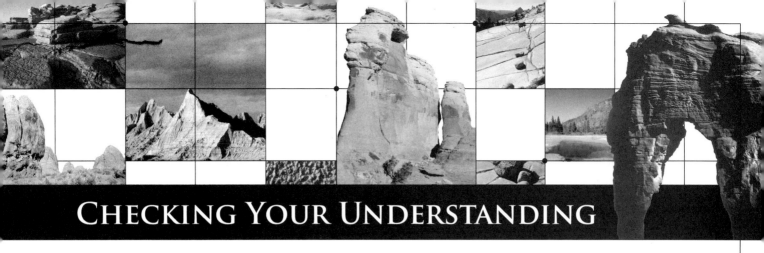

CHECKING YOUR UNDERSTANDING

1. What is the difference between a concretion and a rounded sedimentary feature?

2. Why do uniformitarian scientists view rounded sedimentary structures as concretions?

3. Why should we consider that rounded sedimentary features were possibly created during the Flood?

4. What can these rounded features tell us about the geologic conditions during the time they were deposited and buried?

5. Where should we expect to find rounded sedimentary features? Concretions?

6. Why are some rounded features larger than others? Why are some concretions larger than others?

7. What does the size of a rounded sedimentary feature tell us about possible Flood water conditions?

CHAPTER 8 *Defining Ripple Marks in Biblical History*

INTRODUCTION

Ripple marks can be formed in many different types of sedimentary materials and they occur throughout the rock record. They are often used to support uniformitarian preconceived paleoenvironments that purportedly existed for long periods of time. However, ripple marks are nothing more than sedimentary features reflective of air or water movement. Their size and scale can provide valuable information in assessing conditions of deposition. The scientific analysis of ripple marks extends well beyond the scope of this chapter. Our evaluation of these features will be limited to an overview of the smaller-scale features, recognizing that ripple marks are scalable to sand waves and even larger dune sizes. The varied sedimentary forms of ripples include (progressing in size): micro-ripples, ripples, sand waves, dunes, antidunes, hummocks, and bars (see discussion in Stow 2005).

From a biblical perspective, most of the rock record was created under aqueous conditions during the Flood. Therefore, we should expect to see sedimentary features indicative of water movement in much of the strata. Ripple marks created by aqueous processes support this interpretation. They also form today, so contemporary studies of geological processes can help us understand the mechanics of their formation in the past. Armed with a general knowledge of ripple marks, it is hoped that the reader will gain a better understanding of how these sedimentary features support a biblical interpretation of earth history.

Ripple Marks

Ripple marks are physical structures created in loose sediment by the surface friction of moving wind or water. They are best visualized as small-scale sand waves or dunes. In many instances, the shape of a ripple can provide information about current strength, intensity, and direction. Ripples range in size from 1.5 inches to almost 24 inches (crest-to-crest), and up to 2.4 inches in height (Reineck and Singh 1980). They can be used to estimate water current velocity where no other means of making this determination is possible (Rubin and McCulloch 1980).

The complex and varying nature of water or air currents acting on the small, loose particles produces a wide array of ripple crest patterns. The general progression of ripple crests moves from straight-crested (linear) through sinuous-crested to isolated (i.e., linguoid-crested) forms based on the complexity of flow velocity (Nichols 1999). However, this is a simplification as ripple marks can take many forms. For example, Ricci-Lucchi (1995) recognized 8 ripple-crested forms while Collinson and Thompson (1989) identified 11 (Figure 8-1). Through computer modeling, Rubin (1987) identified approximately 78 possible ripple mark and cross-bedded dune forms.

Individual ripple crest symmetry provides information related to the direction of water or air movement and its energy (Collinson and Thompson 1989; Pettijohn and Potter 1964; Potter and Pettijohn 1977; Reineck and Singh 1980; Ricci-Lucchi 1995; Selley 1988). Ripples with perfect symmetry reflect oscillatory wind/water movement (i.e., bi-directional), while asymmetrical ripples reflect current flow in a single direction (Stow 2005). They can also form into complex shapes indicative of multi-directional water or air movement (Figure 8-2).

Figure 8-1. Diagram showing changes in ripple mark development with increased water flow velocity (modified from Nichols 1999, Figure 4.9, p. 45).

Ripples can form in many different environments under a variety of conditions (e.g., Friedman and Sanders 1978; Harms and others 1975, 1982; Lewis and McConchie 1994; Middleton 1965; Scholle and Spearing 1982; Scholle and others 1983). They have been used by uniformitarian scientists to support the concept of long-term water and/or air movement extending into earth's deep

Figure 8-2. Ripple marks preserved in the Pottsville Formation south of Birmingham, Alabama. The many layers contain different types of ripple marks reflective of changing water current direction and intensity. Scale in inches and centimeters.

past (e.g., Bigarella 1973; Brown 1970; Pettijohn 1975; Pettijohn and others 1987; Potter and Pettijohn 1977; Rubin 1987).

DIFFERENCES BETWEEN WATER-FORMED AND AIR-FORMED RIPPLES

The differences between water-formed and air-formed small-scale ripples are negligible. So any attempt to determine the original depositional setting must then shift to other larger-scale features, such as sand dunes, that uniformitarian scientists contend can clearly demonstrate the past environment. It is also not unusual to find small-scale ripple marks

superimposed on sand dunes that occur either above or underwater.

Sand dune morphology is believed to provide distinctive features that can aid in determining if the paleosetting was subaerial or subaqueous. These features include dune shape, size, nature of the internal cross-bedding, angle of repose (Mann and Kanagy 1990), and the avalanching of noncohesive sand on the dune slip face (Hunter 1977; McKee 1945). The geologic evidence to support many of these preconceptions in the rock record comes solely from the uniformitarian perspective. In the absence of body fossil evidence, many times the paleosetting is interpreted as eolian (e.g., desert) simply because of the investigator's personal preference. Even when the evidence is questionable or ambiguous, many uniformitarian scientists often stick to their existing theories.

This conflict between personal belief and experimental data is seen in the analysis of fossilized trackways in the Coconino Sandstone from the Grand Canyon (Figure 8-3). The Coconino Sandstone contains cross-bedded sands, ripple marks, and vertebrate trackways and has traditionally been interpreted by uniformitarian scientists as an ancient desert (Matthes 1932; McKee 1945, 1947, 1979). For many years, Brand (1977, 1978, 1979, 1996) and Brand and Tang (1991)

have examined the trackways in the Coconino to determine if they actually formed underwater. They conducted experiments where salamanders were introduced into a tank with water circulating across loose sand particles. As the salamanders moved

Figure 8-3. Footprints of an unknown vertebrate move from the lower left toward the upper right. The tracks follow along a straight-crested ripple mark (dark diagonal line) in the Coconino Sandstone. These footprints are consistent with a subaqueous setting (see Brand 1992, 1996; Brand and Tang 1991). The Flood would have created opportunities for moving water and sediments to be preserved rapidly enough to capture and preserve ephemeral features such as ripple marks and footprints. Scale in inches and centimeters.

Figure 8-4. Water-generated ripple marks in the Pottsville Formation south of Birmingham, Alabama. The symmetry of these ripples shows that they are linguoid ripples with the former current moving from right to left. Scale in inches and centimeters.

across the sand, they produced tracks that were essentially the same as those found preserved in the Coconino Sandstone (Brand 1992, 1996; Brand and Tang 1991). However, some uniformitarian scientists rejected this experimental evidence[1] because of their preconceived paleoenvironment (Lockley et al 1992). An excellent overview of the controversy is provided by creationists Snelling and Austin (1992).

WATER-FORMED RIPPLES AND PALEOCURRENT ANALYSIS

Water-formed ripple marks provide no clue to the depth in which they formed (Pettijohn 1975), as they extend from the shoreline to the deepest parts of the ocean (Heezen and Hollister 1971; Faugères and Stow 1993; Stow and Lovell 1979; Stow and others 2002). However, their shape and size can provide important information about the direction, intensity, and strength of the water current that created them (Figure 8-4).

Uniformitarian scientists generally assume that ripple marks found in lithified strata can be used to define water movement occurring over extended periods of time. For example, Pelletier (1958) reported on ripple marks found in strata in Maryland and Pennsylvania that exhibit a consistent ripple direction from the upper Devonian (Catskill) to the

Pennsylvanian (Pottsville) — a period of time allegedly spanning almost 200 million years! This is an incredible length of time even by uniformitarian standards, as demonstrated by Pettijohn's (1975, p. 520) statement:

> The stability or persistence of a particular paleocurrent system through time is indeed one of the astonishing results of paleocurrent measurements.

Despite their ephemeral nature, ripple marks can do more for uniformitarian geoscientists than define extended periods of earth history. They can also convey information about sea water circulation patterns and the tectonic stability of continental shelves. Pettijohn (1975, p. 521) stated:

> . . . the stability of paleocurrent systems has been demonstrated in many cases and that such stability through time implies the existence of stable tectonic elements with their consequent slopes that govern erosion, transport, and sedimentation for long periods of time.

Using ripple marks to infer a stable continent position relative to sea level, the passing of long periods of time, and unchanging sediment source areas is clearly expected within the uniformitarian world view. However, this is not the only way of understanding and interpreting ripple marks found in the rock record.

A YOUNG-EARTH FLOOD FRAMEWORK

The young-earth Flood framework would define the majority of the ripple marks found in the rock record as having formed during the Flood, although some may have been buried and preserved in both pre- and post-Flood settings. Information drawn directly from the rock record would be necessary to make any specific determination. Our depositional environment would largely occur within an aqueous setting and over a brief period of time. Any reworking of the sedimentary materials would be reflective of changing geologic energy and could also take the form of cross-beds and ripple marks. Hence, ripple marks can provide creationists with additional information related to changing aqueous flow patterns and depositional settings. For example, ripple marks found in the uniformitarian Late Cretaceous epeiric seaway sediments extending across North America can also be understood as features formed as Flood water slowly withdrew to the deepening oceanic basins (Froede 1995a; Froede and Williams 1997).

During the Flood, water moved across the earth's surface driven by winds and global tectonism (see Barnette and Baumgardner 1994) creating in places ripple marks that would be buried and preserved. Areas of uplift on the submerged continents would form barriers to the movement of Flood water. Sediments eroded from the areas of uplift would be transported and deposited consistent with the Floodwater flow patterns adjacent to the submerged barrier. Ripple marks that might form on the exposed surfaces of these deposits would then conform to Floodwater movement. With continued deposition, the ripple mark orientation would reflect a consistent water current direction extending across hundreds of vertical feet of sediments. This setting would then reflect continuous sedimentation and consistent Floodwater current movement, and not millions of years of uniformitarian epeiric sea water circulation.

For example, the Appalachian Mountains were probably uplifted during an early part of the Flood (Lower Flood Event Division). The uplifted rocks were eroded, and the resulting detritus was removed and deposited into adjacent basins. The submerged Appalachian Mountains restricted Flood water from flowing in a general east/west direction. Instead, the water was forced to move either north or south around the uplifted barrier. Water currents then created ripple marks on the sediments as they were added to the deepening basins (Figure 8-5). This would explain why Pelletier (1958) noted consistent water current direction (determined from ripple marks) purportedly extending for almost 200 million years. In some cases, these submerged continental barriers could have created conditions of deepwater current circulation that might have been separate and distinct from surface currents. Hence, ripple marks might prove useful in defining complex Floodwater flow patterns between sedimentary basins and adjacent areas of uplift.

Ripple marks are also exposed in various layers of upturned strata in the Western United States.

Figure 8-5. Well-defined ripple marks from the Sequatchie Formation exposed at Ringgold, Georgia. These features reflect the movement of Flood water possibly influenced by the uplifting Appalachian Mountains to the east. Scale in inches and centimeters.

Figure 8-6. Ripple marks from the Dakota sandstone found west of Denver, Colorado, provide direct evidence that this area was underwater at one time. A creationist interpretation would suggest that the ripples formed early during the Flood and then later became exposed with the uplift of the Rocky Mountains during a later stage of the Flood (Holroyd 1995). Scale in inches and centimeters.

The uplift associated with the formation of the modern Rocky Mountains (Middle/Upper Flood Event Division) accelerated erosion, which removed sufficient overburden to expose these features at the ground surface (Figure 8-6). Much of the paleocurrent information derived from ripple marks found in the Western United States remains to be resolved (Figure 8-7). However, these features could prove useful in understanding Floodwater movement and tectonic uplift in areas around the Rocky Mountains during the Flood.

CONCLUSIONS

Because of our modern knowledge of the mechanics of ripple formation in sediments, these features are useful in reconstructing earth history. However, as with many other phenomena, interpretation is driven primarily by the world view rather than the actual data. Thus, most if not all uniformitarian historical reconstructions using ripple marks would not agree with the biblical framework. We would view these features from the rock record as physical evidence in support of the global Flood. Additionally, creationists can employ ripple marks to possibly reconstruct current direction and energy expended during the various stages of the Flood. Their direction would aid in determining the timing

Figure 8-7. Very pronounced ripples in the Aguja Sandstone in the Big Bend area of Texas. The size of these wave crests suggests that strong water currents were moving in a top-to-bottom direction. Scale in inches and centimeters.

and preserve these features. This setting is not unexpected during the Flood.

While ripple marks are ephemeral sedimentary features reflective of flow direction, they can provide the investigator with important information regarding current strength, intensity, and direction. Creationists can use these structures to investigate circulatory patterns and areas of tectonic uplift during the time of the global Flood.

of tectonism of locally or regionally submerged barriers on the submerged continents.

The burial and preservation of ripple marks requires rapid sedimentation; otherwise, these fragile sedimentary features would be reworked or eroded. In some cases, the now-lithified ripple marks appear to form on massive flat to near-flat surfaces. This would require large-scale water current movement coupled with high rates of sedimentation sufficient to bury

Endnotes

1. This incident illustrates how a researcher's world view defines how data are interpreted. It also demonstrates the human condition to stay with the comfortable and familiar rather than carefully weighing the evidence and changing the interpretation to fit the data. Unfortunately, to change any dominant geological interpretation usually requires almost overwhelming evidence to the contrary and requires many years to accomplish. This does not occur very often and is one reason why there are so many incorrect ideas within the geological sciences.

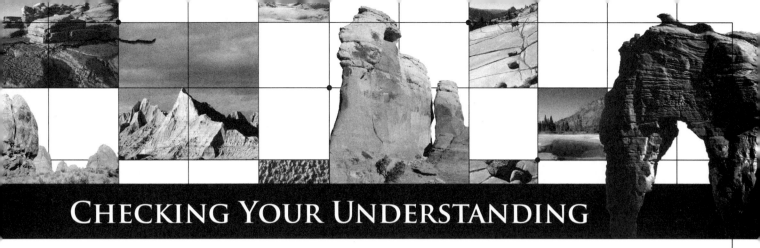

CHECKING YOUR UNDERSTANDING

1. Ripple marks come in a variety of shapes and sizes. What is the largest ripple form? The smallest? Where might we expect to find them?

2. Are ripple marks limited to forming only in water?

3. Can ripple marks form on sand dunes?

4. What do ripple marks tell us about wind or water movement? How many types of ripple marks are there?

5. How are ripple marks useful in the young-earth Flood framework?

6. How can we tell the difference between ripple marks formed in air or underwater?

7. Do vertebrate trackways in rippled sand force us to accept a desert setting? Why is the trackway across ripple marks in Figure 2-5 interpreted by uniformitarian scientists as having formed underwater when the trackway along the ripple crest in Figure 8-3 is defined as eolian?

CHAPTER 9

Defining Bentonites, Metabentonites and Tonsteins in Biblical History

INTRODUCTION

Volcanic eruptions have contributed significant volumes of pyroclastic sediments to the rock record (Axelrod 1981; Carey 1991; Fisher and Smith 1991; Lockley and Rice 1990; Rampino 1991; Rice 1990; Ross 1928, 1955; Ross and others 1928; Smith and Lowe 1991). Evidence of past volcanic ashfalls are found in many stratigraphic sections all across the globe. In many cases, these pyroclastic layers indicate large-scale, catastrophic, eruptive events unlike anything occurring on earth today. For uniformitarian scientists, ash layers are often used to provide radiometric information necessary to assign the volcanic deposit and adjacent strata to their geologic time scale.

During a volcanic eruption, ash is hurled into the atmosphere. Upon losing its buoyant heat energy, it then falls over a wide area. Because the volcanic minerals are not stable at surface conditions and the ash particles have a proportionately large surface area, they begin to chemically alter, first through the process of devitrification and then by the chemical breakdown of the minerals. The end result is the complete destruction of the original glass shard fabric (Pettijohn 1975). The resulting clay is further modified depending on its depth of burial, exposure to migrating subsurface brines, and changing pH/Eh conditions within the subsurface.

Bentonites, metabentonites, and tonsteins are all clays derived from volcanic ash. They are considered important stratigraphic markers to uniformitarian scientists because they often cover broad areas and they are radiometrically datable. Can these volcanic clays be used by young-earth creationists in defining earth history? Can they be tied to the biblical time scale? A review of these various ash-derived clays will help us understand their role in defining the passage of time and how they can be interpreted within the young-earth Flood framework.

Grain size (mm)	Epiclastic fragments	Pyroclastic fragments	
256	Boulders (and "blocks")	Course	Blocks and Bombs
64	Cobble	Fine	Blocks and Bombs
2	Pebble	Lapilli	
1/16	Sand	Course	Ash
1/256	Silt	Fine	Ash
	Clay	Fine	Ash

Table 9-1. Particle sizes of volcaniclastic materials can be related to the type of volcanic eruption and its subsequent weathering. Bentonites, metabentonites, and tonsteins comprise the ash portion of the table. Weathered ash is transformed to silt-to-clay-size particles that are similar to those derived from other source rocks. Hence, it is difficult to pin down a volcanic origin without additional evidence (derived from Williams and McBirney 1979, p. 127).

VOLCANIC ASHFALLS

Besides the usual steam and gas emissions, volcanic eruptions result in the generation of pyroclastic materials of various particle sizes (Table 9-1). Bentonites, metabentonites, and tonsteins are derived from rhyolitic to dacitic ashfalls originating from plinian-to-ultaplinian types of volcanic eruptions (Figure 9-1). According to uniformitarian scientists, these two powerful and explosive types of eruptions are capable of supplying enough volcanic ash to provide the thickness and areal extent of large volcanic deposits found in the rock record (Carey and Sigurdsson 1989; Carey and Sparks 1986; Heiken and Wohletz 1985; Pyle 1989; Slaughter and Hamil 1970; Walker 1973). But in some cases, the thickness of the altered ash layers is evidence of volcanism on a scale far exceeding that observed in modern times (Haynes 1994). Uniformitarian scientists believe that volcanic eruptions are short-term events relative to their time scale, but that they occur in cycles spanning tens to thousands of years. With the rise of neocatastrophism, they have also suggested that a few large eruptions have caused climate change sufficient to alter the path of evolution (e.g., Axelrod 1981; Lockley and Rice 1990).

Once deposited, ash can be chemically and physically altered, usually to some type of clay, based on its composition and the depositional environment in which it falls (Fisher and Schmincke 1984; Price and Duff 1969; Weaver 1958). This alteration is usually so severe that geologists generally will not accept a volcanic origin of the clay without conclusive proof, such as contained glass shards. Technological advances now allow tests based on chemistry, heavy minerals content, and trace element fingerprinting to help in ascertaining the origin of clays (Brookins and Rigby 1987; Delano and others 1994; Fisher and Schmincke 1984; Haynes 1994; Huff 1983; Kolata and others 1987, 1996; Weaver 1963). These are exciting developments for creationists because they open the possibility that more clay layers will be identified as volcanically derived, and thereby reflect their catastrophic origin. A volcanic origin for many of the clay layers

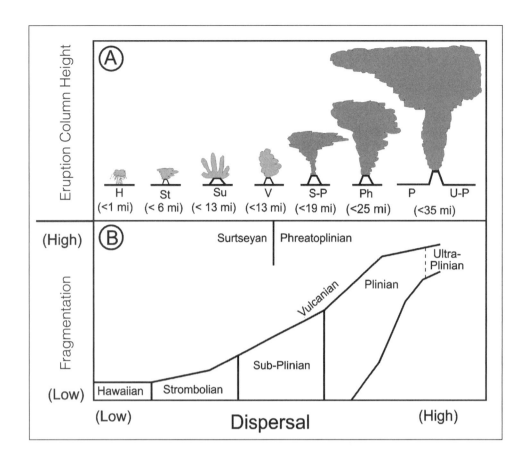

Figure 9-1. Different types of volcanic eruptions. (A) shows the eruption height (in miles) of the different eruptive styles. The letters beneath each volcano correspond to the eruption types in (B), which show the relationship between areal dispersion of the different types of volcanic eruptions compared to the amount of fragmentation (a function of explosivity) of the volcanic ejecta (modified from Cas and Wright 1987, p. 130).

found within the subsurface would require dramatic changes to existing uniformitarian theories of slowly changing paleoenvironments.

Many geologists have suggested that there are greater volumes of volcanically derived materials composing the rock record than are currently recognized or acknowledged (Buie 1964; Fisher and Schmincke 1984; Froede 1994d, 1996; Grim 1958; Patterson and Buie 1974; Reynolds 1966, 1970; Ross 1955; Weaver 1963, 1989). The identification of former ash layers could help resolve some clay origin questions, and could play a significant role in further defining the time constraints necessary to develop the rock record within an area or region.

VOLCANIC ASH AS A DATING TOOL

Both young-earth creationists and uniformitarian scientists recognize that it is not always possible to identify the volcano responsible for a given ashfall. However, this shortcoming does not prevent geologists from using them as stratigraphic markers when they can be correlated across widespread areas (Figure 9-2). Using radioactive age-dating methods, uniformitarian scientists claim that volcanic ash layers are accurate dating tools (Chamley 1989; Haynes 1994; Kauffman and Caldwell 1993; Mathisen and McPherson 1991; Miall 2000). However, that claim is dubious, given the many instances in which fossils are used to recalibrate the radiometric date of the ash (Brooks and others 1976; Stearn and Carroll 1989). Other discrepancies come from (1) the unknown age of the magma melt, and/or (2) the exposure of the buried ash to mineral-rich connate brines which alter its crystalline structure and reset its radiometric age (Elliot and Aronson 1993). Despite the presumption that volcanic ash layers can provide an absolute age-date,

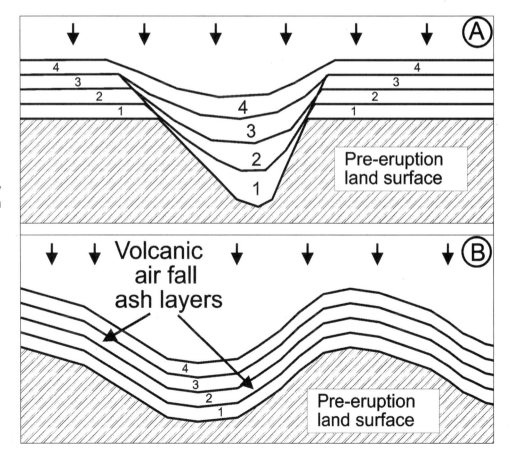

Figure 9-2. Ashfalls conform to preexisting topography. The age of each ash layer can be determined by superposition; #1 is the oldest and #4 is the youngest. Ashfalls slump and thicken in valleys (A), but are evenly layered on flat surfaces (B). In both cases, wind direction (current direction if subaqueous) and distance from the source play major roles in the spreading, reworking, and subsequent deposition of the ash layers (modified from Fisher and Schmincke 1984, p. 147).

Figure 9-3. Bentonite exposed along Dawson Creek, Big Bend National Park, Texas. Diagenesis has produced color banding that uniformitarian scientists assert are individual paleosols, even though the soil's high acidic content severely restricts plant growth and diversity. In reality, this massive volcanic deposit was created, transported, and deposited during the Flood.

they are often calibrated against some paleontological data set.

By themselves, ash deposits do not prove or even suggest the passage of vast periods of time. Rather, the surrounding non-volcanic strata and fossils are used by uniformitarian scientists to support this interpretation. The alteration of an ash to clay also suggests the passage of time, but that duration will vary considerably depending upon the rate of devitrification and diagenesis. While ash layers reflect catastrophic short-term events, it is the interpretive framework employed by the individual who examines the adjacent strata that will dictate how these deposits are applied to their world view.

BENTONITES

Bentonites are laterally widespread, clay-rich, thin beds that are of *probable* volcanic origin (Chamley 1989; Fisher and Schmincke 1984; Grim and Güven 1978; Moore and Reynolds 1997). The uncertainty lies in the fact that bentonite can form in several different ways. Grim and Güven (1978, p. 127) have identified the origin of bentonite by the following means:

1. Alteration of volcanic ash or tuff essentially *in situ.*

2. Hydrothermal alteration, generally of igneous rocks.

3. Deuteric alteration of igneous material.

4. Miscellaneous and uncertain modes of origin, including instances where no precise mode of origin can be established.

According to Chamley (1989, p. 412), the most relevant arguments in support of bentonite being derived from an altered volcanic ash are:

1. Thinness usually less than 4 inches (10 cm) associated with continuous to near-continuous lateral form exceeding tens to hundreds of miles (or km).

2. Sharp lower and upper contacts with adjacent sedimentary rocks.

3. Presence of frequent vitroclastic textures and of locally unaltered vitric tuffs.

4. Local existence of lateral gradation from unaltered ash-rich sediment to altered clay-rich sediment.

5. Occurrence of some relict minerals originating under high-temperature conditions. These minerals, which usually do not exist in adjacent sediments, may include biotite, rutile, sanidine, sphene, zircon, and other species.

Figure 9-4. Massive ash layers exposed in Death Valley, California. These deposits indicate extensive historical eruptions, and their morphology suggests that they formed subaqueously during the Flood, only to be later modified subaerially during the Ice Age Timeframe.

Despite other possibilities, the best explanation for most of the bentonite found in a sedimentary setting is from the alteration of an ash or tuff (Figure 9-3). Bentonite is found in strata spanning from the upper Paleozoic to the present (Grim and Güven 1978). Weaver (1989) stated that bentonites occur in sediments as young as Late Pliocene, but most occur in lower Pliocene to upper Miocene age strata. Individual beds range in thickness from a few inches to tens of feet.

The dominant clay minerals in bentonites are the smectites (Chamley 1989; Moore and Reynolds 1997). Bentonite can vary in its mineral composition to include smectite-bentonite, kaolinite-bentonite, and illite-bentonite. With increasing depth of burial, both smectite-bentonites and kaolinite-bentonites tend to be altered to illite-smectite, illite, and even chlorite (Chamley 1989). Hence, the recognition of altered volcanic ash layers becomes increasingly enigmatic with each transformation of the clay mineral.

According to Einsele (1992, p. 67), the history of a volcanic ash can be understood from:

> . . . phreatomagmatic eruptions and co-ignimbrite processes. The pyroclasts and hydroclasts settle not only through air, but also through lake water and sea water. Thus, they generate widespread thin ash layers which are often well preserved in depressions on land, and in parts of the sea. Bentonite layers (tonsteins) in marine and

Figure 9-5. Photograph from Zabriskie Point, Death Valley, California, showing the bedding (accented by diagenesis) of former lake bed deposits which are composed of altered ash layers. These deposits probably occurred both during and after the Flood.

Figure 9-6. A K-bentonite layer (Millbrig) along the Red Mountain Expressway, Birmingham, Alabama. This volcanic ash layer covers hundreds of square miles — an eruption of monumental scale. The ash is sandwiched by massive carbonate layers, suggesting the eruption occurred during the Flood. Whether the eruption occurred above or under water has not been resolved. Scale in inches and centimeters.

lake sediments as well as in coal-bearing sequences are mostly derived from former volcanic ash.

Although bentonite occurs in freshwater environments (Figures 9-4 and 9-5), the majority of bentonites are identified as being formed under marine conditions (in many cases identified by the marine fossils contained within them). The preservation and subsequent identification of the altered ash layers within the rock record is a function of the amount of sediment mixing along with the intensity of bioturbation (Einsele 1992). Groundwater

chemistry is also a major factor in the preservation of the buried bentonitic layers (Weaver 1989).

In several investigations using scanning electron microscopy, many bentonites still retained well-preserved relict textures of pumice pyroclasts and glass shards (Heiken and Wohletz 1985). However, further alteration destroys these remaining evidences, rendering the volcanic origin of the clay as doubtful.

METABENTONITES

According to Grim and Güven (1978, p. 158), metabentonites:

. . . are reported in many formations of Paleozoic age. In general, these materials are composed of illite-smectite mixed-layer minerals, so that the material does not have the physical properties of bentonites. The metabentonites have been looked upon essentially as altered volcanic ash to which potassium has been added later, giving rise to the illite component and the loss of bentonite properties.

Significant work has been conducted on the Ordovician metabentonites (i.e., K-bentonites) of eastern North America and northern Europe (Figures 9-6, 9-7, 9-8a, and 9-8b) (Haynes 1994; Huff and Kolata 1990; Huff and others 1992, 1996; Kolata and others 1996; Samson and others 1989). Several uniformitarian geoscientists have suggested that these ash layers provide such reliable radiometric dates that they can be used to recalibrate the conodont and graptolite index fossils used to age-date the strata (Goldman and others 1994; Haynes 1994; Mitchell and others 1994).

The origin of the Ordovician-age K-bentonitic beds began as volcanic ash layers that were buried to various depths and subjected to moderate amounts of heat (Haynes 1994; Kolata and others 1996). Within this setting, the ash was transformed to a bentonite and was later subjected to potassium-rich groundwater (Hay and others 1988; Haynes 1994). The potassium was incorporated in the clay structure, resulting in a significant reduction in the swelling capability of the clay — the primary physical characteristic of smectite-rich bentonite. Tectonic and erosional forces served to eventually uplift and remove the overburden of strata covering the K-bentonites, leaving them exposed at or near the ground surface.

TONSTEINS

The term "tonstein" (German for claystone) refers to a kaolinite-dominated, thin claystone bed interbedded with coal-bearing strata. Many tonsteins are believed to be of volcanic origin (Cas and Wright 1987; Fisher and Schmincke 1984), and are commonly associated with coal deposits as underclays,

Figure 9-7. A K-bentonite layer (Deicke) exposed within the Colvin Mountain Sandstone at Greensport Gap, Alabama. The altered ash layer is behind the scale. Scale in inches and centimeters.

Figure 9-8a. A K-bentonite layer (Millbrig) exposed at the Big Ridge roadcut on Interstate 59, northeast of Gadsden, Alabama. The volcanic ashfall layer is immediately behind the white scale bar which is 6 inches (15 cm) high.

One Inch

Figure 9-8b. A close-up view of the Millbrig tuffaceous ash collected from this outcrop. According to uniformitarian scientists, this ash has remained relatively unaltered for approximately 450 million years. Given the ease with which volcanic ash alters, it is more plausible that it is only a few thousand years old. Note the large black biotite crystals in the ashfall tuff matrix. Scale at bottom in centimeters with inch scale bar at top left.

fireclays, and flint clays (e.g., Bohor and Triplehorn 1993; Chesnut 1983; Loughnan 1970; Lyons and others 1992, 1994; Price and Duff 1969; Rice and others 1994; Spears 1970; Spears and Kanaris-Sotiriou 1979; Spears and Rice 1973; Triplehorn and Bohor 1981).

The kaolinitic composition of many tonsteins is believed to indicate that they formed in a freshwater setting. Their close association with coal seams led uniformitarian scientists to interpret them as forming in a freshwater coastal swamp (Figure 9-9). However, acids generated by decomposing plants would have played a major role in diagenesis, regardless of the purported paleoenvironment.

Uniformitarian scientists claim that tonsteins play an important role in defining the origin of coal deposits. These clays have been suggested to represent the former soils in which the swamps existed over the course of millions of years. However, additional evidence in support of this interpretation is generally lacking. A volcanic origin for tonsteins would create serious problems for the uniformitarian autochthonous model for the origin of coal.

A YOUNG-EARTH FLOOD FRAMEWORK

The biblical geologic framework would predict significant volcanism during and for some

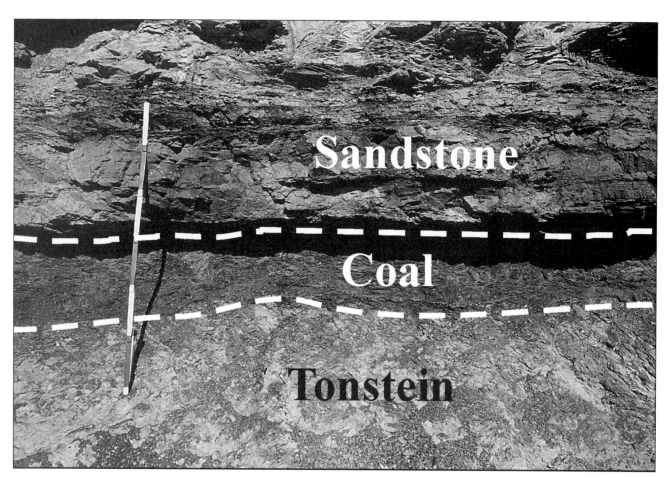

Figure 9-9. A tonstein clay layer beneath a coal layer exposed along Tennessee State Highway 30, east of Spencer, Tennessee. This clay layer has been interpreted as the soil of an ancient coastal swamp (Jones 1977). However, the evidence in support of it being a paleosol is lacking, and a volcanic origin for this tonstein would prove fatal to the current uniformitarian paleoenvironmental reconstruction. Scale in six-inch (15 cm) divisions.

time after the Flood. It is not unreasonable to imagine the initiation of large-scale volcanic eruptions with the advent of the Flood (e.g., Froede 2000; Froede and others 1998a; Reed 2000). Eruptions would have begun subaerially only to be later inundated by the rising Flood water. Subaqueous eruptions would have sent volcanic material into the surrounding water to be carried away by currents. With the ongoing eruption of pyroclastic materials, some of the volcanoes could eventually extend above the Flood water, thus allowing ash generated by the plinian-to-ultraplinian eruptions to travel with air currents until heat loss and gravity brought it back to earth. Ash alteration would reflect both its depositional and diagenetic environments. According to Weaver (1989, p. 378):

> . . . much of the fine, fresh glass in marine sediments may have a subaerial origin, whereas those altered to smectite are more likely to be from submarine explosions.

Bentonite — a smectitic clay — could have originated from subaqueous volcanic eruptions, as it is often found in marine strata. Whether the ash fell on exposed land surfaces or into receding Flood water might be determined by the ashfall geometry and the chemistry of the clay deposit. Subaerial volcanic eruptions likely diminished throughout the Ice Age Timeframe in their explosivity, size, and scale. We see this today from the few continental-scale ash layers that we find exposed in recently derived surficial sediments and strata.

Volcaniclastic layers are initially highly porous and permeable. Once deposited and buried, they would be subject to flushing by large volumes of connate water as the sediments dewatered with the withdrawal of Flood water. The buried volcaniclastics would have experienced a wide variety of changing subsurface conditions. Probably the greatest impact on the materials would have occurred with changes in pH/Eh conditions. As ash devitrifies, it releases large quantities of silica and metals into solution. These dissolved minerals could have contributed to the replacement of calcareous and/or woody material buried in the subsurface (Figure 9-10) (see Froede 1994a; Howe and others 2003; Williams 1993; Williams and Howe 1993; Williams and others 1993, 1995, 1998) or they could precipitate along lithologic contacts due to changing pH/Eh conditions within the subsurface (e.g., Altschuler and others 1963; Kolata and others 1996).

Within the biblical framework, we should view volcanic ash layers as lithostratigraphic units subject to movement by Flood water (if subaqueous) or wind patterns (if subaerial). The biblically defined geologic age for an ash layer would be dependent on changing geologic energy as exemplified by both overlying and underlying rocks, sediments, and possibly fossils. Only through a site-specific investigation can we accurately pursue an age determination for an ash deposit within the biblical framework of earth history.

CONCLUSIONS

It is well documented that volcanic events have contributed significant volumes of pyroclastic sediments to the global rock record. Indeed, the volcaniclastic contribution is probably greater than currently understood. This is because an unknown amount of fine-grained ash first altered to smectite, and later to illite, and is largely unrecognized in rocks classified as shale (Fisher and Schmincke 1984; Grim 1958; Ross 1955; Weaver 1963).

Volcanically derived clays include bentonite, kaolinite, illite, chlorite, etc. It is possible that a single layer of ash could alter to different types of clay across a broad area due to variations in subsurface chemistry. It is also possible that one layer of ash could be re-worked and redeposited in a manner suggesting two distinct volcanic eruptions. Remember that we are dealing with an aqueous setting and rapidly changing geologic conditions during the Flood Event Timeframe (Figure 1-6) when we would expect the greatest vol-ume of volcanic ash to be added to the rock record. This is why the chemical fingerprinting

Figure 9-10. A large petrified tree trunk is weathering out of a bentonite of the Aguja Formation along Dawson Creek, Big Bend National Park, Texas (see Williams and Goette 1998). Preservation of such objects is made possible by the breakdown of the volcanic ash and the release of free silica which replaces the organic material. The trunk was buried during the Flood and later uncovered by erosion. Weathering is slowly disintegrating it into smaller pieces. Scale in inches and centimeters.

of clays derived from ash layers could prove to be so vital and important to the young-earth Flood frame-work. It is possible that chemical fingerprinting may identify a large-scale ashfall that crosses one or more uniformitarian time boundaries. If proven true, this would falsify that part of the time scale.

The biblical approach places greater emphasis on changing geologic energy as a means to define the Flood and its effect on the depositional setting, rath-er than on the evolutionary stage of fossils found in adjacent strata. Hence, the preservation and extent of an ash deposit would tie directly to the geologic energy at the time these ash layers were deposited. Subsequent alteration would depend on depth of burial, organic content of associated layers, and groundwater pH/Eh conditions, and not on pur-ported, long-term, uniformitarian geologic processes.

Volcanic strata also show great promise in help-ing define the withdrawal rate of Flood water from the continents. Using ash layers as isochrons within the young-earth Flood framework could possibly divide the rock record in several different ways — all depending on the changing geologic energy levels of the surrounding sediments. For example, the Late Cretaceous bentonites found within the Western North American Interior Seaway might be useful in determining the Floodwater withdrawal rate in re-lationship to the establishment of Flood/post-Flood environments (Froede 1995a). Much work remains to be conducted in identifying, defining, and refin-ing the use of volcanic ash layers within the biblical framework.

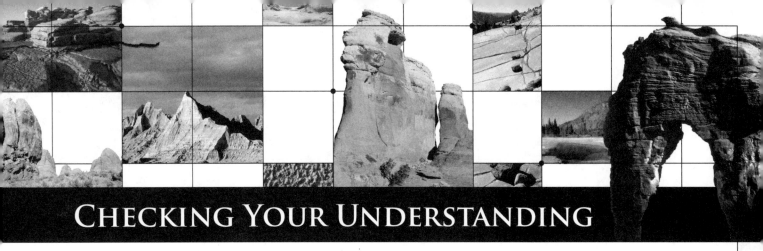

CHECKING YOUR UNDERSTANDING

1. What kind of uniformitarian age-dating methods can be applied to volcanic ash layers?

2. What makes them so valuable in defining the uniformitarian geologic time scale?

3. Can volcanic ash alter in the subsurface? What causes this to occur?

4. When in biblical history might we expect the greatest volume of ash to be added to the rock record? Why?

5. Can a volcano erupt underwater? What would happen to the resulting ash-size materials?

6. How can we identify former ash deposits from the clay layers we find in the subsurface today?

7. Why is the identification of clay and ash deposits derived from volcanic eruptions so important to the biblical account of earth history?

CHAPTER 10 *Defining Turbidites in Biblical History*

INTRODUCTION

Turbidites are one of several types of sedimentary deposits formed by gravity flow (Figure 10-1). They are created subaqueously from turbidity currents. Being denser than sea water, turbidity currents flow from their point of initiation down to the sea floor. While under transport, the suspended sediments act to erode the seabed in places and deposit additional sediments at other locations. Considerable volumes of sediment can be moved and deposited in this manner. Within the spectrum of gravity-flow deposits, turbidites probably represent the largest volume of sedimentary materials in the rock record.

Turbidity currents are typically initiated when a mechanical force (e.g., earthquake, impact, tectonic uplift) causes the loose sediments to destabilize, and they flow downhill like an avalanche of snow. Both creationists and uniformitarian scientists agree that turbidity currents are quickly generated, rapidly moving sediment flows that result in the formation of strata within days, hours, or even minutes. As such, they are examples of locally catastrophic geologic events. Strata generated by turbidity currents can exhibit a broad range of sedimentary features. Creationists need to understand turbidity currents and turbidites because they fit very well into many of the expected depositional settings within the young-earth Flood framework.

FLYSCH DEPOSITS

Originally, turbidite deposits were known as "flysch deposits." "Flysch" is the old and somewhat vague term used to describe a turbidite formation,

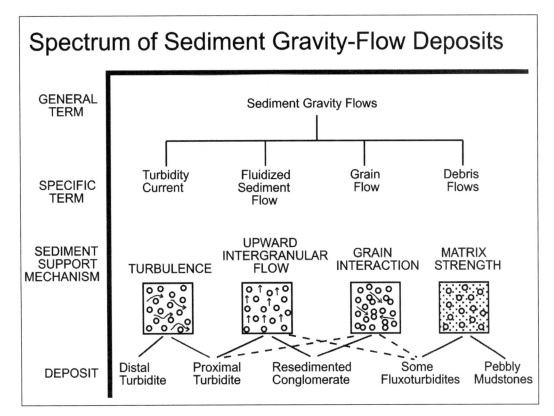

Figure 10-1. Classification of subaqueous sediment gravity-flows. Turbidity currents form just one portion of the wide spectrum of sediment gravity-flow (from Middleton and Hampton 1976).

and "greywacke" was used to identify the rock type (Stow and others 1996). European geologists were the first to identify flysch beds as turbidite deposits, defining them as a specific marine facies (Hsü 1970). Flysch deposits had long been noted in many of earth's geosynclinal basins, and were commonly identified as being submarine or deep-sea fan deposits (Mutti 1974; Nelson and Nilsen 1974; Normark 1974; Whitaker 1974). Prior to the theory of plate tectonics, geologists interpreted marine sedimentation by the "geosynclinal" theory, and much of this older work remains relevant (e.g., Briggs 1974; Enos 1969; Lajoie 1970; McBride 1966; Morris 1974; Mutti and Lucchi 1972; Picha and Niem 1974; Poole 1974). Today, the term "flysch deposit" is more commonly used interchangeably with "turbidite deposit." For the purposes of this chapter, the term "turbidite" will be used unless discussing the older concept of flysch facies. The term "geosyncline" has been dropped from usage by most

geologists due to a shift toward the concept of plate tectonics.

HISTORY OF TURBIDITY CURRENT RESEARCH

The mechanisms and processes responsible for the creation of turbidite deposits were resolved late in the 20th century. Prior to this time, their mode of deposition was poorly understood. Through a combination of field studies and laboratory experiments, the mystery of turbidites was resolved.

First identified in the late 1820s by a geologist working with Italian strata, turbidite deposits were poorly defined (Hsü 1970). However, major advances in the study of turbidity currents and their potential erosional energy occurred following the 1929 earthquake under the Atlantic Ocean off Newfoundland, Canada. The earthquake's energy destabilized sediments on a portion of the continental shelf. The sediments then flowed eastward under

Low Density Turbidity Current Deposits

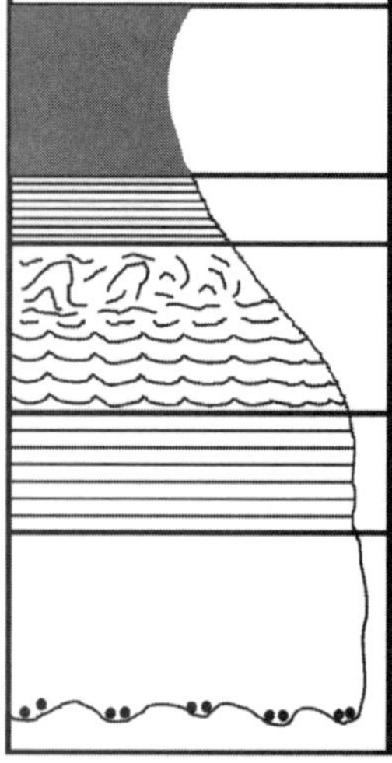

LITHO/SEDIMENTARY STRUCTURE	GRAIN SIZE	BOUMA (1962) DIVISIONS	INTERPRETATION
	Mud	E - Laminated to homogeneous mud	Deposition from low-density tail of turbidity current ± setting of pelagic or hemipelagic particles
	Silt	D - Upper mud/silt laminae	Shear sorting of grains & flocs
	Sand	C - Ripples, climbing ripples, wavy or convoluted laminae	Lower part of lower flow regime of Simons et al (1965)
	Sand	B - Plane laminae	Upper flow regime plane bed
	Course Sand	A - Structureless or graded sand to granule	Rapid deposition with no traction transport, possible quick (liquefied) bed

Figure 10-2. The idealized Bouma turbidite sequence. The divisions are used as a facies description and to specify the various stratigraphic layers within turbidites (from Edwards 1993, p. 7, Figure 1.3).

the power of gravity down the continental slope. The avalanching sediments snapped a succession of undersea telegraph cables, enabling scientists to estimate the speed of the sediment as approximately 42 miles per hour (Piper and others 1988). This event documented for the first time what many geologists believe was a turbidity current. To better understand what happened, various laboratory experiments were conducted in an attempt to duplicate the conditions and results of the undersea earthquake.

Many years later, various undersea well-core studies were conducted to examine the resulting turbidite deposit from the 1929 earthquake. This work was performed to define the link between turbidity current flow processes and the resulting deposits (e.g., Clarke and others 1990; Heezen and others 1954; Heezen and Ewing 1952; Lowe 1976a, 1976b; Piper and others 1985, 1988; Shor and others 1990).

In 1950, Kuenen and Migliorini published what many view as the most important article on turbidites (Walker 1973). This paper sparked a large-scale effort to identify and investigate turbidite deposits

in the field. Bouma (1962) later published a small but important book that defined the concept of a turbidite facies and its lithologic sequence. As the result of his groundbreaking work, the turbidite facies became known as the Bouma sequence (Figure 10-2). The Bouma sequence was used for many years to describe turbidite deposits and facies. However, according to Stow and others (1996, p. 396), research in the 1970s revealed:

> . . . the Bouma sequence was found to be strictly applicable to medium-grained sand-mud turbidites. Consequently, parallel sequence models were developed for both coarse-grained (conglomeratic) turbidites and fine-grained (mud-rich) turbidites.

In the years that followed, much research was conducted in an attempt to identify and interpret the many different turbidite depositional settings. However, the primary focus of these investigations has been on the deep-sea or submarine fan environment (Bowen and others 1993; Einsele 1991;

Howell and Normark 1982; Mutti 1985a; Stanley and Kelling 1978) and the basin margin setting for carbonates (Brown and Loucks 1993; Cook and Mullins 1983; Eberli 1991).

Several proposals have been made suggesting a shift away from modern deep-sea turbidite depositional environments. Various scientists have suggested that turbidite research focus on the resulting particle size (Lowe 1982; Pickering and others 1986; Piper and Stow 1991; Reading 1991; Reading and Richards 1994; Stow and Shanmugam 1980). However, this proposal does not adequately resolve the problems with current models and terminology (Normark and Barnes 1983/1984; Normark and others 1983/1984, 1993). Hence, turbidites and the processes that form them remain open for further investigation and interpretation.

SEDIMENTARY GRAVITY-FLOW DEPOSITS

Turbidites are only one type of sedimentary gravity-flow deposit — a process that has been the focus of much research (Allen 1971; Hampton 1972; Hiscott 1994b; Kuenen and Menard 1952; Lowe 1976a, 1976b; Middleton 1966a, 1966b, 1967; Middleton and Hampton 1976; Zeng and Lowe 1997a, 1997b). However, the marine setting and the uniqueness of the events that generate turbidity currents make it a difficult subject of modern study. As a result, there is still much unknown about turbidity currents and turbidites. Even today, sediment movement dynamics and the resulting stratification are still under investigation.

Figure 10-3. Classic turbidites from the Marathon Basin, Texas. These turbidite deposits are composed of alternating sandstones and shales. They were deposited, lithified, and then upturned during the Flood (Froede and others 1998b; Howe and Froede 1999; Howe and Williams 1994). Scale in six-inch (15-cm) divisions.

Figure 10-4. Alternating layers of sandstone and shale in turbidite deposits of the Rockwood Formation turned on end by orogenic processes following their emplacement. Both the turbidites and tectonism would have occurred during different divisions within the Flood Event Timeframe. The outcrop is located at Whiteoak Mountain northeast of Chattanooga, Tennessee. See Wilson (1986) for additional information.

TURBIDITE SEDIMENT TYPES AND FACIES

Turbidites compose much of the rock record in many areas, and they cover large portions of many of the world's basins (Horn and others 1972; Lucchi and Valmori 1980; Pilkey 1988; Pilkey and others 1980). Turbidite deposits can be composed of many different types of sediments. The sediment type is a function of the source area. Various depositional models have been developed to explain turbidites by their sedimentary components, e.g., muds, silts, sands, and conglomerates (see Bouma and Stone 2000; Einsele 1992; Hartley and Prosser 1995; Miall 2000; Stow and others 1996; Walker 1992). Different environments generate different types of sediment, either clastic or carbonate. When subjected to gravity flow, these sediments show a variety of sedimentary structures and stratigraphic sequences (Figures 10-3 through 10-6).

According to Walker (1992, p. 242), turbidite facies have been divided into five main facies: 1) classical turbidites, 2) massive sandstones, 3) pebbly mudstones,

Figure 10-5. Alternating turbidite-deposited layers of limestone and shale of the Stones River Formation of the Chickamauga Group north of Gadsden, Alabama. Tool marks and sole casts form traces on the bottoms of many of the limestone layers, indicating that some scouring did occur during their emplacement. Note person in foreground for scale. See Neathery and Drahovzal (1986) for further information about this outcrop.

Figure 10-6. These alternating layers of sandstone and shale were derived from turbidity currents. These layers are part of the Red Mountain Formation. Tool marks are found along the bottom surface of many of the sandstone layers, and they reflect a scouring event in association with the deposition of many of the turbidite sands. The outcrop is located north of Ringgold, Georgia. See Rindsberg and Chowns (1986) for a description of this outcrop. Scale in six-inch (15-cm) divisions.

turbidity currents and their deepwater deposits are caused by three different, yet interrelated elements:

(1) the presence of a delta or other system that constructs a relatively thick, wide shelf sedimentary unit, which constitutes the main source of sediment for the deep-water turbidite system, (2) tectonic modification of the shelf declivity leading to shelf sediment failure, and (3) the relative fall of sea level position, which determines the timing of submarine shelf erosion and reworking.

Of course, uniformitarian scientists interpret these three components within the context of deep

4) conglomerates, and 5) pebbly mudstones, debris flows, slumps, and slides.

Each of these facies varies somewhat depending on their depositional setting and composition — whether clastic, carbonate, or organic debris. The current focus in turbidite research is on their facies and depositional environments, especially variations of shelf-fed and/or deltaic depositional environments. According to Peres (1993, p. 93),

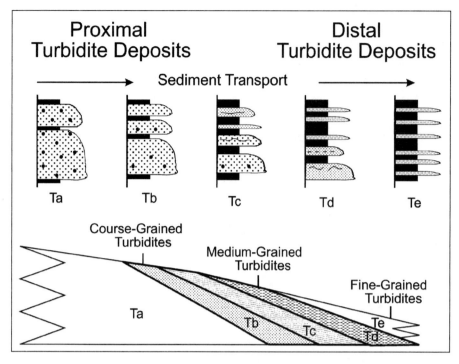

Figure 10-7. Diagram illustrating the downgradient changes (covering many miles) in internal structure and thickness of a high- to low-density turbidity current deposit. This figure shows the classic transition from proximal to distal facies (following the Bouma sequence — see Figure 10-2) which develop within the submarine fan model. However, these same types of deposits can form laterally to each other as channel and overbank deposits. Modified from Tucker (1991, p. 83, Figure 2.96).

beds contain coarse-grained and larger particle sizes than the distal fine-grained sediments found in the lower reaches of the resulting fan. Hence, one turbidity current can deposit a wide variety of sediment types and sizes, all depending on the source area, the energy level of the flow, and the distance traveled.

Stacked sequences of turbidites often exhibit graded bedding, either normal or reversed, throughout their thickness. Work by Hiscott (1994a) reveals that in some cases multiple stacks of graded beds might reflect the passage of a *single* large turbidity current with strongly fluctuating hydrodynamic conditions and vigorous burst/sweep cycles.

This is bad news for uniformitarian scientists because it removes the need for multiple turbidity currents (and associated longer time frames). In other words, more of the rock record may have been deposited within a matter of minutes, making assumptions regarding deep time unnecessary.

In the field, geologists determine the difference between proximal and distal turbidite facies by variations in sediment particle size. As the deposit moves away from the source, particle size decreases. But care is needed in that diagnosis. This same particle-size change has been noted moving from sediments deposited in the main channels of the turbidite, which carry most of the heavier load, to laterally adjacent overbank deposits, which are composed of finer-grained materials (Howell and

time, present-day geologic processes, and current rates of sedimentation.

PROXIMAL VERSUS DISTAL DEPOSITS

Because turbidites are sediments transported from one place to another, they can be thought of as resedimentation deposits. Acting under the force of gravity, a turbidity current will flow downslope, sometimes at great speed. During its travel, the flow will deposit its suspended sedimentary load as a function of energy and particle size. Coarser grains are deposited first, then finer grains, and lastly, the smallest grains. The resulting turbidite layers show this decrease in particle size (Figure 10-7). There is a horizontal as well as vertical distribution; proximal

Normark 1982). Furthermore, the rock record is falsifying most uniformitarian model assumptions as current research is focused on modern submarine fan deposits, but many turbidites in outcrop do not share the same features! Not only has this created some consternation about differences between proximal and distal turbidites facies (Howell and Normark 1982), but it is another illustration of the shortcomings of the principle of uniformitarianism.

TRACE FOSSILS

Trace fossils are the tracks, trails, burrows, and borings of various creatures preserved in the rocks (see Cowart and Froede 1994; Frey 1975). They are useful in identifying different turbidite facies. Seilacher (1962) distinguished between two different trace maker environments commonly associated with turbidites: (1) pre-event trace fossil associations, and (2) post-event assemblages (see also Einsele 1992; Froede and Cowart 1996). Of course, it would be illogical/impossible for trace-making creatures to conduct normal business within the midst of a sediment avalanche! Therefore, trace fossils associated with turbidity current deposits must have formed either before or after the event.

Early research concentrated on classifying trace fossils as paleo-depth indicators (Seilacher 1964, 1967), but subsequent studies refuted this idea

Figure 10-8a. An outcrop of the Pennington Formation exposed at Dougherty Gap, Georgia. The exposed section consists of alternating layers of sandstone and shale with current ripple marks along the top surface of many of the sandstone layers and tool marks and traces cast at the base of sandstone. This sequence probably formed as Flood-induced turbidity currents swept antediluvian sediments from the rapidly rising Appalachians to the east. Scale in six-inch (15-cm) divisions.

(Bishop and Brannen 1993; Bottjer and Droser 1992; Bromley 1990; Ekdale 1988; Frey 1971, 1975; Frey and others 1990; Goldring 1993; Wetzel 1991). We cannot overlook the possibility that some of the trace makers might have been displaced and so their traces may occur out of place compared to where they might have lived. As a result, caution must be exercised in using traces in any attempt to determine paleo-depth without additional evidence (Figures 10-8a and 10-8b) (Cowart and Froede 1994; Froede and Cowart 1996).

Some modern examples lead geologists to suspect that turbidite facies indicate bathymetry. Depth is generally inferred from sediment particle size, bedding, and trace fossils. But there is a problem — none of these can accurately and consistently yield valid bathymetry. To make matters worse, it is easy to confuse distal turbidite deposits and tempestites because of the similarities between trace fossils and sedimentology in both settings (Einsele and Seilacher 1991). While many different types of traces have been found in association with turbidite deposits (Burton and Link 1991; Chamberlain 1978; D'Alessandro and others 1986; Frey and others 1990; Wetzel 1991), there are still too many uncertainties to confidently predict the paleoenvironmental setting solely from trace fossils.

Figure 10-8b. A close-up view of the underside of a sandstone layer shows animal behavioral traces cast into its base. This occurred when a sand-rich turbidity current scoured into a semi-lithified clay layer. The current then deposited sand, preserving the bioturbated clay traces as casts. Scale in inches and centimeters.

CONTOURITES

Contourites are sedimentary deposits formed by the winnowing and reworking action of bottom currents (Stow and others 1996, 2002). They are usually identified by ripple marks or other similar sedimentary structures along the upper surface of the turbidite (Stanley 1993; Stow and Lovell 1979).

Contourites have been documented within the modern deep-sea basin environment and indicate the movement of water over the sea floor. Presently, contourites are considered an important topic of study as petroleum exploration moves into deeper water (Stow and others 2002), although much remains unknown about them (Faugères and Stow

1993; Stow and others 1996). They demonstrate water movement at depth and sufficient velocity to rework previously deposited materials and are associated with turbidite deposits.

HYPERPYCNAL TURBIDITY CURRENTS

Turbidity current research has also focused on density currents generated at the mouths of rivers where high concentrations of suspended sediments, typically associated with upstream flooding, raise the density of river water above that of sea water, resulting in the discharge of one or more hyperpycnal plumes into adjacent marine basins (Geyer and others 2004; Mulder and Syvitski 1995; Wheatcroft and others 1996). Dense, sediment-laden river water flows beneath sea water, hugging the bathymetric topography. These currents not only transport sediments into deeper water, but also scour and erode preexisting sediments (Mulder and Syvitski 1995; Mulder and others 2003). Hyperpycnal deposits, or hyperpycnites, have been identified as far as 435 miles (700 km) from river mouths in the Sea of Japan (Nakajima 2006).

Hyperpycnites are similar to turbidites; both are created by water currents carrying suspended particles because of their inherent turbulence. The resulting deposit is a coarsening-up sequence during the initial period of discharge followed by a fining-up sequence during the waning period of discharge (Mulder and others 2003). The deposit would ideally show a silt-sand-silt layering of sediments, suggesting that particle settling and traction act simultaneously (Mulder and others 2003). Hyperpycnal flow turbidites can form significant stratigraphic deposits on the continental shelves, slopes, and basin floors (Plink-Björklund and Steel 2004).

Hyperpycnal flows and the resulting hyperpycnites have been modeled by laboratory experiments (Duringer and others 1991; Parsons and others 2001). This work has allowed researchers to document similar stratigraphic sequences on a larger scale in the field (e.g., Edwards and others 2005; Mutti and others 1996, 2000, 2002). Mulder and others (2003) made the important discovery that high-magnitude floods can form erosional interstratal contacts during peak flood conditions. Therefore, hyperpycnal turbidites can generate coarsening-up facies with erosional or sharp contacts between beds that cannot be used to mark sequence boundaries. This is significant for Flood geologists because it shows that a single instantaneous process can generate sediments that were previously interpreted as requiring long periods of time to form. Furthermore, it is an example of the rapid formation of unconformities, which many uniformitarian scientists commonly cite as evidence of the passage of time.

JÖKULHAUP GENERATED TURBIDITY CURRENT DEPOSITS

Another area of active turbidity current research is associated with glacial outbursts, which are called "jökulhaups." The resulting deposits have been identified as hyperpycnal flows (e.g., Aharon 2006; Mulder and others 2003) and classic turbidite sequences (e.g., Begossi and others 2002; Brunner and others 1999). The mechanism used to describe these glacially generated turbidites is similar to that defined for hyperpycnal flows. The catastrophic release of water from glacial melting scours existing sediment along its pathway toward the sea. The dense water-sediment pulse is washed out from the river mouth where its density allows it to flow beneath the marine water, dropping its sedimentary load as it moves basinward. Eventually, the density of the flow decreases and the current slows and then stops. These events are restricted to glacial environments, but in those locales they contribute a significant sediment load to the sea floor, forming thick sequences of turbidite deposits in rapid fashion (e.g., Brunner and others 1999). Of course, in the biblical model, these types of deposits would be restricted to those portions of the rock record formed during and since the Ice Age Timeframe.

TURBIDITY CURRENT MODELS

Mutti (1985b) suggested that too much emphasis has been placed on modeling the various types of turbidite facies — in some cases without sufficient fieldwork. He stated:

> Although every turbidite system is probably unique, underlying general models should exist, such as those described for fluvial and nearshore sediments. Unfortunately, during these years we have spent more time discussing conceptual models than collecting data from which models are necessarily derived. What we need now are **good data**.

This call has been echoed by other turbidite experts, who have complained that while there are many models to explain the various types of turbidity-generated strata, no single model addresses all the differing turbidity-generated sediments found within the rock record (Bouma 1972; Mutti and Normark 1987; Normark and others 1993). Hence, both turbidite deposits and the models explaining them continue to be open to new investigation and interpretation.

TURBIDITE DEPOSIT CHARACTERISTICS

While models used to reconstruct turbidites remain in a state of flux, research to date has identified certain features as being characteristic of turbidite deposits. However, there is enough variation in them and overlap with other types of

sedimentary processes that no one characteristic can provide the means of identifying turbidites in the field. Walker (1992, p. 241) identified four of these characteristics:

1. Sandstones and shales are monotonously interbedded through tens or hundreds of meters of section.

2. Beds tend to have sharp, flat bases, with no indication of erosion of the sea floor on a scale exceeding a few tens of centimeters (i.e., the sea floor was flat and unchannelized).

3. The sharp bases (soles) of the beds have abundant markings, now classified into three types; *tool marks*, which are carved into the underlying mud by rigid objects (sticks, stones, shells); *scour marks*, which are cut into the underlying mud by fluid scour; and *organic marks*, which represent trails and burrows made by organisms and filled in by the turbidity current. Tool and scour marks give an accurate indication of local flow directions.

4. Within the sandstone beds the grain size commonly decreases upward (i.e., graded bedding). . . .

These generalizations form a good starting point from which to begin an investigation of possible turbidite deposits. The literature on turbidites documents many other characteristics commonly associated with the various kinds of deposits.[1] In many cases, a photographic review of the many sedimentary features formed by turbidity currents can prove very helpful in understanding outcrops encountered in the field (e.g., Dzulynski and Walton 1965; Pettijohn and Potter 1964; Reineck and Singh 1980; Ricci-Lucchi 1995).

A Young-Earth Flood Framework

Although creationists have only scratched the surface, the Flood clearly would have redistributed preexisting sediments, florae, and faunae across wide areas. Tectonic forces operating during the Flood created rapid changes in topography, both up and down. With changes in topography came changes in gradient, which led to scour and erosion on the new highs, transport down the new slopes, and deposition in the new basins. Given the catastrophic sea level rise in conjunction with the tectonic events, much of the sedimentation would have been submarine, probably in the form similar to turbidity currents. Of course, this would all have occurred on a scale that cannot be compared to the simple river discharge and slope instability models of uniformitarian scientists. Nor is it unreasonable that scale differences would have created sedimentary features incomprehensible by modern processes.

Periods of stasis (non-deposition) between turbidity current events would have allowed trace makers the opportunity to bioturbate the sediments before the next deposit was emplaced (see Froede and Cowart 1996; Woodmorappe 2006). Also, during periods of non-deposition, Floodwater currents would have created conditions favorable for contourite deposits to form from any previously deposited turbidite sediments.

A significant problem in the uniformitarian approach to turbidites is that most of the present-day models focus on modern deep-sea or submarine fans. While this setting provides a source area and basin, it is not applicable to Flood conditions. For example, most turbidite deposits found on the continents are missing their original upgradient source areas. Where were the original source areas and where did they go? Many times provenance studies — tracking the source of the sediment by their mineral makeup — are used to help identify the source area. Often, the absence of information leads to speculation about a former upgradient area, unsupported by hard data. This is a major shortcoming of the ancient turbidite/submarine fan model. The source sediments must have come from somewhere! This is another area where the Flood aids our understanding of the rock record more than present-day submarine/deep-sea fan models.

The key is a focus on the relationship between turbidites and rapid local/regional tectonics of the Flood. It is similar to the old concept of flysch facies suggested by early European geologists studying the Alps. They noted a relationship between the infilling of basins immediately adjacent to active areas of uplift. We would expect an accelerated version of this concept within the Flood framework. The uniformitarian geologist Lajoie (1970, p. i) spoke directly to this concept when he was describing flysch facies and its development within the uniformitarian system:

> It should be pointed out that the tectonic environment may only have a secondary effect on flysch sediments, the first being on the source area; *in order to form flysch sequences a rapidly rising source may be more important than an unstable environment of sedimentation* (emphasis mine).

During the Flood Event Timeframe, many areas of the crust were rapidly uplifted. Unlithified sediments on top of these rising areas would become unstable, flowing as slumps, debris flows, and turbidity currents into the newly forming basins. Of these three gravity-flow processes, turbidity currents are the best mechanism for moving massive quantities of sediment to adjacent basins. In this depositional setting, there is no stable upgradient source to feed a deep-sea or submarine fan. Rather, a broad area undergoing uplift would provide sediments for potentially multiple pulses of turbidity currents and their large-scale turbidites. Furthermore, this would explain sheet-type turbidites, which are common in the rock record. Many of these Flood-derived turbidites are probably similar to massive scale hyperpycnal flows or jökulhaup events where dense sediment-water slurries flow down into adjacent basins, depositing their sedimentary load along the way (Froede 2004b). Within this setting there is no clearly defined upgradient source area — rather the uplifted continent is the source for the turbidites. Hence, the Flood framework of rapid uplift generating gravity-flow deposits on a massive scale better explains the rock record for many places. While the deep-sea fan model applies to modern processes, it does not provide a useful template for much of the rock record. New ideas regarding catastrophic flooding (i.e., hyperpycnal flows or jökulhaup events) in the formation of density currents holds much promise for the young-earth Flood framework.

CONCLUSIONS

Turbidite deposits have been studied for many years, at modern submarine settings, and in the laboratory. All of this work has resulted in a greater understanding of the mechanisms and sedimentary features formed by gravity-driven currents. However, much research remains to be conducted because no single model can explain the full range of turbidites seen in the field. Recent work on hyperpycnal flows and catastrophic glacial outbursts suggests a different perspective in understanding the formation of turbidite deposits. They provide a fertile area of study consistent with the geologic energy expectations of the Flood.

Turbidites are formed underwater when preexisting sediments become unstable for various reasons. Most turbidites cover many square miles, and individual beds range in thickness from less than one inch to hundreds of feet. Although turbidites can form within minutes, uniformitarian scientists still discuss them in the context of deep time.

The Flood provides a natural explanation for many of the massive turbidites found in the rock record. Cataclysmic tectonism would have rapidly changed the elevation of large parts of the crust. Any sediment, whether antediluvian or initial Flood deposits, on top of these uplifted areas would be subject to instability, and could flow via slumps, debris flows, and turbidity currents into adjacent basins. Any florae and faunae carried along would have been hydrodynamically sorted and redeposited within the turbidite. Time between flows would have allowed trace makers the opportunity to bioturbate the sediments. However, if there was little time between turbidity currents, there would likely be no bioturbation. During this time, contour currents would also have reworked the upper portions of exposed turbidites, creating contourites.

Both uniformitarianism and the young-earth Flood framework suggest that turbidites formed rapidly from preexisting sediments. A biblical approach would focus on their formation primarily during the Flood Event Timeframe (Figure 1-6) and not over the course of hundreds of millions of years. Their magnitude and scale are easily accommodated within the global flood of Genesis. The interpretation of these features in the rock record will depend upon the individual's beliefs regarding earth history. However, there is nothing to prevent their interpretation from following the literal biblical framework.

Endnotes

1. For supplemental information on turbidites, the reader may enjoy these books and articles: Bouma and Brouwer 1964; Bouma and others 1985; Dzulynski and Walton 1965; Edwards 1993; Hartley and Prosser 1995; Nelson and Nilson 1984; Stanley and Swift 1976; Stow 1992; Stow and Piper 1984; Weimer and Link 1991; Weimer and others 1994; and Winn and Armentrout 1995.

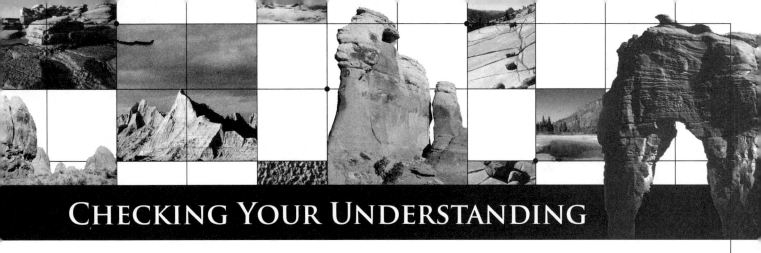

CHECKING YOUR UNDERSTANDING

1. Define the term "turbidity current." What is a turbidite?

2. What conditions are necessary to create suspended sediments of sufficient density that they will flow beneath sea water?

3. How fast can a turbidity current flow?

4. What event in 1929 provided scientists the opportunity to finally understand turbidity currents?

5. What are the differences between proximal turbidite deposits and distal turbidite deposits? What is inferred based on distance traveled? Should we use this relationship without question in our investigations of turbidite deposits?

6. What information can we gain in identifying trace fossils in a turbidite sequence? Can they convey the water depth in which they were formed? What formed them?

7. Jökulhaups and hyperpycnal flows would occur on a river scale. The 1929 earthquake initiated a turbidity current flow from a portion of the continental shelf. What setting might we invoke to explain the even larger scale turbidite deposits that we find adjacent to the Appalachian Mountains or Rocky Mountains? How does this setting differ from uniformitarian expectations?

AFTERWORD

In this monograph, geologist Carl Froede has provided valuable interpretations of many important geological processes and structures, showing them all to be at least persuasive — and often even compelling — evidences for Flood geology. While not intended as a comprehensive textbook or reference book on scriptural geology (and there is still a need for *that*), it will prove invaluable as a supporting collection of case studies based on actual field observations, which illustrate the validity of the basic Flood model.

The traditional uniformitarian geology, which long ago was popularized by James Hutton and Charles Lyell, and then eulogized by Charles Darwin as enabling his system of evolution to appear feasible, is now increasingly being phased out by modern geologists. The neo-catastrophism which is becoming very popular is still not biblical Flood geology, of course, for it perpetuates the myth of billions of years of earth history. The neo-catastrophists (Derek, Ager, Kenneth Hsu, Stephen Gould, et al.) tend to view the geological strata as formed by intermittent catastrophes occurring in an overall context of slow processes that left no record.

Froede, however, has shown that even those structures that are still being cited as evidence of long ages (e.g., paleosols, paleoenvironments) are easily explained in a Flood geology framework. Furthermore, the ubiquitous occurrence of vast turbidite formations throughout the geologic column is shown by him to be *prima facie* evidence of hydraulic catastrophism. When all this is combined with the fact that there is no global unconformity in the column — *which means no worldwide time gap* — it becomes evident that the real testimony of the rocks is to the historical reality of the biblical flood. There is no need to invoke local or regional cataclysm which has been so plainly documented in the records of the Book of Genesis.

But there is great prejudice against this Flood explanation, of course, for it speaks of a righteous Creator who judges and punishes sin. Modern men and women (especially scientific and philosophical intellectuals) do not want this kind of God. It is a remarkable commentary on the "wisdom of this world" (2 Cor. 2:6) that so many people are eagerly willing to believe there have been vast floods all over the planet Mars — where there is no water at all now (one wonders where it all went!) — but refuse to believe in the divinely recorded account of a worldwide Flood on earth, where there is enough water to submerge a smoothed earth to a depth of well over a mile.

Thankfully, Carl Froede is one of a growing number of younger geologists (and may their tribe increase!) who are not ashamed of God's Word and are also well trained and experienced in the earth sciences and are now seeking sacrificially to reinterpret all the geologic data in the context of the literal and divinely inspired record of Scripture. To considerable extent, Froede is plowing new ground, so that some of his analyses may need refinement with further study. Nevertheless, he has made a strong case in every instance, and the overall impact is bound to be impressive, even to die-hard skeptics, if they will only examine the evidence carefully and objectively.

To the Christian believer, Froede's case studies of these important geologic phenomena will be like springs of water in a thirsty land. "For the word of the LORD is right: and all His works are done in truth. . . . Let all the earth fear the LORD: let all the inhabitants of the world stand in awe of Him" (Ps. 33:4–8; NKJV).

To the open-minded non-Christian, one can hope that the discussions in this monograph will encourage him or her to consider seriously the strong evidence for the truth of the Bible and biblical Christianity. Even on such subjects as special creation and the cataclysmic Flood (both of which are rejected by many scientists), the biblical records can be strongly supported by the actual facts of science and history.

There are thousands of scientists today, as well as most founding fathers of science (Newton, Kepler, Bacon, Boyle, Faraday, etc.) who believe in the Bible as the Word of God. There are no demonstrable scientific errors in the Bible, and scores of true scientific insights.

Above all, its record of the incarnation, atoning death and bodily resurrection of God in Christ is historically authentic and eternally true. The Lord Jesus Christ was actually our Creator (John 1:1–3; Col. 1:16; etc.) as well as our sin-bearing Savior (Eph. 1:7; 1 John 1:7–9; etc.), and every reader is well advised to trust in Him for eternal salvation.

Henry M. Morris, Ph.D.

GLOSSARY

allostratigraphy. The area of stratigraphy that deals with the identification of strata that are bound by mappable unconformities.

autochthonous. Formed or produced in place where it is now found. For example, coal is viewed as an autochthonous deposit, as it occurs where its original plants grew and decayed.

ball-and-pillow structure. A sedimentary structure found in sandstones and some limestones, characterized by hemispherical or kidney-shaped masses resembling balls and pillows, and commonly attributed to foundering. These structures are generated in soft sediment.

biostratigraphy. The area of stratigraphy that deals with the distribution of fossils in the stratigraphic record and their organization into units on the basis of their contained fossils.

bioturbation. The disruption of sediments by organisms. Can occur in the form of complete sedimentary layer destruction or as discrete burrows, trails, and traces.

channel lag deposits. Coarse-grained material that is rolled or bounced along the bottom of a channel at a slower rate than the finer-grained material.

clastic. Pertaining to a rock or sediment composed principally of broken fragments that are derived from preexisting rocks or minerals, and that have been transported some distance from their places of origin; also said of the texture of a rock. Usually used in reference to sand, silt, and clay particles and/or rocks.

clastic dike. A sedimentary dike consisting of one or more clastic materials derived from underlying or overlying beds. This is an intrusive sedimentary structure.

co-ignimbrite. A volcanic ash cloud generated as a result of a pyroclastic flow coming into contact with an external water source (surface water body or ground water).

connate water. Water entrapped in the open spaces (i.e., interstices) of sedimentary rock at the time the original sediments were deposited.

conodonts. One of a large number of small, disjunct fossil elements, phosphatic in composition, and commonly tooth-like in form but not in function. Produced in a bilaterally paired, serial arrangement by small marine animals of uncertain affinity. They are commonly believed to be the teeth of certain (extinct?) marine worms.

contemporaneous. Said of things formed at the same time.

contourite. Any sedimentary deposit formed on the continental rise by contour-following bottom currents. In the case of the young-earth Flood model, the author would suggest that contourites formed on and around the submerged continents adjacent to areas of uplift by contour-following bottom currents during the Flood.

density current. For the purposes of this book they are defined as a gravity-induced flow invoked by differences in the concentration of suspended particles.

deuteric. Changes that take place in an igneous magma immediately following its emplacement as a consequence of the reaction of its gases and vapors, along with other components within the magma.

devitrification. The conversion of a volcanic glass to a crystalline material by chemical alteration. This process sometimes results in the release of silica and metals.

diagenesis. All the chemical, physical, and biologic changes undergone by sediment after its initial deposition, plus during and after its lithification.

diastrophism. A general term for all movement of the crust produced by tectonic processes, including the formation of ocean basins, continents, plateaus, and mountain ranges.

distal turbidite deposits. Strata deposited at the furthest position from the source area. The resulting layers are composed of fine-grained particle sizes.

eluviation. The downward movement of soluble or suspended material in a soil, from the A horizon to the B horizon, by ground water percolation.

eolian. Wind processes related to the erosion or deposition of dune sand or loess, including the formation of sedimentary structures such as wind-formed ripple marks and cross-bedding.

epeiric sea. A sea within a continent. The marine water is stirred by currents and tidal forces. This setting is believed to have occurred during the Late Cretaceous when an epeiric seaway extended across North America from Canada to the Gulf of Mexico. A creationist interpretation for this seaway suggests that it formed in association with retreating Flood water (see Froede 1995a).

epiclastics. Earth materials (i.e., sand, silt, and clay-size particles) derived from pre-existing rocks and sediments. Epiclastics are also derived from weathered volcanic sediments. The differences with pyroclastics is one of heat and temperature at the time of formation.

eustatic. Related to worldwide changes in sea level position and impacting all oceans. Can be caused by multiple mechanisms (e.g., tectonism, ice cap melt, alpine glacial melt, isostasy).

facies. The aspect, appearance, and characteristics of a rock unit, usually reflecting the conditions of its origin. The sum total of features that reflect the specific environmental conditions under which a given rock was formed or deposited. Can be singular or plural depending upon its usage. For the purposes of this work the term "facies" refers to specific types of environments (e.g., swamp, desert, delta, savannah) and the characteristics of the sediments (e.g., sandstone, mud, silt, clay, limestone) that are found within those settings. The use of the term "facies" within our Flood framework would reflect actual paleoenvironments and associated sediments that existed either during the Antediluvian Timeframe or following the Flood (i.e., from the late-Flood to our present geological settings). We would not use the term "facies" to describe Flood deposits, as it is inconsistent with its defined meaning.

flysch. As used within this work this term is applied to sediments with lithologic and stratigraphic characteristics of a turbidite deposit. They are marine sediments characterized by a thick sequence of poorly fossiliferous, thinly bedded, graded marls and sandy and calcareous shales and muds, rhythmically interbedded with conglomerates, coarse sandstones, and graywackes.

geologic energy. This is a new term used by several young-earth creation scientists to describe a physical process energy which reflects the geological conditions (e.g., erosive force, deposition, tectonism) in operation at any particular period of time (Reed et al. 1996). For example, the onset and early portion of the Flood was a period of high geologic energy and the present age is a period of much lower geologic energy (see Figure 1-10).

geosyncline. A large trough-like or basin-like downwarping of the earth's crust, usually associated with an adjacent area of uplift, in which a thick succession of sedimentary and volcanic rocks accumulated.

glauconite. A dull-green earthy or granular mineral of the mica group. As a clay, it is recognized as being diagenetically derived from iron-rich sources. One suggested source is an iron-rich (i.e., mafic) volcanic ash (Jeans et al. 1982).

glauconitic. Said of a mineral aggregate that contains glauconite, resulting in the characteristic green color (e.g., glauconitic shale or clay).

gleying. A soil developed under conditions of poor drainage, resulting in the reduction of iron and other elements and in gray colors and mottles.

graded bedding. A type of bedding in which each layer displays a gradual change in particle size. Normal graded bedding is when the particles exhibit coarse grains at the base to fine grains at the top. Reverse graded bedding is the opposite of normal graded bedding. Graded bedding may form under conditions in which the velocity of the prevailing current declines in a gradual manner, as by deposition from a single short-lived turbidity current.

graptolites. A colonial marine organism characterized by a tiny cup or tube-shaped, highly resistant exoskeleton of organic composition, arranged with other individuals along one or more branches to form a colony.

hydroclasts. Volcanic materials formed during eruptions due to the contact of hot magma with an external source of water.

hydrostatic pressure. The pressure exerted by water at any given point in a body of water at rest.

illuviation. The accumulation, in a lower soil horizon, of soluble or suspended material that was transported from an upper horizon by the process of eluviation.

imbrication. A sedimentary fabric characterized by disk-shaped or elongated fragments dipping in a preferred direction at an angle to the bedding. It is commonly displayed by pebbles on a stream bed, where flowing water tilts the pebbles so that their flat surfaces dip upstream. This is best visualized as sediments arranged like shingles on a roof: one partially on top of another and oriented in the same direction.

indurated. Said of a rock or sediment hardened or lithified by pressure, compaction, cementation, and/or heat.

in situ. In the natural or original position.

isostasy. Related to crustal equilibrium. Changes in isostasy result in either uplift or depression and sea level position will vary accordingly.

law of faunal assemblages. A general law in geology which holds that similar assemblages of fossil organisms (floras and faunas) indicate similar geologic ages for the rocks that contain them.

law of faunal succession. Key "index fossils" can be linked to specific strata of a certain age. The changes marked by these index fossils are believed to occur in a recognizable order (via evolution) in succeeding sedimentary layers. This concept provides a means to establish order (by way of fossil content) to the many layers of fossil-containing sediments.

law of horizontality. Water-deposited sediments occur horizontally or nearly so, and parallel or nearly parallel to the earth's surface.

law of original continuity. A water-laid stratum, at the time it was formed, must continue laterally in all directions until it thins out as a result of nondeposition or until it abuts against the edge of the original basin of deposition.

law of superposition of strata. Also known as the principle of superposition. Strata are deposited sequentially with younger rock layers above older rock layers unless disturbance has overturned or inverted the rock layers.

lithification. The conversion of a newly deposited sediment into a solid rock, involving such processes as cementation, compaction, and crystallization. It can occur at any time following deposition of the sediments.

lithostratigraphy. The area of stratigraphy that deals with the description and systematic organization of the rocks of earth's crust into distinctive named units based on their lithologic character and stratigraphic relationships.

mottled. A soil that is irregularly marked with spots or patches of different colors, usually indicating poor aeration or seasonal wetness.

neocatastrophism. Also known as "catastrophic uniformitarianism," holds that the periodic catastrophic event may have more effect on the rock record than vast periods of gradual evolution or uniformitarianism (Ager 1993a). A philosophical belief held by many uniformitarian scientists who support such earth-changing catastrophic events as Flood basalt volcanism and meteor/comet impact events. Such catastrophic events, by definition, are outside uniformitarianism.

orogeny. The process of mountain formation. Initiation of uplift could be by crustal compression or magmatic uplift.

palynology. The study of pollen and spores and their dispersal as applied to stratigraphy and paleoecology.

parent material. An unconsolidated material, mineral or organic, from which the solum develops. According to Ellis and Mellor (1995, p. 322), it is the material from which a soil develops by soil-forming processes.

pH/Eh. These letters refer to acid/base (pH) and oxidation/reduction (Eh) conditions. In both of these cases, the water under these chemical conditions serves to alter most materials.

penecontemporaneous. Formed or existing at *almost* the same time (e.g., said of a structure or mineral that was formed immediately after deposition of a sediment but before its consolidation into a rock).

phreatomagmatic activity. Volcanic eruptions generated by the interaction between hot magma and surface and/or ground water (lake, river, sea, or ground water). The water immediately surrounding the magma is heated and volatilized resulting in an explosion. Where significant amounts of volcanic material are ejected from the surface to near surface magmatic source in addition to steam, the activity is said to be phreatomagmatic.

Plinian eruption. An explosive volcanic eruption of pyroclastic ejecta forming a column which may be up to 35 miles (56 km) in height dispersing ejecta over an area of 300 to 3,125 square miles. For example, the vertical eruption following the initial lateral blast of Mount St. Helens was a Plinian type of eruption (see Austin 1991). This type of eruption is typical to many modern explosive volcanoes. In some cases, volcanic ash layers have been identified within certain strata as reflecting eruptions that were many orders of magnitude above modern Plinian eruptions. These larger-scale older eruptions are identified as ultra-Plinian.

primary structure. In sedimentary rocks, the term refers to a structure formed as a result of the conditions of deposition but before lithification (e.g., bedding and ripple marks).

progradation. The outward building of a sedimentary deposit, typically in an aqueous setting, through the accumulation of geologic materials. Examples include advancing deltas or shorelines.

provenance. A place of origin. Specifically, the area from which the constituent materials of a sedimentary rock or facies were derived. Study typically focuses on a particular mineral suite that could be used to link the sediments back to a specific source area.

proximal turbidite deposits. Strata derived from materials closest to the source area. The resulting layers are composed of the coarse-grained and large-sized particles.

pyroclastics. These constitute sand, silt, and clay-size particles formed under eruptive conditions as a result of the degassing of magma, and not as a result of weathering processes.

resedimentation. The sedimentation of material which was deposited from former processes, but later disturbed and subsequently redeposited.

sand boil. A sediment-laden spring that bubbles through overlying sedimentary materials as a result of the difference in hydrostatic pressure. They commonly form along river levees during flood stage with an ejection of sand and water being forced through permeable sands and silts that compose the river levee.

saprolite. A soft, clay-rich, thoroughly decomposed rock formed in place by chemical weathering. Forms in humid, tropical, or subtropical climates. Color is red or brown.

shelf declivity. The inclination of the continental shelf surface. The shelf is generally a mildly dipping feature. Changes in declivity would be caused by uplift, via tectonic processes. With uplift, any unconsolidated sediments lying within this shelf area could be subject to destabilization resulting in the formation of debris flows or with even greater continental tilt, turbidity currents.

sol. A homogeneous suspension of colloidal particles in a fluid. A completely mobile mud is a sol.

solum. The upper part of a soil profile, including the A and B horizons in which soil-forming processes occur.

subaerial. Formed, existing, or taking place on a land surface.

subaqueous. Formed, existing, or taking place underwater.

tectonics. A branch of geology dealing with the broad architecture of the outer part of the earth, that is, the regional assembling of structural or deformational features, a study of their mutual relations, origin, and history. This term also refers to processes related to the movement of the crust of the earth (mountain building, plate spreading/rifting).

thixotropy. The property of certain colloidal substances, e.g., a thixotropic clay, to weaken or change from a gel to a sol when shaken but to increase in strength upon standing. Basically, the clay becomes liquid when subject to a seismic force but afterward it returns to its solid state.

turbidite. Sediment deposited from a turbidity current. It is characterized by graded bedding, moderate sorting, and well-developed primary sedimentary structures, especially lamination.

turbidity current. In this work, the term is used to describe a density current in water; specifically a bottom-flowing current laden with suspended sediment, moving swiftly down a subaqueous slope and spreading horizontally on the floor of the basin. These density slurries are created by unstable sediments being subject to some force or energy whereby they become unstable and flow under the force of gravity.

ultra-Plinian eruption. These are volcanic eruptions in earth's past that are documented only by massive pyroclast deposits. Because the size of the eruption is inferred from the thickness and extent of the volcanic ash layer, much remains unknown about these types of eruptions. Compared to modern day Plinian eruptions, the ultra-Plinian eruptions are believed to have sent pyroclastics higher and further. In some cases, the volcanic ash layers suggest three to five times that of their modern counterparts.

vitric. The term is commonly used in reference to volcanic types of sediments because it refers to a glassy composition.

volcaniclastic. Sand, silt, or clay-size materials derived from a volcanic eruption. Upon devitrification these materials alter to form quartz, feldspar, mica, and zeolites.

Walther's law. The same facies succession of strata that is present vertically also occurs horizontally unless sedimentation discontinues, thereby creating a break in sedimentation and an unconformity boundary.

zeolite. A generic term for a large group of white or colorless (sometimes red or yellow) hydrous aluminosilicates that are analogous in composition to the feldspars, with sodium, calcium, and potassium as their chief metals. They form during and following burial, generally by reaction of pore waters with these aluminosilicates. They are commonly viewed as alteration products of a volcanic ash.

TERMS ARE DERIVED FROM VARIOUS SOURCES, INCLUDING ALLABY AND ALLABY 1999; BATES AND JACKSON 1987; JACKSON 1997; AND NEUENDORF AND OTHERS 2005, UNLESS OTHERWISE NOTED.

REFERENCES

AAPG: American Association of Petroleum Geologists
CENTJ/TJ: Creation Ex Nihilo Technical Journal
CRSQ: Creation Research Society Quarterly
GSA: Geological Society of America
J. Sed. Pet: Journal of Sedimentary Petrology
SEPM: Society of Economic Paleontologists and Mineralogists

Adams, F.D. 1938. *The birth and development of the geological sciences*. New York: Dover Publications.

Ager, D.V. 1963. *Principles of paleoecology*. New York: McGraw-Hill.

———— 1993a. *The nature of the stratigraphical record*. Third edition. New York: J. Wiley.

———— 1993b. *The new catastrophism*. New York: Cambridge University Press.

Aharon, P. 2006. Entrainment of meltwaters in hyperpycnal flows during deglaciation superfloods in the Gulf of Mexico. *Earth and Planetary Science Letters* 241:260–270.

Aigner, T. 1985. *Storm depositional systems*. Lecture notes in earth sciences 3. New York: Springer-Verlag.

Aigner, T., and H.E. Reineck. 1982. Proximality trends in modern storm sands from the Helgoland Bight (North Sea) and their implications for basin analysis. *Senckenbergiana maritima* 14:183–215.

Akin, W.E. 1991. *Global patterns: Climate, vegetation, and soils*. Norman, OK: University of Oklahoma Press.

Akridge, A.J. 2000. DeSoto Falls in DeSoto State Park, Alabama: Evidence for recent formation? *CRSQ* 36:170–176.

Akridge, A.J., and C.R. Froede, Jr. 2000. Rock spires (pseudo-hoodoos) on the Lookout Mountain Syncline. *CRSQ* 36:216–220.

———— 2005. Ashfall Fossil Beds State Park, Nebraska: A post-Flood/Ice Age paleoenvironment. *CRSQ* 42:183–192.

Akridge, A.J., and E.L. Williams. 2001. The Slumgullion earthflow. *CRSQ* 38:101–105.

———— 2005. Cataclysms recorded in a recent geomorphic event: The Gros Ventre slide, Wyoming. *CRSQ* 42:131–138.

Albritton, C.C., Jr. 1986. *The abyss of time: Changing conceptions of the earth's antiquity after the sixteenth century*. New York: St. Martin's Press.

Alexander, L.T., and J.G. Cady. 1962. *Genesis and hardening of laterite in soils*. Soil Conservation Service Technical Bulletin No. 1282. United States Department of Agriculture. Washington, D.C.

Allaby, A., and M. Allaby. 1999. *A dictionary of earth sciences*. Second edition. New York: Oxford University Press.

Allen, J.R.L. 1971. Mixing at turbidity current heads, and its geological implications. *J. Sed. Pet.* 41:97–113.

———— 1982. *Sedimentary structures: Their character and physical basis*. New York: Elsevier.

Altschuler, Z.S., E.J. Dwornik, and H. Kramer. 1963. Transformation of montmorillonite to kaolinite during weathering. *Science* 141:148–152.

Anand, A., and A.K. Jain. 1987. Earthquakes and deformational structures (seismites) in Holocene sediments from the Himalayan-Andaman Arc, India. *Tectonophysics* 133:105–120.

Andrews, P.B. 1970. *Facies and genesis of a hurricane-washover fan, St. Joseph Island, central Texas coast*. Austin, TX: Bureau of Economic Geology Report of Investigations 67.

Anonymous. 1995. Speaking to the earth: An interview with Steven Austin and Kurt Wise. *Bible-Science News* 33(5):17–21.

Asquith, G.B. 1979. *Subsurface carbonate depositional models: A concise review*. Tulsa, OK: PennWell Books.

Astin, T.R. 1986. Septarian crack formation in carbonate concretions from shales and mudstones. *Clay Minerals* 21:617–631.

Auldaney, J. 1992. Asteroids and their connection to the Flood. In Proceedings of the 1992 Twin-Cities Creation Conference, Twin-Cities Creation-Science Association. Northwestern College. Roseville, MN, p. 133–136.

———— 1994. Asteroid hypothesis for dinosaur extinction. *CRSQ* 31:11–12.

Austin, S.A. 1991. *Mount St. Helens: A slide collection for educators*. El Cajon, CA: Geology Education Materials.

———— (editor). 1994. *Grand Canyon: Monument to catastrophe*. Santee, CA: Institute for Creation Research.

Austin, S.A., J.R. Baumgardner, D.R. Humphreys, A.A. Snelling, L. Vardiman, and K.P. Wise. 1994. Catastrophic plate tectonics: A global Flood model of earth history. In Walsh, R.E. (editor). *Proceedings of the Third International Conference on Creationism.* Technical symposium sessions. Pittsburgh, PA: Creation Science Fellowship, p. 609–621.

Austin, S.A., and J.D. Morris. 1986. Tight folds and clastic dikes as evidence for rapid deposition and deformation of two very thick stratigraphic sequences. In Walsh, R.E., C.L. Brooks, and R.S. Crowell (editors). *Proceedings of the First Conference on Creationism.* Technical symposium sessions and additional topics. Pittsburgh, PA: Creation Science Fellowship, p. 3–15.

Austin, S.A., and K.P. Wise. 1994. The Pre-Flood/Flood boundary: As defined in Grand Canyon, Arizona and eastern Mojave Desert, California. In Walsh, R.E. (editor). *Proceedings of the Third International Conference on Creationism.* Technical symposium sessions. Pittsburgh, PA: Creation Science Fellowship, p. 37–47.

Axelrod, D.I. 1981. *Role of volcanism in climate and evolution.* GSA Special Paper 185. Boulder, CO.

Barnette, D.W., and J.R. Baumgardner. 1994. Patterns of ocean circulation over the continents during Noah's flood. In Walsh, R.E. (editor). *Proceedings of the Third International Conference on Creationism.* Technical symposium sessions. Pittsburgh, PA: Creation Science Fellowship, p. 77–86.

Bates, R.L., and J.A. Jackson (editors). 1987. *Glossary of geology.* Third edition. Alexandria, VA: American Geological Institute.

Begossi, R., and J.C. Della Fávera. 2002. Catastrophic floods as a possible cause of organic matter accumulation giving rise to coal. *International Journal of Coal Geology* 52:83–89.

Berggren, W.A., D.V. Kent, M.P. Aubry, and J. Hardenbol (editors). 1995. *Geochronology, time scales and global stratigraphic correlation.* Special publication No. 54. Tulsa, OK: SEPM.

Berthault, G. 1994. Experiments on stratification. In Walsh, R.E. (editor). *Proceedings of the Third International Conference on Creationism.* Technical symposium sessions. Pittsburgh, PA: Creation Science Fellowship, p. 103–110.

——— 2002. Analysis of main principles of stratigraphy on the basis of experimental data. *Lithology and Mineral Resources* 37(5):442–446.

——— 2004. Sedimentological interpretation of the Tonto Group stratigraphy (Grand Canyon Colorado River). *Lithology and Mineral Resources* 37(5):442–446.

Bigarella, J.J. 1973. Paleocurrents and the problem of continental drift. *Geologische Rundschau* 62:447–477.

Birkeland, P.W. 1999. *Soils and geomorphology.* Third edition. New York: Oxford University Press.

Bishop, G.A., and N.A. Brannen. 1993. Ecology and paleoecology of Georgia Ghost shrimp. In Farrell, K.M., C.W. Hoffman, and V.J. Henry, Jr. (editors). *Geomorphology and facies relationships of Quaternary barrier island complexes near St. Mary's, Georgia.* Georgia Geological Society Fieldtrip Guidebook 13(1):19–29.

Blatt, H., G. Middleton, and R. Murray. 1972. *Origin of sedimentary rocks.* Englewood Cliffs, NJ: Prentice-Hall.

Boardman, J. 1985. *Soils and Quaternary landscape evolution.* New York: John Wiley.

Bohor, B.F., and D.M. Triplehorn. 1993. *Tonsteins: Altered volcanic-ash layers in coal-bearing sequences.* Boulder, CO: GSA Special Paper 285.

Bottjer, D.J., and M.L. Droser. 1992. Paleoenvironmental patterns of biogenic sedimentary structures. In Maples, C.G., and R.R. West (editors). *Trace fossils.* Knoxville, TN: The Paleontological Society Short Courses in Paleontology Number 5, p. 130–144.

Bouma, A.H. 1962. *Sedimentology of some flysch deposits: A graphic approach to facies interpretation.* New York: Elsevier.

——— 1972. Recent and ancient turbidites and contourites. *Transactions of the Gulf Coast Association of Geological Societies* 22:205–221.

Bouma, A.H., and A. Brouwer (editors). 1964. *Turbidites.* Developments in Sedimentology No. 3. New York: Elsevier.

Bouma, A.H., W.R. Normark, and N.E. Barnes (editors). 1985. *Submarine fans and related turbidite systems.* New York: Springer-Verlag.

Bouma, A.H., and C.G. Stone (editors). 2000. *Fine-grained turbidite systems.* Tulsa, OK: American Association of Petroleum Geologists Memoir 72.

Bourgeois, J. 1980. A transgressive shelf sequence exhibiting hummocky stratification: The Cape Sebastian Sandstone (Upper Cretaceous), southwestern Oregon. *J. Sed. Pet* 50:681–702.

Bourman, R.P. 1993a. Modes of ferricrete genesis: Evidence from southeastern Australia. *Zeitschrift für Geomorphologie* 37:77–101.

——— 1993b. Perennial problems in the study of laterite: A review. *Australian Journal of Earth Sciences* 40:387–401.

——— 1996. Towards distinguishing transported and in situ ferricretes: Data from southern Australia. *AGSO Journal of Australian Geology and Geophysics* 16(3):231–241.

Bourman, R.P., A.R. Milnes, and J.M. Oades. 1987. Investigations of ferricretes and related surficial ferruginous materials in parts of southern and eastern Australia. *Zeitschrift für Geomorphologie* 64:1–24.

Bourman, R.P., and C.D. Ollier. 2002. A critique of the Schellman definition and classification of "laterite." *Catena* 47:117–131.

Bowen, D.W., P. Weimer, and A.J. Scott. 1993. The relative success of siliclastic sequence stratigraphic concepts in exploration: Examples from incised valley fill and turbidite systems reservoirs. In Weimer, P., and H.W. Posamentier (editors). *Siliciclastic sequence stratigraphy: Recent developments and applications.* Tulsa, OK: American Association of Petroleum Geologists Memoir 58, p. 15–42.

Bown, T.M., and M.J. Kraus. 1981a. Lower Eocene alluvial paleosols (Willwood Formation, northwest Wyoming, U.S.A.) and their significance for paleoecology, paleoclimatology, and basin analysis. *Palaeogeography, Palaeoclimatology, Palaeoecology* 34:1–30.

———— 1981b. Vertebrate fossil-bearing paleosol units (Willwood Formation, Lower Eocene, northwest Wyoming, U.S.A.): Implications for taphonomy, biostratigraphy, and assemblage analysis. *Palaeogeography, Palaeoclimatology, Palaeoecology* 34:31–56.

———— 1987. Integration of channel and floodplain suites, I. Developmental sequence and lateral relations of alluvial paleosols. *J. Sed. Pet.* 57:587–601.

Boyajian, G.E., and C.W. Thayer. 1995. Clam calamity: A recent supratidal storm-deposit as an analog for fossil shell beds. *Palaios* 10:484–489.

Braithwaite, C.J.R. 1973. Reefs: Just a problem of semantics? *AAPG Bulletin* 57:1100–1116.

Brand, L. 1977. Coconino Sandstone (Permian) fossil vertebrate footprints — paleoecological implications. *AAPG Bulletin* 61:771.

———— 1978. Footprints in the Grand Canyon. *Origins* 5(2):64–82.

———— 1979. Field and laboratory studies on the Coconino Sandstone (Permian) vertebrate footprints and their paleoecological implications. *Palaeogeography, Palaeoclimatology, Palaeoecology* 28:25–38.

———— 1992. Comment and reply on "Fossil vertebrate footprints in the Coconino Sandstone (Permian) of northern Arizona: Evidence for underwater origin." *Geology* 20:668–670.

———— 1996. Variations in salamander trackways resulting from substrate differences. *Journal of Paleontology* 70:1004–1010.

Brand, L., and T. Tang. 1991. Fossil vertebrate footprints in the Coconino Sandstone (Permian) of northern Arizona: Evidence for underwater origin. *Geology* 19:1201–1204.

Braunstein, J. (compiler). 1973. *Paleoecology.* Tulsa, OK: AAPG Reprint Series 6.

———— (compiler). 1974. *Facies and the reconstruction of environments.* Tulsa, OK: American Association of Petroleum Geologists Reprint Series 10.

Brett, C.E., and G.C. Baird (editors). 1997. *Paleontological events: Stratigraphic, ecological, and evolutionary implications.* New York: Columbia University Press.

Brewer, R. 1976. *Fabric and mineral analysis of soils.* Second edition. New York: John Wiley.

Briggs, G. 1974. Carboniferous depositional environments in the Ouachita Mountains-Arkoma Basin area of southeastern Oklahoma. in Briggs, G. (editor). *Carboniferous of the Southeastern United States.* Boulder, CO: GSA Special Paper 148, p. 225–239.

Bromley, R.G. 1990. *Trace fossils: Biology and taphonomy.* Boston, MA: Unwin Hyman.

Brookins, D.G., and J.K. Rigby, Jr. 1987. Geochronologic and geochemical study of volcanic ashes from the Kirtland Shale (Cretaceous), San Juan Basin, New Mexico. In Fassett, J.E., and J.K. Rigby, Jr. (editors). *The Cretaceous-Tertiary Boundary in the San Juan and Raton Basins, New Mexico and Colorado.* Boulder, CO: GSA Special Paper 209, p. 105–110.

Brooks, C., D.E. James, and S.R. Hart. 1976. Ancient lithosphere: Its role in young continental volcanism. *Science* 193:1086–1094.

Brown, W.R. 1970. Investigations of the sedimentary record in the Piedmont and Blue Ridge of Virginia. In Fisher, G.W., F.J. Pettijohn, J.C. Reed, Jr., and K.N. Weaver (editors). *Studies of Appalachian geology.* New York: Wiley, p. 335–349.

Brown, W.T., Jr. 2001. *In the beginning: Compelling evidence for Creation and the Flood.* Seventh edition. Phoenix, AZ: Center for Scientific Creation.

Brown, A.A., and R.G. Loucks. 1993. Influence of sediment type and depositional processes on stratal patterns in the Permian basin-margin Lamar Limestone, McKittrick Canyon, Texas. In Loucks, R.G., and J.F. Sarg (editors). *Carbonate sequence stratigraphy: Recent developments and applications.* Tulsa, OK: American Association of Petroleum Geologists Memoir 57, p. 133–156.

Brunner, C.A., W.R. Normark, G.G. Zuffa, and F. Serra. 1999. Deep-sea sedimentary record of the late Wisconsin cataclysmic floods from the Columbia River. *Geology* 27:463–466.

Buchanan, F. 1807. *A journey from Madras through the countries of Mysore, Canara and Malabar.* Volume 2. London: East India Company.

Büdel, J. 1982. *Climatic geomorphology.* Translated by L. Fischer and D. Busche. Princeton, NJ: Princeton University Press.

Buie, B.F. 1964. Possibility of volcanic origin of the Cretaceous sedimentary kaolin of South Carolina and Georgia [abs.]. In Bradley, W.F. (editor). *Clays and clay minerals.* Proceedings of the Twelfth National Conference on Clays and Clay Minerals, p. 195. New York: Macmillan.

Buol, S.W., F.D. Hole, and R.J. McCracken. 1980. *Soil genesis and classification.* Second edition. Iowa State University Press. Ames, IA.

Burton, B.R., and P.K. Link. 1991. Ichnology of fine-grained mixed carbonate-siliclastic turbidites, Wood River Formation, Pennsylvanian-Permian, south-central Idaho. *Palaios* 6:291–301.

Burst, J.F. 1965. Subaqueously formed shrinkage cracks in clay. *J. Sed. Pet.* 35:348–353.

Buurman, P. 1980. Palaeosols in the Reading Beds (Paleocene) of Alum Bay, Isle of Wright, U.K. *Sedimentology* 27:593–606.

Campbell, J.M. 1917. Laterite. *Mineral Magazine* 17:67-77, 120–128, 171–179, 220–229.

Cant, D.J., and F.J. Hein (editors). 1987. *Approaches to interpretation of sedimentary environments.* Tulsa, OK: SEPM Reprint Series 11.

Carey, S.N. 1991. Transport and deposition of tephra by pyroclastic flows and surges. In Fisher, R.V. and G.A. Smith (editors). *Sedimentation in volcanic settings.* Tulsa, OK: SEPM Special Publication No. 45, p. 39–57.

Carey, S., and H. Sigurdsson. 1989. The intensity of plinian eruptions. *Bulletin of Volcanology* 51:28–40.

Carey, S., H. Sigurdsson, and R.S.J. Sparks. 1986. Quantitative models of the fallout and dispersal of tephra from volcanic eruption columns. *Bulletin of Volcanology* 48:109–125.

Cas, R.A.F., and J.V. Wright. 1987. *Volcanic successions modern and ancient.* New York: Chapman and Hall.

Catuneanu, O. 2006. *Principles of sequence stratigraphy.* New York: Elsevier.

Chamberlain, C.K. 1978. *A guidebook to the trace fossils and paleoecology of the Ouachita Geosyncline.* Tulsa, OK: SEPM.

Chamley, H. 1989. *Clay Sedimentology.* New York: Springer-Verlag.

Chan, M.A., W.T. Parry, and J.R. Bowman. 2000. Diagenetic hematite and manganese oxides and fault-related fluid flow in Jurassic sandstones, southeastern Utah. *AAPG Bulletin* 84:1281–1310.

Chesnut, D.R. 1983. *Source of the volcanic ash deposit (flint clay) in the fire clay coal of the Appalachian Basin.* Lexington, KY: Kentucky Geological Survey Open File Report OF-83-03.

Chronic, H. 1984. *Pages of stone: Geology of Western National Parks and Monuments. Part 1: Rocky Mountains and Western Great Plains.* Seattle, WA: The Mountaineers.

Clare, K.E. 1960. *Roadmaking gravels and soils in Central Africa.* Overseas Bulletin No. 12. Middlesex, England: Department of Scientific and Industrial Research. Road Research Laboratory.

Clarke, G.R. 1957. *The study of the soil in the field.* Fourth edition. London: Oxford University Press.

Clarke, J.E.H., A.N. Shor, D.J.W. Piper, and L.A. Mayer. 1990. Large-scale current-induced erosion and deposition in the path of the 1929 Grand Banks turbidity current. *Sedimentology* 37:613–629.

Clifton, H.E. 1988. Sedimentologic relevance of convulsive geologic events. In Clifton, H.E. (editor). *Sedimentologic consequences of convulsive geologic events.* Boulder, CO: GSA Special Paper 229, p. 1–5.

Coffin, H.G., and R.H. Brown. 1983. *Origin by design.* Washington, DC: Review and Herald.

Cohee, G.V., M.F. Glaessner, and H.D. Hedberg (editors). 1978. *Contributions to the geologic time scale.* Tulsa, OK: American Association of Petroleum Geologists Studies in Geology 6.

Collinson, J.D., and D.B. Thompson. 1989. *Sedimentary structures.* New York: Chapman and Hall.

Colman, S.M., and D.P. Dethier (editors). 1986. *Rates of chemical weathering of rocks and minerals.* New York: Academic Press.

Conkin, J.E., B. Conkin, and L. Steinrock. 1998. *Middle Devonian type Jeffersonville Limestone at the Falls of the Ohio.* Louisville, KY: University of Louisville Studies in Paleontology and Stratigraphy.

Cook, H.E., and H.T. Mullins. 1983. Basin margin environment. In Scholle, P.A., and D. Spearing (editors). *Sandstone depositional environments.* Tulsa, OK: American Association of Petroleum Geologists Memoir 31, p. 539–617.

Cowart, J.H., and C.R. Froede Jr., 1994. The use of trace fossils in refining depositional environments and their application to the creationist model. *CRSQ* 31:117–124.

Crimes, T.P., and J.C. Harper (editors). 1970. *Trace fossils.* Liverpool: Seel House Press.

——— 1977. *Trace fossils II.* Liverpool: Seel House Press.

Curran, H.A. 1985. *Biogenic structures: Their use in interpreting depositional environments.* Tulsa, OK: SEPM Special Publication 35.

Curtis, D.M. (compiler). 1976. *Sedimentary processes: Diagenesis.* Tulsa, OK: SEPM Reprint Series 1.

———— 1978. *Environmental models in ancient sediments.* Tulsa, OK: SEPM Reprint Series 6.

Cvancara, A.M. 1995. *A field manual for the amateur geologist.* Revised edition. New York: Wiley.

Cys, J.M., and S.J. Mazzullo (compilers). 1978. *Sedimentary processes: Depositional processes in ancient carbonates.* Tulsa, OK: SEPM Reprint Series 7.

D'Alessandro, A., A.A. Ekdale, and M. Sonnino. 1986. Sedimentologic significance of turbidite ichnofacies in the Saraceno Formation (Eocene), southern Italy. *J. Sed. Pet.* 56:294–306.

Daniels, R.B., and R.D. Hammer. 1992. *Soil geomorphology.* New York: Wiley.

Davis, R.A., Jr., S.C. Knowles, and M.J. Bland. 1989. Role of hurricanes in the Holocene stratigraphy of estuaries: Examples from the Gulf Coast of Florida. *J. Sed. Pet.* 59:1052–1061.

DeCelles, P.G. 1987. Variable preservation of middle Tertiary, coarse-grained, nearshore to outer-shelf storm deposits in Southern California. *J. of Sed. Pet.* 57:250–264.

Delano, J.W., S.J. Tice, C.E. Mitchell, and D. Goldman. 1994. Rhyolitic glass in Ordovician K-bentonites: A new stratigraphic tool. *Geology* 22:115–118.

Diller, J.S. 1889. Sandstone dikes. *GSA Bulletin* 1:411–442.

Dockery, D.T., III. 1980. *The invertebrate macropaleontology of the Clarke County, Mississippi, Area.* Jackson, MS: Mississippi Bureau of Geology Bulletin 122.

———— 1986. The Bashi-Tallahatta section at Mt. Barton, Meridian, Mississippi. In Neathery, T.L. (editor). *Southeastern Section of the GSA: Centennial Field Guide Volume 6,* Boulder, CO, p. 383–386.

Douglass, S.L. 1994. Beach erosion and deposition on Dauphin Island, Alabama, U.S.A. *Journal of Coastal Research* 10:306–328.

Dodd, J.R., and R.J. Stanton Jr. 1990. *Paleoecology: Concepts and applications.* Second edition. New York: Wiley.

Dott, R.H., Jr. 1983. Episodic sedimentation — How normal is average? How rare is rare? Does it matter. *J. Sed. Pet.* 53:5–23.

Dott, R.H., Jr. and J. Bourgeois. 1982. Hummocky stratification: Significance of its variable bedding sequences. *GSA Bulletin* 93:663–680.

Driese, S.G., C.I. Mora, and K.R. Walker (editors). 1992. *Paleosols, paleoweathering surfaces, and sequence boundaries.* Knoxville, TN: University of Tennessee Department of Geological Sciences Studies in Geology 21.

Dubar, J.R., and D.W. Beardsley. 1961. Paleoecology of the Choctawhatchee deposits (Late Miocene) at Alum Bluff, Florida. *Southeastern Geology* 2:155–189.

Duck, R.W. 1995. Subaqueous shrinkage cracks and early sediment fabrics preserved in Pleistocene calcareous concretions. *Journal of the Geological Society of London* 152:151–156.

Duke, W.L. 1985. Hummocky cross-stratification, tropical hurricanes and intense winter storms. *Sedimentology* 32:167–194.

Duke, W.L., R.W.C. Arnott, and R.J. Cheel. 1991. Shelf sandstones and hummocky cross-stratification: New insights on a stormy debate. *Geology* 19:625–628.

Dunham, R.J. 1970. Stratigraphic reefs versus ecological reefs. *AAPG Bulletin* 54:1931–1932.

Duringer, P., J.C. Paicheler, and J.L. Schneider. 1991. Un courant d'eau peut-il générer des turbidites? Résultats d'expérimentations analogiques. *Marine Geology* 99:231–246.

Dzulynski, S., and E.K. Walton. 1965. *Sedimentary features of flysch and greywackes.* Developments in Sedimentology 7. New York: Elsevier.

Eberli, G.P. 1991. Calcareous turbidites and their relationship to sea-level fluctuations and tectonism. In Einsele, G., W. Ricken, and A. Seilacher (editors). *Cycles and events in stratigraphy.* New York: Springer-Verlag, p. 340–359.

Edwards, D.A. 1993. *Turbidity currents: Dynamics, deposits and reversals.* Lecture notes in earth sciences No. 44. New York: Springer-Verlag.

Edwards, C.M., D.M. Hodgson, S.S. Flint, and J.A. Howell. 2005. Contrasting styles of shelf sediment transport and deposition in a ramp margin setting related to relative sea-level change and basin floor topography, Turonian (Cretaceous) Western Interior of central Utah, USA. *Sedimentary Geology* 179:117–152.

Einsele, G. 1991. Submarine mass flow deposits and turbidites. In Einsele, G, W. Ricken, and A. Seilacher (editors). *Cycles and events in stratigraphy.* New York: Springer-Verlag, p. 313–339.

———— 1992. *Sedimentary basins: Evolution, facies, and sediment budget.* New York: Springer-Verlag.

———— 1998. Event stratigraphy: Recognition and interpretation of sedimentary event horizons. In Doyle, P., and M.R. Bennett (editors). *Unlocking the stratigraphic record: Advances in modern stratigraphy*. New York: Wiley, p. 145–193.

Einsele, G., and A. Seilacher. 1991. Distinction of tempestites and turbidites. In Einsele, G., W. Ricken, and A. Seilacher (editors). *Cycles and events in stratigraphy*. New York: Springer-Verlag, p. 377–382.

Ekdale, A.A. 1988. Pitfalls of paleobathymetric interpretations based on trace fossil assemblages. *Palaios* 3:464–472.

Elliot, W.C., and J.L. Aronson. 1993. The timing and extent of illite formation in Ordovician K-bentonites at the Cincinnati Arch, the Nashville Dome and north-eastern Illinois basin. *Basin Research* 5:125–135.

Ellis, S., and A. Mellor. 1995. *Soils and environment*. New York: Routledge.

Ellwood, B.B. 1996. *Geology and America's National Park areas*. Upper Saddle River, NJ: Prentice Hall.

Emanuel, K.A. 1995. Hypercanes: A possible link in global extinction scenarios. *Journal of Geophysical Research* 100(D7):13,755-13,765.

———— 2003. Tropical cyclones. *Annual Review of Earth and Planetary Sciences* 31:75–104.

Emery, D., and K.J. Myers. 1996. *Sequence stratigraphy*. Cambridge, MA: Blackwell Science.

Enos, P. 1969. Anatomy of a flysch. *J. Sed. Pet.* 39:680–723.

Ettensohn, F.R., N. Rast, and C.E. Brett (editors). 2002. *Ancient seismites*. Boulder, CO: GSA Special Paper 359.

Fairbridge, R.W. 1963. Eustatic changes in sea level. In Ahrens, L.H. (editor). *Physics and chemistry of the earth*. Volume 4. New York: Pergamon Press, p. 99–185.

———— 1976. Shellfish-eating preceramic Indians in coastal Brazil. *Science* 191:353–359.

Faugères, J.C., and D.A.V. Stow. 1993. Bottom-current-controlled sedimentation: A synthesis of the contourite problem. *Sedimentary Geology* 82:287–297.

Faulkner, D. 1999. A biblically-based cratering theory. *CENTJ* 13(1):100–104.

Fedo, C.M., H.W. Nesbitt, and G.M. Young. 1995. Unraveling the effects of potassium metasomatism in sedimentary rocks and paleosols, with implications for paleoweathering conditions and provenance. *Geology* 23:921–924.

Feldmann, R.M. 1990. Theodore Roosevelt National Park. In Harris, A.G., and E. Tuttle (editors). *Geology of national parks*. Fourth edition. Dubuque, IA: Kendall/Hunt Publishing, p. 124–131.

Fenwick, I. 1985. Paleosols: Problems of recognition and interpretation. In Boardman, J. (editor). *Soils and Quaternary landscape evolution*. New York: John Wiley, p. 3–21.

Ferguson, J., R.V. Burne, and L.A. Chambers. 1983. Iron mineralization of peritidal carbonate sediments by continental groundwaters, Fisherman Bay, South Australia. *Sedimentary Geology* 34:41–57.

Fischer, J.M. 1994. A giant meteorite impact and rapid continental drift. In Walsh, R.E. (editor). *Proceedings of the Third International Conference on Creationism, technical symposium sessions*. Pittsburgh, PA: Creation Science Fellowship, p. 185–197.

Fisher, R.V., and H.U. Schmincke. 1984. *Pyroclastic rocks*. New York: Springer-Verlag.

Fisher, R.V., H.U. Schmincke, and G.A. Smith. 1991. Volcanism, tectonics and sedimentation. In Fisher, R.V. and G.A. Smith (editors). *Sedimentation in volcanic settings*. Tulsa, OK: SEPM Special Publication 45, p. 1–5.

Foss, J.E., and A.V. Segovia. 1984. Rates of soil formation. In LaFleur, R.G. (editor). *Groundwater as a geomorphic agent*. Winchester, MA: Allen and Unwin.

Foster, V.M. 1940. *Lauderdale County mineral resources*. Geology by V.M. Foster and tests by T.E. McCutcheon. Jackson, MS: Mississippi Geological Survey Bulletin 41.

Frey, R.W. 1971. Ichnology — The study of fossil and recent lebensspuren. In Perkins, B.F. (editor). *Trace fossils: A field guide to selected localities in Pennsylvanian, Permian, Cretaceous, and Tertiary rocks of Texas and related papers*. pp. 91-125. Miscellaneous Publication 71-1. Baton Rouge, LA: Louisiana State University School of Geoscience.

———— 1975. *The study of trace fossils*. New York: Springer-Verlag.

Frey, R.W., S.G. Pemberton, and T.D.A. Saunders. 1990. Ichnofacies and bathymetry. *Journal of Paleontology* 64:155–158.

Friedman, G.M. (editor). 1969. *Depositional environments in carbonate rocks*. Tulsa, OK: SEPM Special Publication 14.

Friedman, G.M., and J.E. Sanders. 1978. *Principles of sedimentology*. New York: John Wiley.

Froede, C.R., Jr. 1994a. Fossil wood of Big Bend National park. *CRSQ* 30:187–189.

———— 1994b. Comments on "Underwater Mudcracks" by M.J. Oard, 1994, *CRSQ* 30:213–214. *CRSQ* 31:71–72.

———— 1994c. Sequence stratigraphy and creation science. *CRSQ* 31:138–147.

———— 1994d. A post-Flood (Early Ice Age?) paleoenvironment in Mississippi. *CRSQ* 31:182–186.

———— 1995a. Late Cretaceous epeiric sea or retreating Floodwater? *CRSQ* 32:13–16.

———— 1995b. A proposal for a creationist geological timescale. *CRSQ* 32:90–94.

———— 1995c. Dauphin Island, Alabama: Evidence for rapid erosion. *CRSQ* 32:143–148.

———— 1996. A theory for the volcanic origin of radioactive shales and clays: Examples from the Southeastern United States. *CRSQ* 33:160–168.

———— 1997a. Letter to the editor. *CENTJ* 11(1):40–43.

———— 1997b. Dauphin Island, Alabama: Radiocarbon dating and questions about age. *CRSQ* 33:238–239.

———— 1997c. Cloudland Canyon State Park, Georgia: 300 million years of erosion? *CRSQ* 34:38–43.

———— 1997d. The Flood Event/Ice Age Stratigraphic Boundary on the United States Southeastern Coastal Plain. *CRSQ* 34:75–83.

———— 1997e. An unconformity boundary exposed at the lower Tornillo Creek bridge, Big Bend National Park, Brewster County, Texas, U.S.A. *CRSQ* 34:147–153.

———— 1998a. Sequence stratigraphy, stratigraphic time, and the Flood. *CRSQ* 35:100–103.

———— 1998b. *Field studies in catastrophic geology.* Technical monograph #7. Chino Valley, AZ: Creation Research Society Books.

———— 1999. The Florida Keys: Evidence in support of slow Floodwater retreat, Part I: The Upper Keys. *CRSQ* 35:186–192.

———— 2000. Submarine volcanism: Part I — Subaqueous basalt eruptions and lava flows. *CRSQ* 37:22–35.

———— 2002a. Extraterrestrial bombardment of the Inner Solar System: A review with questions and comments based on new information. *CRSQ* 38:209–212.

———— 2002b. Rhizolith evidence in support of a late Holocene sea-level highstand at least 0.5 m higher than present at Key Biscayne, Florida. *Geology* 30:203–206.

———— 2003. Dust Storms from the Sub-Saharan African Continent: Implications for plant and insect dispersion in the post-Flood world. *CRSQ* 39:237–244.

———— 2004a. Eroded Appalachian mountain siliciclastics as a source for the Navajo Sandstone. *TJ* 18(2):3–5.

———— 2004b. Jökullhlaups and catastrophic coal formation. *CRSQ* 38:209–212.

———— 2005a. The Tertiary stratigraphy surrounding Americus, Georgia: Evidence in support of the young-earth Flood framework. *CRSQ* 42:85–90.

———— 2005b. The impact of Hurricane Georges (September 28, 1998) across Dauphin Island, Alabama. *Southeastern Geology* 44(1):45–51.

———— 2006a. A large cliff scarp exposure of beach-nourished sands along the St. Andrew Bay Channel, Florida: Evidence for the rapid formation of siliciclastic stratigraphy. *CRSQ* 43:180–186.

———— 2006b. Spur and groove coral reef morphology. *CRSQ* 42:268–271.

———— 2006c. Neogene sand-to-pebble size siliciclastic sediments on the Florida Peninsula: Sedimentary evidence in support of the Genesis Flood. *CRSQ* 42:229–240.

———— 2006d. A Hurricane Frederic-generated storm-surge deposit exposed along a surf-zone foredune scarp on Dauphin Island, Alabama, U.S.A. *Journal of Coastal Research* 22(2):371–376.

———— 2006e. The impact that Hurricane Ivan (September 16, 2004) made across Dauphin Island, Alabama. *Journal of Coastal Research* 22(3):561–573.

Froede, C.R., Jr. and A.J. Akridge. 2003. Isolated areas of pulpit rocks on the Lookout Mountain synclinal ridge: Possible origin and development. *Southeastern Geology* 41(4):225–228.

Froede, C.R., Jr. and J. Brelsford. 1998. Speculation regarding the albedo of the antediluvian moon. *CRSQ* 35:166–167.

Froede, C.R., Jr. and J.H. Cowart. 1996. Dougherty Gap: Evidence for a turbidity current paleoenvironment. *CRSQ* 32:202–214.

Froede, C.R., Jr. and D.B. DeYoung. 1996. Impact events within the young-earth Flood model. *CRSQ* 33:23–34.

Froede, C.R., Jr. and R.O. Howard, Jr. 2002. The occurrence of septaria and non-septarian concretions in the Upper Cretaceous Blufftown Formation, southwestern Georgia, U.S.A., and their relationship to synsedimentary seismicity. *Southeastern Geology* 41(1):63–73.

Froede, C.R., Jr., G.F. Howe, J.K. Reed, and J.R. Meyer. 1998a. A preliminary report on the Precambrian Pikes Peak Iron Formation, Yavapai County, Arizona. *CRSQ* 35:15–22.

Froede, C.R., Jr., G.F. Howe, E.L. Williams, and R.L. Goette.1998b. Flysch/turbidite deposits and translational sliding in the Marathon Basin, Texas. *CRSQ* 35:95–98.

Froede, C.R., Jr. and J.K. Reed. 1999. Assessing creationist stratigraphy with evidence from the Gulf of Mexico. *CRSQ* 36:51–60.

Froede, C.R., Jr. and B.R. Rucker. 2006. Iron Mountain, Santa Rosa County, Florida: A paleogroundwater table inverted relief feature. *Southeastern Geology* 44(3):137–145.

Froede, C.R., Jr. and E.L. Williams. 1997. Large-scale ripple marks in the Lower Cretaceous rocks of Texas. *CRSQ* 33:238.

———— 1999. The Wetumpka impact crater, Elmore County, Alabama: An interpretation within the young-earth Flood model. *CRSQ* 36:32–37.

———— 2003. Grand Falls, Arizona: Evidence of missing uniformitarian time. *CRSQ* 40:182–188.

Froede, C.R., Jr., E.L. Williams, and J. Brelsford.1998. Panola Mountain, Georgia: Exfoliation evidence in support of Flood exposure. *CRSQ* 35:41–44.

Frye, J.C., and A.B. Leonard. 1967. Buried soils, fossil mollusks, and late Cenozoic paleoenvironments. In Teichert, C. and E.L. Yochelson (editors). *Essays in paleontology and stratigraphy.* R.C. Moore Commemorative Volume. Lawrence, KS: University of Kansas Special Publication 2, p. 429–444.

Furniss, G., N.W. Hinman, G.A. Doyle, and D.D. Runnells. 1999. Radiocarbon-dated ferricrete provides a record of natural acid rock drainage and paleoclimatic changes. *Environmental Geology* 37:102–106.

Gardner, J.A. 1926-1944. *The molluscan fauna of the Alum Bluff Group of Florida.* U.S. Geological Survey Professional Paper 142, parts 1-4, 1926; part 5, 1928; part 6, 1937; part 7, 1944.

Garner, P. 1996a. Where is the Flood/post-Flood Boundary? Implications of dinosaur nests in the Mesozoic. *CENTJ* 10(1):101–106.

———— 1996b. Continental Flood basalts indicate a pre-Mesozoic Flood/post-Flood boundary. *CENTJ* 10(1):114–127.

Garton, M. 1996. The pattern of fossil tracks in the geological record. *CENTJ* 10(1):82–100.

Gautier, D.L. (editor). 1986. *Roles of organic matter in sediment diagenesis.* Tulsa, OK: SEPM Special Publication 38.

Gerasimov, I.P. 1971. Nature and originality of paleosols. In Yaalon, D.H. (editor). *Paleopedology: Origin, nature, and dating of paleosols.* Israel Universities Press, p. 15–27.

Geyer, W.R., P.S. Hill, and G.C. Kineke. 2004. The transport, transformation and dispersal of sediment by buoyant coastal flows. *Continental Shelf Research* 24:927–949.

Gish, D.T. 1995. *Evolution: The fossils still say no!* El Cajon, CA: Institute for Creation Research.

Glinka, K.D. 1914. *Die typen der bodenbildung, ihre klassification und geographische verbreitung.* Berlin: Borntraeger.

Gohau, G. 1990. *A history of geology.* Revised and translated by Carozzi, A.V., and M. Carozzi. New Brunswick, NJ: Rutgers University Press.

Goldman, D., C.E. Mitchell, S.M. Bergström, J.W. Delano, and S. Tice. 1994. K-bentonites and graptolite biostratigraphy in the Middle Ordovician of New York State and Quebec: A new chronostratigraphic model. *Palaios* 9:124–143.

Goldring, R. 1993. Ichnofacies and facies interpretation. *Palaios* 8:403–405.

Goodbred, S.L., Jr. and A.C. Hine 1995. Coastal storm deposition: Salt-marsh response to a severe extratropical storm, March 1993, west-central Florida. *Geology* 23:679–682.

Goudie, A. 1995. *The changing earth: Rates of geomorphological processes.* Cambridge, MA: Blackwell.

Gould, S.J. 1989. *Wonderful life: The Burgess Shale and the nature of history.* New York: W.W. Norton & Company.

Grabau, A.W. 1960. *Principles of stratigraphy.* Volume two. New York: Dover.

Gradstein, F.M., J.G. Ogg, and A.G. Smith (editors). 2004. *A geologic time scale 2004.* New York: Cambridge University Press.

Greene, M.T. 1982. *Geology in the nineteenth century.* Ithaca, NY: Cornell University Press.

Grim, R.E. 1958. Concept of diagenesis in argillaceous sediments. *AAPG Bulletin* 42:246–253.

Grim, R.E., and N. Güven. 1978. *Bentonites: Geology, mineralogy, properties and uses.* Developments in sedimentology 24. New York: Elsevier.

Hamblin, A.P., and R.G. Walker. 1979. Storm dominated shallow marine deposits: The Fernie-Kootenay (Jurassic) transition, southern Rocky Mountains. *Canadian Journal of Earth Sciences* 16:1673–1690.

Hallam, A. 1981. *Facies interpretation and the stratigraphic record.* San Francisco: Freeman.

Hampton, M.A. 1972. The role of subaqueous debris flow in generating turbidity currents. *J. Sed. Pet.* 42:775–793.

Harland, W.B., R.L. Armstrong, A.V. Cox, L.E. Craig, A.G. Smith and D.G. Smith. 1990. *A geologic time scale — 1989.* New York: Cambridge University Press.

Harms, J.C., J.B. Southard, and R.G. Walker. 1982. *Structures and sequences in clastic rocks.* Lecture Notes for Short Course No. 9. Tulsa, OK: SEPM.

Harms, J.C., J.B. Southard, D.R. Spearing, and R.G. Walker. 1975. *Depositional environments as interpreted from primary sedimentary structures and stratification sequences*. Lecture Notes for Short Course 2. Tulsa, OK: SEPM.

Harrassowitz, H. 1930. Boden des tropischen region. Laterit und allitscher (lateritisher) rotlehm. In Blanck, E. (editor). *Handbuch der bodenlehre*. Volume 3. Berlin: J. Springer, p. 387–436.

Hartley, A.J., and D.J. Prosser (editors). 1995. *Characterization of deep marine clastic systems*. Geological Society Special Publication 94. Bath, UK: Geological Society of London.

Hastings, E.L., and L.D. Toulmin. 1963. *Summary of Paleocene and Eocene stratigraphy and economic geology of Southeastern Alabama*. Tenth Annual Field Trip Guidebook for the Southeastern Geological Society. Tallahassee, FL: Southeastern Geological Society.

Hay, R.L., M. Lee, D.R. Kolata, J.C. Matthews, and J.P. Morton. 1988. Episodic potassic diagenesis of Ordovician tuffs in the Mississippi Valley area. *Geology* 16:743–747.

Hayes, M.O. 1967. *Hurricanes as geological agents: Case studies of Hurricanes Carla, 1961, and Cindy, 1963*. Austin, TX: Texas Bureau of Economic Geology Report of Investigations 61.

Hays, M.O., and J.C. Boothroyd. 1969. Storms as modifying agents in the coastal environment. In Davis, R.A., Jr. (editor). 1987. *Beach and nearshore processes*. Tulsa, OK: SEPM Reprint Series 12, p. 25–39.

Haynes, J.T. 1994. *The Ordovician Deicke and Millbrig K-bentonite beds of the Cincinnati Arch and the southern valley and ridge province*. Boulder, CO: GSA Special Paper 290.

Hedtke, R. 1971. A geo-ecological explanation of the fossil record based upon divine creation. *CRSQ* 7:214–221.

Heezen, B.C., D.B. Ericson, and M. Ewing. 1954. Further evidence for a turbidity current following the 1929 Grand Banks earthquake. *Deep-Sea Research* 1:193–202.

Heezen, B.C. and M. Ewing. 1952. Turbidity currents and submarine slumps, and the 1929 Grand Banks earthquake. *American Journal of Science* 250:849-873.

Heezen, B.C. and C.D. Hollister. 1971. *The face of the deep*. New York: Oxford University Press.

Heiken, G., and K. Wohletz. 1985. *Volcanic ash*. Los Angeles, CA: University of California Press.

Hesselbo, S.P., and T.J. Palmer. 1992. Reworked early diagenetic concretions and the bioerosional origin of a regional discontinuity within British Jurassic marine mudstones. *Sedimentology* 39:1045–1065.

Hiscott, R.N. 1994a. Traction-carpet stratification in turbidites — fact or fiction? *Journal of Sedimentary Research* A64:204–208.

——— 1994b. Loss of capacity, not competence, as the fundamental process governing deposition from turbidity currents. *Journal of Sedimentary Research* A64:209–214.

Hobbs, W.H. 1907. Some topographic features formed at the time of earthquakes and the origin of mounds in the Gulf Plain. *American Journal of Science* 173:245–256.

Holliday, V.T., C.R. Ferring, and P. Goldberg. 1993. The scale of soil investigations in archaeology. In Stein, J.K., and A.R. Linse (editors). *Effects of scale on archaeological and geoscientific perspectives*. Boulder, CO: GSA Special Paper 283, p. 29–37.

Holroyd, E.W., III. 1995. *Dinosaur Ridge on a young earth*. Self published. Arvada, CO.

Holt, R.D. 1996. Evidence for a Late Cainozoic Flood/post-Flood Boundary. *CENTJ* 10(1):128–167.

Horn, D.R., J.I. Ewing, and M. Ewing. 1972. Graded-bed sequences emplaced by turbidity currents north of 20_N in the Pacific, Atlantic and Mediterranean. *Sedimentology* 18:247–275.

Horstemeyer, M.F., and J.R. Baumgardner. 2003. What initiated the Flood cataclysm? In Ivey, R.L., Jr. (editor). *Proceedings of the Fifth International Conference on Creationism*. Technical symposium sessions. Pittsburgh, PA: Creation Science Fellowship, p. 155–163.

Hounslow, M.W. 1997. Significance of localized pore pressure to the genesis of septarian concretions. *Sedimentology* 44:1133–1147.

Howe, G.F., and C.R. Froede Jr. 1999. The Haymond Formation Boulder Beds of Marathon Basin, West Texas: Theories on origin and catastrophic deposition. *CRSQ* 36:17–25.

Howe, G.F., and E.L. Williams. 1994. The evolution of geological origins theories: Part I — The Haymond interbeds, Marathon Basin, Texas. *CRSQ* 31:25–31.

Howe, G.F., E.L. Williams, and C.R. Froede, Jr. 2003. The possible origin of fossil wood and pollen in the Aguja and Javelina Formations, Big Bend National Park, Texas. *CRSQ* 40:44–52.

Howell, D.G., and W.R. Normark. 1982. Sedimentology of submarine fans. In Scholle, P.A., and D. Spearing (editors). *Sandstone depositional environments*. Tulsa, OK: American Association of Petroleum Geologists Memoir 31, p. 365–404.

Hsü, K.J. 1970. The meaning of the word flysch — A short historical search. In Lajoie, J. (editor). *Flysch sedimentology in North America*. Waterloo, Ontario: The Geological Association of Canada Special Paper 7, p. 1–11.

Huff, W.D. 1983. Correlation of Middle Ordovician K-bentonites based on chemical fingerprinting. *Journal of Geology* 91:657–669.

Huff, W.D., S.M. Bergström and D.R. Kolata. 1992. Gigantic Ordovician volcanic ash fall in North America and Europe: Biological, tectonomagmatic, and event-stratigraphic significance. *Geology* 20:875–878.

Huff, W.D., and D.R. Kolata. 1990. Correlation of the Ordovician Deicke and Millbrig K-bentonites between the Mississippi Valley and the Southern Appalachians. *AAPG Bulletin* 74:1736–1747.

Huff, W.D., D.R. Kolata, S.M. Bergström, and Y.S. Zhang. 1996. Large-magnitude Middle Ordovician volcanic ash falls in North America and Europe: Dimensions, emplacement and post-emplacement characteristics. *Journal of Volcanology and Geothermal Research* 73:285–301.

Hunt, C.B. 1972. *Geology of soils: Their evolution, classification, and uses*. San Francisco, CA: Freeman.

Hunter, R.E. 1977. Basic types of stratification in small eolian dunes. *Sedimentology* 24:361–387.

Hunter, R.E., and H.E. Clifton. 1982. Cyclic deposits and hummocky cross-stratification of probable storm origin in Upper Cretaceous rocks of the Cape Sebastian Area, Southwestern Oregon. *J. Sed. Pet.* 52:127–143.

Imbrie, J., and N. Newell (editors). 1964. *Approaches to paleoecology*. New York: Wiley.

Ingram, S.L. 1991. The Tuscahoma-Bashi section at Meridian, Mississippi: First notice of lowstand deposits above the Paleocene-Eocene TP2/Te1 sequence boundary. *Mississippi Geology* 11(4):9–14.

Isphording, W.C., and G.W. Isphording. 1991. Identification of ancient storm events in buried Gulf Coast sediments. *Transactions of the Gulf Coast Association of Geological Societies* 41:339–347.

Jackson, J.A. 1997. *Glossary of geology*. Fourth edition. Alexandria, VA: American Geological Institute.

Jeans, C.V., R.J. Merriman, J.G. Mitchell, and D.J. Bland. 1982. Volcanic clays in the Cretaceous of southern England and northern Ireland. *Clay Minerals* 17:105–156.

Jenny, H. 1941. *Factors of soil formation: A system of quantitative pedology*. New York: Dover.

Jones, M.J. 1977. *Field guide to the geology of the Fall Creek Falls Area*. Nashville, TN: Tennessee Division of Geology.

Julien, P.Y., Y. Lan, and G. Berthault 1993. Experiments on stratification of heterogeneous sand mixtures. *Bulletin of the Geological Society of France* 164(5):649–660.

Karlén, W., A. Bodin, J. Kuylenstierna, and J.O. Näslund. 1995. Climate of northern Sweden during the Holocene. In Finkl, C.W., Jr. (editor). *Holocene cycles: Climate, sea levels, and sedimentation*, Special issue No. 17, Journal of Coastal Research. Ft. Lauderdale, FL: Coastal Education and Research Foundation, p. 49–54.

Kauffman, E.G., and W.G.E. Caldwell. 1993. The Western Interior Basin in time and space. In Caldwell, W.G.E., and E.G. Kauffman (editors). *Evolution of the Western Interior Basin*. St. John's, Newfoundland: Geological Association of Canada Special Paper 39, p. 1–30.

Keen, T.R., and R.L. Slingerland. 1993. Four storm-event beds and the tropical cyclones that produced them: A numerical hindcast. *J. Sed. Pet.* 63:218–232.

Kimberley, M.M. 1990. Paleosols. In Magill, F.N. (editor). *Magill's survey of science*. Earth science series, volume 4. Englewood Cliffs, NJ: Salem Press, p. 2011–2017.

Klevberg, P. 1999. The philosophy of sequence stratigraphy: Part I — Philosophic background. *CRSQ* 36: 72–80.

——— 2000. The philosophy of sequence stratigraphy: Part II — Application to stratigraphy. *CRSQ* 37:36–46.

Klevberg, P., and R. Bandy. 2003a. Postdiluvial soil formation and the question of time, Part I. Pedogenesis. *CRSQ* 39:252–268.

——— 2003b. Postdiluvial soil formation and the question of time, Part II. Time. *CRSQ* 40:99–116.

——— In press. The "problem" of soils. In Oard, M.J., and J.K. Reed (editors). *Rock solid answers: Responses to popular objections to biblical geology*. Green Forest, AR: Master Books.

Klevberg, P., and M.J. Oard. 2005. Drifting interpretations of the Kennedy gravel. *CRSQ* 41:289–315.

Klevberg, P., R. Bandy, and M.J. Oard. 2007. The "problem" of paleosols. In Oard, M.J., and J.K. Reed (editors). *Rock solid answers: Responses to popular objections to biblical geology*. Green Forest, AR: Master Books.

Klevberg, P., M.J. Oard, and R. Bandy. 2003. Are paleosols really ancient soils? *CRSQ* 40:134–149.

Kolata, D.R., J.K. Frost, and W.D. Huff. 1987. Chemical correlation of K-bentonite beds in the Middle Ordovician Decorah Subgroup, upper Mississippi Valley. *Geology* 15:208–211.

Kolata, D.R., W.D. Huff, and S.M. Bergström. 1996. *Ordovician K-bentonites of eastern North America*. Boulder, CO: GSA Special Paper 313.

Kraus, M.J. 1987. Integration of channel and floodplain suites, II. Vertical relations of alluvial paleosols. *J. Sed. Pet.* 57:602–612.

———— 1992. Mesozoic and Tertiary paleosols. In Martini, I.P., and W. Chesworth (editors). *Weathering, soils and paleosols.* Developments in earth surface processes No. 2. New York: Elsevier, p. 525–542.

———— 1999. Paleosols in clastic sedimentary rocks: Their geologic applications. *Earth-Science Reviews* 47:41–70.

Kraus, M.J., and T.M. Bown. 1993. Short-term sediment accumulation rates determined from Eocene alluvial paleosols. *Geology* 21:743–746.

Kreisa, R. 1981. Storm-generated sedimentary structures in subtidal marine facies with examples from the middle to upper Ordovician of southwestern Virginia. *J. Sed. Pet.* 51:823–848.

Kuenen, P.H. 1958. Experiments in geology. *Transactions of the Geological Society of Glasgow* 23:1–28.

Kuenen, P.H., and H.W. Menard. 1952. Turbidity currents, graded and non-graded deposits. *J. Sed. Pet.* 22:83–96.

Kuenen, P.H., and C.I. Migliorini. 1950. Turbidity currents as a cause of graded bedding. *Journal of Geology* 58:91–127.

Kumar, N., and J.E. Sanders. 1976. Characteristics of shoreface storm deposits: Modern and ancient. *J. Sed. Pet.* 46:145–162.

Lajoie, J. 1970. Introduction. In Lajoie, J. (editor). *Flysch sedimentology in North America.* Waterloo, Ontario: The Geological Association of Canada Special Paper 7.

Lambert, D. 1988. *The field guide to geology.* New York: Facts on File.

Lamplugh, G.W. 1902. Calcrete. *Geological Magazine* 9:575.

Laudan, R. 1987. *From mineralogy to geology: The foundations of a science, 1650–1830.* Chicago, IL: University of Chicago Press.

Lee, H.J., S.S. Chun, J.H. Chang, and S.J. Han. 1994. Landward migration of isolated shelly sand ridge (chenier) on the macrotidal flat of Gomso Bay, west coast of Korea: Controls of storms and typhoon. *Journal of Sedimentary Research* A64:886–893.

Lehman, T.H. 1989. Upper Cretaceous (Maastrichtian) paleosols in Trans-Pecos Texas. *GSA Bulletin* 101:188–203.

———— 1990. Paleosols and the Cretaceous/Tertiary transition in the Big Bend region of Texas. *Geology* 18:362–364.

Lewis, D.W., and D. McConchie. 1994. *Practical Sedimentology.* New York: Chapman and Hall.

Lewis, D.W., and L. Marquardt. 1995. *A field guide to Dinosaur Ridge.* Second edition. Golden , CO: Friends of Dinosaur Ridge.

Lewis, D.W., and A. Rice (editors). 1990. *Volcanism and fossil biotas.* Boulder, CO: GSA Special Paper 244.

Lockley, M.G., D.B. Loope, and L.R. Brand 1992. Comment and reply on "Fossil vertebrate footprints in the Coconino Sandstone (Permian) of northern Arizona: Evidence for underwater origin." *Geology* 20:666–670.

Loughnan, F.C. 1970. Flint clay in the coal-barren Triassic of the Sydney basin, Australia. *J. Sed. Pet.* 40:822–828.

Lowe, D.R. 1976a. Grain flow and grain flow deposits. *J. Sed. Pet.* 46:188–199.

———— 1976b. Subaqueous liquefied and fluidized sediment flows and their deposits. *Sedimentology* 23:285–308.

———— 1982. Sediment gravity flows: II. Depositional models with special reference to the deposits of high-density turbidity currents. *J. Sed. Pet.* 52:279–297.

Lyons, P.C., W.F. Outerbridge, D.M. Triplehorn, H.T. Evans, Jr., R.D. Congdon, M. Capiro, J.C. Hess, and W.P. Nash. 1992. An Appalachian isochron: A kaolinized Carboniferous air-fall volcanic-ash deposit (tonstein). *GSA Bulletin* 104:1515–1527.

Lyons, P.C., D.A. Spears, W.F. Outerbridge, R.D. Congdon, and H.T. Evans Jr. 1994. Euramerican tonsteins: Overview, magmatic origin, and depositional-tectonic implications. *Palaeogeography, Palaeoclimatology, Palaeoecology* 106:113–134.

Machette, M.N. 1978. Dating Quaternary faults in the Southwestern United States by using buried calcic paleosols. *United States Geological Survey Journal of Research* 6:369–381.

Mack, G.H., W.C. James, and H.C. Monger. 1993. Classification of paleosols. *GSA Bulletin* 105:129–136.

Mahaney, W.C. 1978. *Quaternary soils.* Norwich, England: Geo Abstracts. University of East Anglia.

Maignien, R. 1966. *Review of research on laterites.* Paris, France: United Nations Educational, Scientific and Cultural Organization.

Mann, A.W., and C.D. Ollier. 1985. Chemical diffusion and ferricrete formation. *Catena* 6:151–157.

Mann, C.J., and S.P. Kanagy II. 1990. Angles of repose that exceed modern angles. *Geology* 18:358–361.

Martini, I.P., and W. Chesworth. 1992. Reflections on soils and paleosols. In Martini, I.P., and W. Chesworth (editors). *Weathering, soils and paleosols.* Developments in earth surface processes 2. New York: Elsevier, p. 3–16.

Mathisen, M.E., and J.G. McPherson. 1991. Volcaniclastic deposits: Implications for hydrocarbon exploration. In Fisher, R.V., and G.A. Smith (editors). *Sedimentation in volcanic settings.* Tulsa, OK: SEPM Special Publication 45, p. 27–36.

Matthes, F.E. 1932. Personal communication to McKee. Quoted in: McKee, E.D. 1933.

Maxwell, R.A., J.T. Lonsdale, R.T. Hazzard, and J.A. Wilson. 1967. *Geology of Big Bend National Park, Brewster County, Texas.* Austin, TX: Bureau of Economic Geology Bulletin No. 6711.

McBride, E.F. 1966. *Sedimentary petrology and history of the Haymond Formation (Pennsylvanian), Marathon Basin, Texas.* Austin, TX: Texas Bureau of Economic Geology Report of Investigation No. 57.

———— 1974. Significance of color in red, green, purple, olive, brown, and gray beds of Difunta Group, northeastern Mexico. *J. Sed. Pet.* 44:760–773.

McFarlane, M.J. 1976. *Laterite and landscape.* New York: Academic Press.

McIlreatch, I.A., and Morrow, D.W. (editors). 1990. *Diagenesis.* Geoscience Canada Reprint Series 4, St. John's, Newfoundland: Geological Association of Canada.

McKee, E.D. 1933. The Coconino Sandstone — Its history and origin. Carnegie Institute of Washington, D.C., *Contributions to Palaeontology* VII, 440:77–115.

———— 1945. Small-scale structures in the Coconino Sandstone of northern Arizona. *Journal of Geology* 53:313–325.

———— 1947. Experiments on the development of tracks in fine cross-bedded sand. *J. Sed. Pet.* 17:23–28.

———— 1979. Ancient sandstones considered to be eolian. In McKee, E.D. (editor). *A study of global sand seas.* Washington, DC: U.S. Geological Survey Professional Paper 1052, p. 187–238.

McKerrow, W.S. (editor). 1978. *The ecology of fossils.* Cambridge, MA: The MIT Press.

McLane, M. 1995. *Sedimentology.* New York: Oxford University Press.

Miall, A.D. 2000. *Principles of sedimentary basin analysis.* New York: Springer-Verlag.

Middleton, G.V. (editor). 1965. *Primary sedimentary structures and their hydrodynamic interpretation.* Tulsa, OK: SEPM Special Publication 12.

———— 1966a. Experiments on density and turbidity currents: I. Motion of the head. *Canadian Journal of Earth Sciences* 3:523–546.

———— 1966b. Experiments on density and turbidity currents: II. Uniform flow of density currents. *Canadian Journal of Earth Sciences* 3:627–637.

———— 1967. Experiments on density and turbidity currents: III. Deposition of sediment. *Canadian Journal of Earth Sciences* 4:475–505.

Middleton, G.V., and M.A. Hampton. 1976. Subaqueous sediment transport and deposition of sediment gravity flows. In Stanley, D.J., and D.J.P. Swift (editors). *Marine sediment transport and environmental management.* New York: Wiley, p. 197–218.

Milnes, A.R., R.P. Bourman, and R.W. Fitzpatrick. 1987. Petrology and mineralogy of "laterites" in southern and eastern Australia and southern Africa. *Chemical Geology* 60:237–250.

Milnes, A.R., R.P. Bourman, and K.H. Northcote. 1985. Field relationships of ferricretes and weathered zones in southern south Australia: A contribution to "laterite" studies in Australia. *Australian Journal of Soil Research* 23:441–465.

Mississippi Geological Society. 1983. *Field trip roadlog: Tertiary and Upper Cretaceous Depositional environments of central Mississippi and west-central Alabama.* Gulf Coast Association of Geological Societies Annual Meeting, Jackson, MS. Austin, TX: Earth Enterprises.

Mitchell, C.E., D. Goldman, J.W. Delano, S.D. Samson, and S.M. Bergström. 1994. Temporal and spatial distribution of biozones and facies relative to geochemically correlated K-bentonites in the Middle Ordovician Taconic foredeep. *Geology* 22:715–718.

Moore, D.M., and R.C. Reynolds, Jr. 1997. *X-ray diffraction and the identification and analysis of clay minerals.* New York: Oxford University Press.

Morris, H.M. (editor). 1985. *Scientific creationism.* Second edition. Green Forest, AR: Master Books.

———— 1996. The geologic column and the Flood of Genesis. *CRSQ* 33:49–57.

Morris, J.D. 1994. *The young earth.* Green Forest, AR: Master Books.

Morris, R.C. 1974. Carboniferous rocks of the Ouachita Mountain, Arkansas: A study of facies patterns along the unstable slope and axis of a flysch trough. In Briggs, G. (editor). *Carboniferous of the Southeastern United States.* Boulder, CO: GSA Special Paper 148, p. 241–279.

Morris, S.C. 1998. *The crucible of creation: The Burgess Shale and the rise of animals.* New York: Oxford University Press.

Mortenson, T. 1997. British scriptural geologists in the first half of the nineteenth century: Part 1. Historical setting. *CENTJ* 11(2):221–252.

———— 2003. The early 19th century British "scriptural geologists:" Opponents of the emerging old-earth theories of geology. In Ivey, R.L., Jr. (editor). *Proceedings of the Fifth International Conference on Creationism. Technical symposium sessions.* Pittsburgh, PA: Creation Science Fellowship, p. 155–163.

———— 2004. *The great turning point: The church's catastrophic mistake on geology — Before Darwin.* Green Forest, AR: Master Books.

———— 2006. The historical development of the old-earth geological timescale. In Reed, J.K., and M.J. Oard (editors). *The geologic column: Perspectives within diluvial geology.* Chino Valley, AZ: CRS Books, p. 7–30.

Morton, R.A. 1988. Nearshore responses to great storms. In Clifton, H.E. (editor). *Sedimentologic consequences of convulsive geologic events.* Boulder, CO: GSA Special Paper 229, p. 7–22.

Mulder, T., and J.P. Syvitski. 1995. Turbidity currents generated at river mouths during exceptional discharges to the world oceans. *Journal of Geology* 103:285–299.

Mulder, T., J.P. Syvitski, S. Migeon, J.C. Faugères, and B. Savoye. 2003. Marine hyperpycnal flows: Initiation, behavior and related deposits. A review. *Marine and Petroleum Geology* 20:861–882.

Müller, A.H. 1979. Fossilization (Taphonomy). In Robison, R.A., and C. Teichert (editors). *Treatise on invertebrate paleontology: Part A, Introduction.* Boulder, CO: GSA.

Munson, P.J., C.A. Munson, and E.C. Pond. 1995. Paleoliquefaction evidence for a strong Holocene earthquake in south-central Indiana. *Geology* 23:325–328.

Mutti, E. 1974. Examples of ancient deep-sea fan deposits from Circum-Mediterranean geosynclines. In Dott, R.H., Jr., and R.H. Shaver (editors). *Modern and ancient geosynclinal sedimentation.* Tulsa, OK: SEPM Special Publication 19, p. 92–105.

———— 1985a. Turbidite systems and their relations to depositional sequences. In Zuffa, G.G. (editor). *Provenance of arenites.* Boston, MA: D. Reidel Publishing.

———— 1985b. *Ancient turbidite systems: Models and problems.* Tulsa, OK: AAPG Films.

Mutti, E., G. Davoli, R. Tinterri, and C. Zavala. 1996. The importance of ancient fluvio-deltaic systems dominated by catastrophic flooding in tectonically active basins. *Memorie di Scienze Geologiche* 48:233–291.

Mutti, E., and W.R. Normark. 1987. Comparing examples of modern and ancient turbidite systems: Problems and concepts. In Leggett, J.K., and G.G. Zuffa (editors). *Marine clastic sedimentology: Concepts and case studies.* Boston, MA: Graham and Trotman, p. 1–38.

Mutti, E., and F. Ricci-Lucchi. 1972. Le torbiditi del `Apennino settentrionale: Introduzione all ´analisi di facies: Memoir Society Geology Italy 11:161–199. English translation: Turbidites of the Northern Apennines: Introduction to facies analysis. *International Geology Review.* 1978. 20:125–166.

Mutti, E., F. Ricci-Lucchi, and M. Roveri. 2002. *Revisiting turbidites of the Marnoso-Arenacea Formation and their basin-margin equivalents: Problems with classic models.* Excursion guidebook of the turbidite workshop. Parma, Italy: Parma University.

Mutti, E., R. Tinterri, D. Di-Biase, L. Fava, N. Mavilla, S. Angella, and L. Calabrese. 2000. Delta-front facies associations on ancient flood-dominated fluvio-deltaic systems. *Espana* 13(2):165–190.

Nakajima, T. 2006. Hyperpycnites deposited 700 km away from river mouths in the central Japan Sea. *Journal of Sedimentary Research* 76:60–73.

Neathery, T.L., and J.A. Drahovzal. 1986. Middle and Upper Ordovician stratigraphy of the southernmost Appalachians. In Neathery, T.L. (editor). *Southeastern Section of the Geological Society of America: Centennial Field Guide Volume 6,* Boulder, CO, p. 167–172.

Nelson, C.H., and T.H. Nilson. 1974. Depositional trends of modern and ancient deep-sea fans. In Dott, R.H., Jr., and R.H. Shaver (editors). *Modern and ancient geosynclinal sedimentation,* pp. 69-91. Tulsa, OK: SEPM Special Publication 19.

———— 1984. *Modern and ancient deep-sea fan sedimentation.* Tulsa, OK: SEPM Short Course 14.

Neuendorf, K.K.E., J.P. Mehl Jr., and J.A. Jackson. 2005. *Glossary of geology.* Fifth edition. Alexandria, VA: American Geological Institute.

Neumann-Mahlkau, P. 1976. Recent sand volcanoes in the sand of a dike under construction. *Sedimentology* 23:421–425.

Nevins, S.E. 1972. Is the Capitan Limestone a fossil reef? In Howe, G.F. (editor). *Speak to the earth: Creation studies in geoscience.* Chino Valley, AZ: CRS Books, p. 16–59.

Newsom, J.F. 1903. Clastic dikes. *GSA Bulletin* 14:227–268.

Nichols, G.1999. *Sedimentology and stratigraphy.* Malden, MA: Blackwell Science.

Normark, W.R. 1974. Submarine canyons and fan valleys: Factors affecting growth patterns of deep-sea fans. In Dott, R.H., Jr., and R.H. Shaver (editors). *Modern and ancient geosynclinal sedimentation*, pp. 56-68. Tulsa, OK: SEPM Special Publication 19.

Normark, W.R., and N.E. Barnes. 1983/1984. Aftermath of COMFAN–Comments, not solutions. *Geo-Marine Letters* 3:223-224.

Normark, W.R., E. Mutti, and A. Bouma. 1983/1984. Problems in turbidite research: A need for COMFAN. *Geo-Marine Letters* 3:53–56.

Normark, W.R., H. Posamentier, and E. Mutti. 1993. Turbidite systems: State of the art and future directions. *Reviews of Geophysics* 31:91–116.

North American Commission on Stratigraphic Nomenclature. 2005. North American stratigraphic code. *AAPG* 89:1547–1591.

Northrup, B.E. 1986. A walk through time: A study in harmonization. In Walsh, R.E., C.L. Brooks, and R.S. Crowell (editors). *Proceedings of the First International Conference on Creationism, volume II*. Pittsburgh, PA: Creation Science Fellowship, p. 147–156.

———— 1990a. Identifying the Noahic Flood in historical geology: Part one. In Walsh, R.E., and C.L. Brooks (editors). *Proceedings of the First International Conference on Creationism. Volume I*. Pittsburgh, PA: Creation Science Fellowship, p. 173–179.

———— 1990b. Identifying the Noahic Flood in historical geology: Part two. In Walsh, R.E., and C.L. Brooks (editors). *Proceedings of the First International Conference on Creationism. Volume I*. Pittsburgh, PA: Creation Science Fellowship, p. 181–188.

Norton, S.A. 1973. Laterite and bauxite formation. *Economic Geology* 68:353–361.

Oard, M.J. 1990. *An ice age caused by the Genesis Flood*. El Cajon, CA: Institute for Creation Research.

———— 1994. Underwater "Mudcracks." *CRSQ* 30:213–214.

———— 2006. The geological column is a general Flood order with many exceptions. In Reed, J.K., and M.J. Oard (editors). *The geologic column: Perspectives within diluvial geology*. Chino Valley, AZ: CRS Books, p. 99–121.

Oard, M.J., J. Hergenrather, and P. Klevberg. 2005. Flood transported quartzites — east of the Rocky Mountains. *TJ* 19(3):76–90.

Oldham, R.D. 1893. *A manual of the geology of India*. Second edition. Calcutta, India.

Ollier, C.D. 1991. Laterite profiles, ferricrete and landscape evolution. *Zeitschrift für Geomorphologie* 35:165–173.

Ollier, C.D., and R.W. Galloway. 1990. The laterite profile, ferricrete and unconformity. *Catena* 17:97–109.

Owen, G. 1996. Experimental soft-sediment deformation: Structures formed by the liquefaction of unconsolidated sands and some ancient examples. *Sedimentology* 43:279–293.

Pain, C.F., and C.D. Ollier. 1992. Ferricrete in Cape York Peninsula, North Queensland. *BMR Journal of Australian Geology and Geophysics* 13:207–212.

———— 1995. Inversion of relief — a component of landscape evolution. *Geomorphology* 12:151–165.

Parker, R.B. 1986. *The tenth muse: The pursuit of earth science*. New York: Charles Scribner's Sons.

Parks, W.S. 1990. The role of meteorites in a creationist cosmology. *CRSQ* 26:144–146.

Parsons, K.M., and C.E. Brett. 1991. Taphonomic processes and biases in modern marine environments: An actualistic perspective on fossil assemblage preservation. In Donovan, S.K. (editor). *The processes of fossilization*. New York: Columbia University Press, p. 22–65.

Parsons, J.D., J.W. Bush, and J.P.M. Syvitski. 2001. Hyperpycnal plume formation from riverine outflows with small sediment concentrations. *Sedimentology* 48:465–478.

Pasley, D. 1972. *Field guide — field trip #1; Windley's Key Quarry (Key Largo Limestone)*. American Quaternary Association Second National Conference. Rosenstiel School of Marine and Atmospheric Science. Miami, FL: University of Miami.

Paton, T.R., G.S. Humphreys, and P.B. Mitchell. 1995. *Soils: A new global view*. New Haven, CT: Yale University Press.

Patterson, S.H., and B.F. Buie. 1974. *Field conference on kaolin and fuller's earth*. Atlanta, GA: Society of Economic Geologists, Georgia Geological Survey Guidebook No. 14.

Pavlow, A.P. 1896. On dikes of Oligocene sandstone in the neocomian clays of the District of Alatyr, in Russia. *Geological Magazine* 33:49–53.

Pelletier, B.R. 1958. Pocono paleocurrents in Pennsylvania and Maryland. *GSA Bulletin* 69:1033–1064.

Peres, W.E. 1993. Shelf-fed turbidite system model and its application to the Oligocene deposits of the Campos Basin, Brazil. *AAPG Bulletin* 77:81–101.

Perse, J.D. 2000. *Geology and significance of a large ferricrete deposit in Handcart Gulch, Park County, Colorado*. Masters thesis. The Ohio State University.

Peterson, U. 1971. Laterite and bauxite formation. *Economic Geology* 66:1070–1071.

Pettijohn, F.J. 1962. Paleocurrents and paleogeography. *AAPG Bulletin* 46:1468–1493.

———— 1975. *Sedimentary rocks*. New York: Harper and Row.

Pettijohn, F.J., and P.E. Potter. 1964. *Atlas and glossary of primary sedimentary structures*. New York: Springer-Verlag.

Pettijohn, F.J., P.E. Potter, and R. Siever. 1987. *Sand and sandstone*. Second edition. New York: Springer-Verlag.

Phillips, J.D. 1999. Edge effects in geomorphology. *Physical Geography* 20:53–66.

———— 2000. Rapid development of ferricretes on a subtropical valley side slope. *Geografiska Annaler* 82A(1):69–78.

Phillips, J.D., M. Lampe, R.T. King, M. Cedillo, R. Beachley, and C. Grantham. 1997. Ferricrete formation in the North Carolina Coastal Plain. *Zeitschrift für Geomorphologie* 41:67–79.

Picha, F., and A.R. Niem. 1974. Distribution and extent of beds in flysch deposits, Ouachita Mountains, Arkansas and Oklahoma. *J. Sed. Pet.* 44:328–335.

Pickering, K.T., D.A.V. Stow, M.P. Watson, and R.N. Hiscott. 1986. Deep-water facies, processes and models: A review and classification scheme for modern and ancient sediments. *Earth-Science Reviews* 23:75–174.

Pilkey, O.H. 1988. Basin plains: Giant sedimentation events. In Clifton, H.E. (editor). *Sedimentologic consequences of convulsive geologic events*, pp. 93-99. Boulder, CO: GSA Special Paper 229.

Pilkey, O.H., S.D. Locker, and W.J. Cleary. 1980. Comparison of sand-layer geometry on flat floors of 10 modern depositional basins. *AAPG Bulletin* 64:841–856.

Pimentel, N.J., V.P. Wright, and T.M. Azevedo. 1996. Distinguishing early groundwater alteration effects from pedogenesis in ancient alluvial basins: Examples from the Palaeogene of southern Portugal. *Sedimentary Geology* 105:1–10.

Piper, D.J.W., and D.A.V. Stow. 1991. Fine-grained turbidites. In Einsele, G., W. Ricken, and A. Seilacher (editors). *Cycles and events in stratigraphy*. New York: Springer-Verlag, p. 360–376.

Piper, D.J.W., A.N. Shor, and J.E.H. Clarke. 1988. The 1929 "Grand Banks" earthquake, slump, and turbidity current. In Clifton, H.E. (editor). *Sedimentologic consequences of convulsive geologic events*. Boulder, CO: GSA Special Paper 229, p. 77–92.

Piper, D.J.W., A.N. Shor, J.A. Farre, S. O'Connell, and R. Jacobi. 1985. Sediment slides and turbidity currents on the Laurentian Fan: Sidescan sonar investigations near the epicenter of the 1929 Grand Banks earthquake. *Geology* 13:538–541.

Plaziat, J.C., B.H. Purser, and E. Philobbos. 1990. Seismic deformation structures (seismites) in the syn-rift sediments of the NW Red Sea (Egypt). *Bulletin de la Société géologique de France* (8), VI, 3:419–434.

Plink-Björklund, P., and R.J. Steel. 2004. Initiation of turbidity currents: Outcrop evidence for Eocene hyperpycnal flow turbidites. *Sedimentary Geology* 165:29–52.

Plumlee, G.S., J.E. Gray, M.M. Roeber Jr., M. Coolbaugh, M. Flohr, and G. Whitney. 1995. The importance of geology in understanding and remediating environmental problems at Summitville. In Posey, H.H., J.A. Pendleton, and D. Van Zyl (editors). *Proceedings: Summitville Forum '95*. Special Publication 38. Denver, CO: Colorado Geological Survey.

Poole, F.G. 1974. Flysch deposits of Antler foreland basin, western United States. In Dickinson, W.R. (editor). *Tectonics and sedimentation*. Tulsa, OK: SEPM Special Publication 22, p. 58–85.

Pope, M.C., J.F. Read, R. Baumbach, and H.J. Hofmann. 1997. Late Middle to Late Ordovician seismites of Kentucky, southwest Ohio and Virginia: Sedimentary recorders of earthquakes in the Appalachian basin. *GSA Bulletin* 109:489–503.

Potter, P.E., and F.J. Pettijohn. 1977. *Paleocurrents and basin analysis*. Second edition. New York: Springer-Verlag.

Potter, P.E., and W.A. Pryor. 1961. Dispersal centers of Paleozoic and later clastics of the Upper Mississippi Valley and adjacent areas. *GSA Bulletin* 72:1195–1250.

Pratt, B.R. 1994. Seismites in the Mesoproterozoic Altyn Formation (Belt Supergroup), Montana: A test for tectonic control of peritidal carbonate cyclicity. *Geology* 22:1091–1094.

———— 1996. Septarian fissures in marine carbonate concretions: Origin through cracking and shrinkage during syndepositional earthquakes. *GSA Abstracts with Programs* 28:A–407.

———— 1998a. Syneresis cracks: Subaqueous shrinkage in argillaceous sediments caused by earthquake-induced dewatering. *Sedimentary Geology* 117:1–10.

———— 1998b. Molar-tooth structure in Proterozoic carbonate rocks: Origin from synsedimentary earthquakes, and implications for the nature and evolution of basins and marine sediment. *GSA Bulletin* 110(8):1028–1045.

——— 2001. Septarian concretions: Internal cracking caused by synsedimentary earthquakes. *Sedimentology* 48:189–213.

Price, N.B., and P.McL.D. Duff. 1969. Mineralogy and chemistry of tonsteins from Carboniferous sequences in Great Britain. *Sedimentology* 13:45–69.

Pullan, R.A. 1967. A morphological classification of lateritic ironstones and ferruginized rocks in northern Nigeria. *Nigerian Journal of Science* 1:161–173.

Pyle, D.M. 1989. The thickness, volume and grainsize of tephra fall deposits. *Bulletin of Volcanology* 51:1–15.

Raiswell, R. 1971. The growth of Cambrian and Liassic concretions. *Sedimentology* 17:147–171.

Raiswell, R., and Q.J. Fisher. 2000. Mudcrack-hosted carbonate concretions: A review of growth mechanisms and their influence on chemical and isotopic composition. *Journal of the Geological Society of London* 157:239–251.

Rampino, M.R. 1991. Volcanism, climatic change, and the geological record. In Fisher, R.V., and G.A. Smith (editors). *Sedimentation in volcanic settings*. Tulsa, OK: Society for Sedimentary Geology Special Publication 45, p. 9–18.

Ransome, F.L. 1901. *A report on the economic geology of the Silverton Quadrangle, Colorado*. United States Geological Survey Bulletin 182, Series A, Economic Geology 12, Washington, D.C.

Raymond, D.E., W.E. Osborne, C.W. Copeland, and T.L. Neathery. 1988. *Alabama stratigraphy*. Circular 140. Tuscaloosa, AL: Geological Survey of Alabama.

Reading, H.G. 1991. The classification of deep-sea depositional systems by sediment calibre and feeder systems. *Quarterly Journal of the Geological Society of London* 148:427–430.

——— (editor). 1996. *Sedimentary environments: Processes, facies, and stratigraphy*. Third edition. New York: Blackwell Science.

Reading, H.G., and M. Richards. 1994. Turbidite systems in deep-water basin margins classified by grain size and feeder system. *AAPG Bulletin* 78:792–822.

Reed, J.K. 2000. *The North American Midcontinent Rift System: An interpretation within the biblical worldview*. Monograph No. 9. Chino Valley, AZ: CRS Books.

——— 2001. *Natural history in the Christian Worldview: Foundation and framework*. Monograph No. 11. Chino Valley, AZ: CRS Books.

——— 2002. Reinventing stratigraphy at the Palo Duro Basin. *CRSQ* 39:25–39.

——— 2004. The geology of the Kansas basement: Part II. *CRSQ* 40:229–239.

——— 2005. Strategic stratigraphy: Reclaiming the rock record! *TJ* 19(2):119–127.

Reed, J.K., and C.R. Froede Jr. 1997. A biblical Christian framework for earth history research Part III — Constraining geologic models. *CRSQ* 33:285–292.

——— 2003. The uniformitarian stratigraphic column — shortcut or pitfall for creation geology. *CRSQ* 40:90–98.

Reed, J.K., C.R. Froede Jr., and C.B. Bennett. 1996. The role of geologic energy in interpreting the stratigraphic record. *CRSQ* 33:97–101.

Reed, J.K., P. Klevberg, and C.R. Froede Jr. 2006a. Toward an empirical stratigraphy. In Reed, J.K., and M.J. Oard (editors). *The geologic column: Perspectives within diluvial geology*. Chino Valley, AZ: CRS Books, p. 31–51.

——— 2006b. Interpreting the rock record without the uniformitarian geologic column. In Reed, J.K., and M.J. Oard (editors). *The geologic column: Perspectives within diluvial geology*. Chino Valley, AZ: CRS Books, p. 123–143.

Reed, J.K., and M.J. Oard (editors). 2006. *The geologic column: Perspectives within diluvial geology*. Chino Valley, AZ: CRS Books.

Reineck, H.E., and I.B. Singh. 1980. *Depositional sedimentary environments*. Second edition. New York: Springer-Verlag.

Reinhardt, J., and W.R. Sigleo. 1983. Mesozoic paleosols: Examples from the Chattahoochee River Valley. In Carrington, T.J. (editor). *Current studies of Cretaceous formations in eastern Alabama and Columbus, Georgia*. Twentieth Annual Field Trip Guidebook for the Alabama Geological Society. Tuscaloosa, AL: Alabama Geological Society, p. 3–10.

——— (editors). 1988. *Paleosols and weathering through geologic time: Principles and applications*. Boulder, CO: GSA Special Paper 216.

Retallack, G.J. 1981. Fossil soils: Indicators of ancient terrestrial environments. In Niklas, K.J. (editor). *Paleobotany, paleoecology, and evolution, volume 1*. New York: Praeger.

——— 1983a. A paleopedological approach to the interpretation of terrestrial sedimentary rocks: The mid-Tertiary fossil soils of Badlands National Park, South Dakota. *GSA Bulletin* 94:823–840.

——— 1983b. *Late Eocene and Oligocene paleosols from Badlands National Park, South Dakota*. Boulder, CO: GSA Special Paper 193.

———— 1984. Completeness of the rock and fossil record: Some estimates using fossil soils. *Paleobiology* 10:59–78.

———— 1986. Fossil soils as grounds for interpreting long-term controls on ancient rivers. *J. Sed. Pet.* 56:1–18.

———— 1990. *Soils of the past: An introduction to paleopedology.* London, UK: HarperCollins Academic.

———— 1992a. Paleozoic paleosols. In Martini, I.P., and W. Chesworth (editors). Weathering, soils and paleosols. Developments in earth surface processes No. 2. New York, NY: Elsevier, p. 543–564.

———— 1992b. Paleosols and changes in climate and vegetation across the Eocene/Oligocene boundary. In Prothero, D.R., and W.A. Berggren (editors). *Eocene-Oligocene climatic and biotic evolution.* Princeton, NJ: Princeton University Press, p. 382–398.

———— 1993. Classification of paleosols: Discussion and reply. *GSA Bulletin* 105:1635–1637.

———— 1994. A pedotype approach to latest Cretaceous and earliest Tertiary paleosols in eastern Montana. *GSA Bulletin* 106:1377–1397.

———— 1997. *A colour guide to paleosols.* New York: Wiley.

Retallack, G.J., and J. Germán-Heins. 1994. Evidence from paleosols for the geological antiquity of rain forest. *Science* 265:499–502.

Retallack, G.J., E.A. Bestland, and T.J. Fremd. 2000. *Eocene and Oligocene paleosols of central Oregon.* Boulder, CO: GSA Special Paper 344.

Reynolds, W.R. 1966. Stratigraphy and genesis of clay mineral and zeolite strata in the Lower Tertiary of Alabama. In Copeland, C.W. (editor). *Facies changes in the Alabama Tertiary.* Alabama Geological Society Fourth Annual Field Trip Guidebook. Tuscaloosa, AL: Alabama Geological Society, p. 26–37.

———— 1970. Mineralogy and stratigraphy of Lower Tertiary clays and claystones of Alabama. *J. Sed. Pet.* 40:829–838.

Ricci-Lucchi, F.R. 1995. *Sedimentographica: Photographic atlas of sedimentary structures.* Second edition. New York: Columbia University Press.

Ricci-Lucchi, F.R., and E. Valmori. 1980. Basin-wide turbidites in a Miocene, over-supplied deep-sea plain: A geometrical analysis. *Sedimentology* 27:241–270.

Rice, A. 1990. The role of volcanism in K/T extinctions. In Lockley, M.G., and A. Rice (editors). *Volcanism and fossil biotas.* Boulder, CO: GSA Special Paper 244, p. 39–56.

Rice, C.L., H.E. Belkin, T.W. Henry, R.E. Zartman, and M.J. Kunk. 1994. The Pennsylvanian fire clay tonstein of the Appalachian basin — Its distribution, biostratigraphy, and mineralogy. In Rice, C.L. (editor). *Elements of Pennsylvanian stratigraphy, Central Appalachian Basin.* Boulder, CO: GSA Special Paper 294, p. 87–104.

Rigby, J.K., and W.K. Hamblin (editors). 1972. *Recognition of ancient sedimentary environments.* Tulsa, OK: SEPM Special Publication 16.

Rindsberg, A.K., and T.M. Chowns. 1986. Ringgold Gap: Progradational sequences in the Ordovician and Silurian of northwest Georgia. In Neathery, T.L. (editor). *Southeastern section of the Geological Society of America: Centennial field guide volume 6.* Boulder, CO: Geological Society of America, p. 159–162.

Ritter, D.F., R.C. Kochel, and J.R. Miller. 1995. *Process geomorphology.* Third edition. Dubuque, IA: Wm.C. Brown Publishers.

Robinson, D.A., and R.B.G. Williams (editors). 1994. *Rock weathering and landform evolution.* New York: Wiley.

Robinson, S.J. 1996. Can Flood geology explain the fossil record? *CENTJ* 10(1):32–69.

Ross, C.S. 1928. Altered Paleozoic volcanic materials and their recognition. *AAPG Bulletin* 12:143–164.

———— 1955. Provenance of pyroclastic materials. *GSA Bulletin* 66:427–434.

Ross, C.S., H.D. Miser, and L.W. Stephenson. 1928. *Water-laid volcanic rocks of early Upper Cretaceous age in southwestern Arkansas, southeastern Oklahoma, and northeastern Texas.* Washington, DC: U.S. Geological Survey Professional Paper 154-F, p. 175–202.

Roth, A.A. 1995. Fossil reefs and time. *Origins* 22(2):86–104.

Rubin, D.M. 1987. *Cross-bedding, bedforms, and paleo-currents.* SEPM Concepts in Sedimentology and Paleontology, Volume 1. Tulsa, OK: SEPM.

Rubin, D.M., and D.S. McCulloch. 1980. Single and superimposed bedforms: A synthesis of San Francisco Bay and flume observations. *Sedimentary Geology* 26:207–231.

Rucker, B.R., and C.R. Froede Jr. 1998. Archaeological and geological evidence of a recent and rapid sea-level rise from sites along coastal Florida. *CRSQ* 35:54–65.

Rudwick, M.J.S. 1985a. *The meaning of fossils.* Second edition. Chicago, IL: University of Chicago Press.

———— 1985b. *The great Devonian controversy.* Chicago, IL: University of Chicago Press.

Ruellan, A. 1971. The history of soils: Some problems of definition and interpretation. In Yaalon, D.H. (editor). *Paleopedology: Origin, nature, and dating of paleosols.* Jerusalem: Israel Universities Press, p. 3–13.

Rugg, S.H. 1990. Detachment faults in the southwestern United States — Evidence for a short and catastrophic Tertiary Period. In Walsh, R.E., and C.L. Brooks (editors). *Proceedings of the Second International Conference on Creationism. Volume II.* Pittsburgh, PA: Creation Science Fellowship, p. 217–229.

Ruhe, R.V. 1965. Quaternary paleopedology. In Wright, H.E., Jr., and D.G. Frey (editors). *The Quaternary of the United States.* Princeton. NJ: Princeton University Press, p. 755–764.

Russell, I.C. 1889. *Sub-aerial decay of rocks and origin of red colour in certain formations.* Washington, DC: U.S. Geological Survey Bulletin 52.

Salvador, A. (editor). 1994. *International stratigraphic guide.* Second edition. Boulder, CO: GSA.

Sanchez, T.A., and S.L. Douglass. 1994. *Alabama shoreline change rates: 1970–1993.* College of Engineering Report No. 94-1. Mobile, AL: University of South Alabama.

Samson, S.D., P.J. Patchett, J.C. Roddick, and R.R. Parrish. 1989. Origin and tectonic setting of Ordovician bentonites in North America: Isotopic and age constraints. *GSA Bulletin* 101:1175–1181.

Schaetzl, R.J., and S. Anderson. 2005. *Soils: Genesis and geomorphology.* New York: Cambridge University Press.

Schäfer, W. 1972. *Ecology and paleoecology of marine environments.* Translated by I. Oertel and edited by G.Y. Craig. Chicago, IL: University of Chicago Press.

Scheven, J. 1990. The Flood/Post-Flood boundary in the fossil record. In Walsh, R.E., and C.L. Brooks (editors). *Proceedings of the Second International Conference on Creationism. Volume II.* Pittsburgh, PA: Creation Science Fellowship, p. 247–266.

Schiebout, J.A. 1979. An overview of the terrestrial early Tertiary of southern North America — Fossil sites and paleopedology. *Tulane Studies in Geology and Paleontology* 15:75–93.

Schmidt, W. 1986. Alum Bluff, Liberty County, Florida. In Neathery, T.L. (editor). *Southeastern section of the Geological Society of America, Centennial Field Guide Volume 6.* Boulder, CO: GSA, p. 355–357.

Scholle, P.A., and P.R. Schluger (editors). 1979. *Aspects of diagenesis.* SEPM Special Publication 26. Tulsa, OK: SEPM.

Scholle, P.A., and D.R. Spearing (editors). 1982. *Sandstone depositional environments.* Tulsa, OK: AAPG Memoir 31.

Scholle, P.A., D.G. Bebout, and C.H. Moore (editors). 1983. *Carbonate depositional environments.* Tulsa, OK: AAPG Memoir 33.

Schwarz, T. 1994. Ferricrete formation and relief inversion: An example from central Sudan. *Catena* 21:257–268.

Scotchman, I.C. 1991. The geochemistry of concretions from the Kimmeridge Clay Formation of southern and eastern England. *Sedimentology* 38:79–106.

Scott, G. 1930. *Ripple marks of large size in the Fredericksburg rocks west of Fort Worth, Texas.* The University of Texas Bulletin Number 3001. Austin, TX: Bureau of Economic Geology, p. 53–56.

Secord, J.A. 1986. *Controversy in Victorian geology: The Cambrian-Silurian dispute.* Princeton, NJ: Princeton University Press.

Seilacher, A. 1962. Paleontological studies on turbidite sedimentation and erosion. *Journal of Geology* 70:227–234.

———— 1964. Biogenic sedimentary structures. In Imbrie, J., and N. Newell (editors). *Approaches to paleoecology.* New York: Wiley, p. 296–316.

———— 1967. Bathymetry of trace fossils. *Marine Geology* 5:413–428.

———— 1969. Fault-graded beds interpreted as seismites. *Sedimentology* 13:155–159.

———— 1984a. Storm beds: Their significance in event stratigraphy. In Seibold, E., and J.D. Meulenkamp (editors). *Stratigraphy: Quo vadis?* Tulsa, OK: AAPG Studies in Geology 16, p. 49–54.

———— 1984b. Sedimentary structures tentatively attributed to seismic events. *Marine Geology* 55:1–12.

Seilacher, A., and T. Aigner. 1991. Storm deposition at the bed, facies, and basin scale: The geologic perspective. In Einsele, G., W. Ricken, and A. Seilacher (editors). *Cycles and events in stratigraphy.* New York: Springer-Verlag, p. 249–267.

Selley, R.C. 1988. *Applied sedimentology.* New York: Academic Press.

Shor, A.N., D.J.W. Piper, J.E.H. Clarke, and L.A. Mayer. 1990. Giant flute-like scour and other erosional features formed by the 1929 Grand Banks turbidity current. *Sedimentology* 37:631–645.

Silvestru, E. 2006. A long and winding way. In Reed, J.K., and M.J. Oard (editors). *The geologic column: Perspectives within diluvial geology.* Chino Valley, AZ: CRS Books, p. 89–98.

Singer, A. 1975. A Cretaceous laterite in the Negev Desert, southern Israel. *Geological Magazine* 112:151–162.

Singer, M.J., and D.R. Munns. 1991. *Soils: An introduction.* New York: Macmillan Publishing.

Slaughter, M., and M. Hamil. 1970. Model for deposition of volcanic ash and resulting bentonite. *GSA Bulletin* 81:961–968.

Smith, F.G.W. 1971. *Atlantic reef corals: A handbook of the common reef and shallow-water corals of Bermuda, the Bahamas, Florida, the West Indies, and Brazil.* Coral Gables, FL: University of Miami Press.

Smith, N. 1994. *Official guide to the National Museum of Natural History/National Museum of Man.* Washington, DC: Smithsonian Institution Press.

Smith, G.A., and D.R. Lowe. 1991. Lahars: Volcano-hydrologic events and deposition in the debris flow — Hyperconcentrated flow continuum. In Fisher, R.V., and G.A. Smith (editors). *Sedimentation in volcanic settings.* Tulsa, OK: Society for Sedimentary Geology Special Publication 45, p. 59–70.

Smyers, N.B., and G.L. Peterson. 1971. Sandstone dikes and sills in the Moreno Shale, Panoche Hills, California. *GSA Bulletin* 82:3201–3208.

Snelling, A.A. 1997. The editor comments. *CENTJ* 11(1):44–45.

Snelling, A.A., and S.A. Austin. 1992. Startling evidence for Noah's flood: Footprints and sand dunes in a Grand Canyon sandstone! *Creation Ex Nihilo Magazine* 15(1):46–50.

Snelling, A.A., M. Ernst, E. Scheven, J. Scheven, S.A. Austin, K.P. Wise, P. Garner, M. Garton, and D. Tyler. 1996. The geological record. *CENTJ* 10(3):333–334.

Snelling, N.J. (editor). 1985. *The chronology of the geological record.* The Geological Society Memoir 10. Boston, MA: Blackwell Scientific Publications.

Spears, D.A. 1970. A kaolinite mudstone (tonstein) in the British coal measures. *J. Sed. Pet.* 40:386–394.

Spears, D.A., and R. Kanaris-Sotiriou. 1979. A geochemical and mineralogical investigation of some British and other European tonsteins. *Sedimentology* 26:407–425.

Spears, D.A., and C.M. Rice. 1973. An Upper Carboniferous tonstein of volcanic origin. *Sedimentology* 20:281–294.

Specht, R.W., and R.L. Brenner. 1979. Storm-wave genesis of bioclastic carbonates in upper Jurassic epicontinental mudstones, east-central Wyoming. *J. Sed. Pet.* 49:1307–1322.

Spencer, W.R. 1994. The origin and history of the solar system. In Walsh, R.E. (editor). *Proceedings of the Third International Conference on Creationism. Technical symposium sessions.* Pittsburgh, PA: Creation Science Fellowship, p. 513–524.

Spencer, W.R., and M.J. Oard. 2004. The Chesapeake Bay impact and Noah's Flood. *CRSQ* 41:206–215.

Stanley, D.J. 1993. Model for turbidite-to-contourite continuum and multiple process transport in deep marine settings: Examples in the rock record. *Sedimentary Geology* 82:241–255.

Stanley, D.J., and G. Kelling (editors). 1978. *Sedimentation in submarine canyons, fans, and trenches.* Stroudsburg, PA: Dowden, Hutchinson & Ross.

Stanley, D.J., and D.J.P. Swift (editors). 1976. *Marine sediment transport and environmental management.* New York: Wiley.

Stearn, C.W., and R.L. Carroll. 1989. *Paleontology: The record of life.* New York: John Wiley.

Steila, D., and T.E. Pond. 1989. *The geography of soils.* Savage, MD: Rowman and Littlefield Publishers.

Stow, D.A.V. (editor). 1992. *Deep-water turbidite systems.* Reprint Series Volume 3 of the International Association of Sedimentologists. Boston, MA: Blackwell Scientific.

——— 2005. *Sedimentary rocks in the field: A color guide.* Burlington, MA: Elsevier Academic Press.

Stow, D.A.V., and J.P.B. Lovell. 1979. Contourites: Their recognition in modern and ancient sediments. *Earth-Science Reviews* 14:251–291.

Stow, D.A.V., and D.J.W. Piper. 1984. *Fine-grained sediments: Deep-water processes and facies.* Boston, MA: Blackwell Scientific.

Stow, D.A.V., C.J. Pudsey, J.A. Howe, J.C. Faugères, and A.R. Viana (editors). 2002. *Deep-water contourite systems: Modern drifts and ancient series, seismic and sedimentary characteristics.* Memoir No. 22. London: Geological Society.

Stow, D.A.V., H.G. Reading, and J.D. Collinson. 1996. Deep seas. In Reading, H.G. (editor). *Sedimentary environments: Processes, facies, and stratigraphy.* Third edition. Cambridge, MA: Blackwell Science, p. 395–453.

Stow, D.A.V., and G. Shanmugam. 1980. Sequence of structures in fine-grained turbidites; comparison of recent deep-sea and ancient flysch sediments. *Sedimentary Geology* 25:23–42.

Sullivan, R.D., and S. Voss. 1991. *Picture tour of the National Museum of Natural History.* Washington, DC: Smithsonian Institution Press.

Tanner, P.W.G. 1998. Interstratal dewatering origin for polygonal patterns of sand-filled cracks: A case study from Late Proterozoic metasediments of Islay, Scotland. *Sedimentology* 45:71–89.

———— 2003. Syneresis. In Middleton, G.V. (editor). *Encyclopedia of sediments and sedimentary rocks.* Norwell, MA: Kluwer Academic, p. 718–720.

Tardy, Y. 2000. Laterites. In Hancock, P.L., and B.J. Skinner (editors). *The Oxford companion to the earth.* New York: Oxford University Press, p. 602.

———— 2003. Laterites. In Middleton, G.V. (editor). *Encyclopedia of sediments and sedimentary rocks.* Norwell, MA: Kluwer Academic, p. 408–411.

Taylor, I.T. 1991. *In the minds of men: Darwin and the new world order.* Third edition. Toronto: TFE Publishing.

Toulmin, L.D. 1977. *Stratigraphic distribution of Paleocene and Eocene fossils in the eastern Gulf Coast region.* Geological Survey of Alabama Monograph 13, Volume One. University, AL.

Triplehorn, D.M., and B.F. Bohor. 1981. *Altered volcanic ash partings in the C coal bed, Ferron Sandstone member of the Mancos Shale, Emery County, Utah.* Washington, DC: U.S. Geological Survey Open-File Report 81–775.

Tsujita, C.J. 1995. Origin of concretion-hosted shell clusters in the Late Cretaceous Bearpaw Formation, Southern Alberta, Canada. *Palaios* 10:408–423.

Tucker, M.E. 1991. *Sedimentary petrology: An introduction to the origin of sedimentary rocks.* Second edition. Boston, MA: Blackwell Scientific.

Tuttle, M.P., and E.S. Schweig. 1995. Archeological and pedological evidence for large prehistoric earthquakes in the New Madrid seismic zone, central United States. *Geology* 23:253–256.

Twidale, C.R. 1984. Role of subterranean water in landform development in tropical and subtropical regions. In LaFleur, R.G., (editor). *Groundwater as a geomorphic agent,* pp. 91-134. The Binghamton Symposia in Geomorphology, International Series 13. Winchester, MA: Allen & Unwin.

———— 1990. Weathering, soil development, and landforms. In Higgins, C.G., and Coates, D.R. (editors). *Groundwater geomorphology: The role of subsurface water in earth-surface processes and landforms.* Boulder, CO: GSA Special Paper 252, p. 29–50.

Tyler, D.J. 1996. A post-Flood solution to the chalk problem. *CENTJ* 10(1):107–113.

———— 2006. Recolonization and the Mabbul. In Reed, J.K., and M.J. Oard (editors). *The geologic column: Perspectives within diluvial geology.* Chino Valley, AZ: CRS Books, p. 73–86.

Tyler, D.J., and H.G. Coffin. 2006. Accept the column, reject the chronology. In Reed, J.K., and M.J. Oard (editors). *The geologic column: Perspectives within diluvial geology.* Chino Valley, AZ: CRS Books, p. 53–69.

Unfred, D.W. 1984. Asteroidal impacts and the flood-judgment. *CRSQ* 21:82–87.

United States Department of Agriculture. 1975. *Soil Taxonomy.* Washington, DC: Soil Conservation Service Agriculture Handbook No. 436.

———— 1993. *Soil Survey Manual.* Washington, DC: USDA Handbook No. 18, revised and enlarged.

———— 1994. *Keys to soil taxonomy.* Sixth edition. Washington, DC: Soil Conservation Service.

Ussher, J. 1658. *The annals of the world.* Revised and updated by Pierce, L., and M. Pierce. 2003. Green Forest, AR: Master Books.

Valentine, K.W.G., and J.B. Dalrymple. 1976. Quaternary buried paleosols: A critical review. *Quaternary Research* 6:209–222.

Vardiman, L. 2003. Hypercanes following the Genesis Flood. In Ivey, R.L., Jr. (editor). *Proceedings of the Fifth International Conference on Creationism. Technical Symposium Sessions.* Pittsburgh, PA: Creation Science Fellowship, p. 17–28.

Vardiman, L., A.A. Snelling, and E.F. Chaffin (editors). 2005. *Radioisotopes and the age of the earth.* Volume II. Results of a young-earth creationist research initiative. El Cajon, CA: Institute for Creation Research.

Verosub, K.L., P. Fine, M.J. Singer, J. TenPas. 1993. Pedogenesis and paleoclimate: Interpretation of the magnetic susceptibility record of Chinese loess-paleosol sequences. *Geology* 21:1011–1014.

Walker, G.P.L. 1973. Explosive volcanic eruptions — A new classification scheme. *Geologische Rundschau* 62:431–446.

Walker, R.G. 1973. Mopping up the turbidite mess. In Ginsburg, R.N. (editor). *Evolving concepts in sedimentology.* The Johns Hopkins University Studies in Geology 21, Baltimore, MD: Johns Hopkins University Press, p. 1–37.

———— 1984. Shelf and shallow marine sands. In Walker, R.G. (editor). *Facies models.* Second edition. Geoscience Canada Reprints Series 1. Waterloo, Ontario: Geological Association of Canada, p. 141–170.

———— 1992. Turbidites and submarine fans. In Walker, R.G., and N.P. James (editors). *Facies models: Response to sea level change.* St. John's, Newfoundland: Geological Association of Canada, p. 239–263.

Walker, R.G., and N.P. James (editors). 1992. *Facies models*. Geoscience Canada Reprints Series 1. St. John's, Newfoundland: Geological Association of Canada.

Walker, T. 1994. A Biblical geologic model. In Walsh, R.E. (editor). *Proceedings of the Third International Conference on Creationism, technical symposium sessions*. Pittsburgh, PA: Creation Science Fellowship, p. 581–592.

———— 1996a. The basement rocks of the Brisbane area, Australia: Where do they fit in the Creation model. *CENTJ* 10(2):241–257.

———— 1996b. The Great Artesian Basin, Australia. *CENTJ* 10(3):379–390.

———— 2001. Post-Flood volcanism on the Banks Peninsula, New Zealand. *TJ* 15(1):96–104.

———— 2005. Overview of the model. Accessed from: http://www.biblicalgeology.net/model/overview.html.

Wang, Y. 2003. Coastal laterite profiles at Po Chue Tam, Lantau Island, Hong Kong: The origin and implication. *Geomorphology* 52:335–346.

Waterston, C.D. 1950. Note on the sandstone injections of Eathie Haven, Cromarty. *Geological Magazine* 87:133–139.

Weaver, C.E. 1958. Geologic interpretation of argillaceous sediments: Part I. Origin and significance of clay minerals in sedimentary rocks. *AAPG Bulletin* 42:254–271.

———— 1963. Interpretative value of heavy minerals from bentonites. *J. Sed. Pet.* 33:343–349.

———— 1989. *Clays, muds, and shales*. Developments in Sedimentology 44. New York: Elsevier.

Weide, D.L. (editor). 1985. *Soils and Quaternary geology of the Southwestern United States*. Boulder, CO: GSA Special Paper 203.

Weimer, P., and M.H. Link (editors). 1991. *Seismic facies and sedimentary processes of submarine fans and turbidite systems*. New York: Springer-Verlag.

Weimer, P., A.H. Bouma, and B.F. Perkins (editors). 1994. *Submarine fans and turbidite systems*. Proceedings of the Gulf Coast Section SEPM Foundation Fifteenth Annual Research Conference, Earth Enterprises, Austin, TX.

West, L., and D. Chure. 1994. *Dinosaur: The Dinosaur National Monument Quarry*. Vernal, UT: Dinosaur Nature Association.

Westrop, S.R. 1986. Taphonomic versus ecologic controls on taxonomic relative abundance patterns in tempestites. *Lethaia* 19:123–132.

Wetzel, A. 1991. Ecologic interpretation of deep-sea trace fossil communities. *Palaeogeography Palaeoclimatology Palaeoecology* 85:47–69.

———— 1992. An apparent concretionary paradox. *Zentralblatt für Geologie und Paläontologie*, Teil I, H12:2823–2830.

Wheatcroft, R.A., J.C. Borgeld, R.S. Born, D.E. Drake, E.L. Leithold, C.A. Nittrouer, and C.K. Sommerfield. 1996. The anatomy of an oceanic flood deposit. *Oceanography* 9(3):158–162.

Whitaker, J.H.McD. 1974. Ancient submarine canyons and fan valleys. In Dott, R.H., Jr., and R.H. Shaver (editors). *Modern and ancient geosynclinal sedimentation*. Tulsa, OK: SEPM Special Publication 19, p. 106–125.

Whitcomb, J.C. 1988. *The world that perished*. Second edition. Grand Rapids, MI: Baker Book House.

Whitcomb, J.C., and H.M. Morris. 1961. *The Genesis Flood*. Grand Rapids, MI: Baker Book House.

Whitmore, J.H. 2005. Origin and significance of sand-filled cracks and other features near the base of the Coconino Sandstone, Grand Canyon, Arizona, USA. *CRSQ* 42:163–180.

———— 2007. Modern and ancient reefs. In Oard, M.J., and J.K. Reed (editors). *Rock solid answers: Responses to popular objections to biblical geology*. Green Forest, AR: Master Books.

Williams, E.L. 1993. Fossil wood of Big Bend National Park, Brewster County, Texas: Part II — Mechanism of silicification of wood and other pertinent factors. *CRSQ* 30:106–111.

Williams, E.L., and R. L. Goette. 1998. Trace fossils in petrified wood Big Bend National Park, Texas. *CRSQ* 35: 93–95.

Williams, E.L., R.L. Goette, W. G. Stark and G.T. Matzko. 1998. Fossil wood from Big Bend National Park, Texas (Dawson Creek region): Part V — Origin and diagenesis of clays. *CRSQ* 35:31–38.

Williams, E.L., and G.F. Howe. 1993. Fossil wood of Big Bend National Park, Brewster County, Texas: Part I — Geologic setting. *CRSQ* 30:47–54.

Williams, E.L., G.F. Howe, G.T. Matzko, R.R. White and W.G. Stark. 1993. Fossil wood of Big Bend National Park, Brewster County, Texas: Part III — Chemical tests performed on wood. *CRSQ* 30:169–176.

———— 1995. Fossil wood of Big Bend National Park, Brewster County, TX: Part IV — Wood structure, nodules, paleosols, and climate. *CRSQ* 31:225–232.

Williams, H., and A.R. McBirney. 1979. *Volcanology*. San Francisco, CA: Freeman, Cooper and Company.

Wilson, J.L. 1975. *Carbonate Facies in Geological History.* New York: Springer-Verlag.

Wilson, R.C.L. (editor). 1983. *Residual deposits: Surface related weathering processes and materials.* The Geological Society of London. Boston, MA: Blackwell Scientific.

Wilson, R.L. 1986. Whiteoak Mountain synclinorium, Bradley County, Tennessee. In Neathery, T.L. (editor). *Southeastern Section of the Geological Society of America: Centennial Field Guide Volume 6,* p. 149–152. Boulder, CO.

Winchester, S. 2001. *The map that changed the world: William Smith and the birth of modern geology.* New York: HarperCollins.

Winn, R.D., Jr., and J.M. Armentrout (editors). 1995. *Turbidites and associated deep-water facies.* Tulsa, OK: SEPM Core Workshop 20.

Wise, K.P., and S.A. Austin. 1995. Nautiloid mass-kill event at a hydrothermal mound within the Redwall Limestone (Mississippian), Grand Canyon, Arizona. *GSA Abstracts with Programs* 27:A–369.

Woodmorappe, J. 1980. An anthology of matters significant to creationism and diluviology: Report I. *Studies in Flood Geology.* El Cajon, CA: Institute for Creation Research.

———— 1981. The essential nonexistence of the evolutionary-uniformitarian geologic column: A quantitative assessment. *Studies in Flood geology.* El Cajon, CA: Institute for Creation Research.

———— 1983. A diluvial treatise on the stratigraphic separation of fossils. *Studies in Flood Geology.* El Cajon, CA: Institute for Creation Research.

———— 1993. *Studies in Flood geology.* El Cajon, CA: Institute for Creation Research.

———— 1998. Hypercanes as a cause of the 40-day global Flood rainfall. In Walsh, R.E. (editor). *Proceedings of the Fourth International Conference on Creationism, technical symposium sessions.* Pittsburgh, PA: Creation Science Fellowship, p. 645–658.

———— 1999. *The mythology of modern dating methods.* El Cajon, CA: Institute for Creation Research.

———— 2006. Are soft-sediment trace fossils (ichnofossils) a time problem for the Flood? *Journal of Creation* 20(2):113–122.

Working Group on the Origin and Nature of Paleosols. 1971. Criteria for the recognition and classification of paleosols. In Yaalon, D.H. (editor). *Paleopedology: Origin, nature, and dating of paleosols,* pp. 153-158. INQUA Commission on Paleopedology. Jerusalem: Israel Universities Press.

Wright, V.P. 1986. *Paleosols: Their recognition and interpretation.* Princeton, NJ: Princeton University Press.

———— 1992a. Paleopedology: Stratigraphic relationships and empirical models. In Martini, I.P., and W. Chesworth (editors). *Weathering, soils and paleosols.* Developments in earth surface processes 2. New York: Elsevier, p. 475–499.

———— 1992b. Paleosol recognition: A guide to early diagenesis in terrestrial settings. In Wolf, K.H., and G.V. Chilingarian (editors). *Diagenesis III.* New York: Elsevier, p. 591–619.

Wright, V.P., R.J. Sloan, B. Valero-Garcés, and L.A.J. Garvie. 1992. Groundwater ferricretes from the Silurian of Ireland and Permian of the Spanish Pyrenees. *Sedimentary Geology* 77:37–49.

Yaalon, D.H. 1971. *Paleopedology: Origin, nature, and dating of paleosols.* Jerusalem: Israel University Press.

Zeng, J., and D.R. Lowe. 1997a. Numerical simulation of turbidity current flow and sedimentation: I. Theory. *Sedimentology* 44:67–84.

———— 1997b. Numerical simulation of turbidity current flow and sedimentation: I. Results and geological applications. *Sedimentology* 44:85–104.

Index